Sigma Xi, The Scientific Research Society

FORUM PROCEEDINGS

Global Change and the Human Prospect:
Issues in Population, Science, Technology and Equity
November 16 - 18, 1991

D1413298

Introductory Note: The following papers were prepared for the Sigma Xi Forum in November, 1991. In most cases, the authors submitted a smoothed version of their presentations. In a few instances, the talks were transcribed and revised by the speaker. In addition, the style of referencing in each paper is that used by the author.

Acknowledgements

Special thanks to the members of the Forum Steering Committee (John F. Ahearne, Rita R. Colwell, U.V. Henderson, Donald N. Langenberg, Thomas F. Malone, V. Kerry Smith, Gilbert White, and Robert M. White) for their expert guidance throughout this entire project.

This volume and the Forum itself owe their existence in large part to the efforts of the Forum Coordinator, Nancy Berry.

Funding for the Forum was provided by: the Burroughs Wellcome Company, Carolina Power & Light Company, the Compton Foundation, Duke Power Company, Electric Power Research Institute, Ford Motor Company, General Electric Company, Glaxo Inc., the Johnson Foundation, the John D. and Catherine T. MacArthur Foundation, National Oceanic & Atmospheric Administration, Phillips Petroleum Company, Texaco Foundation, the U.S. Environmental Protection Agency, and Xerox Corporation.

Cover design by Steve Ater.

Copyright © 1992 by Sigma Xi, The Scientific Research Society, Inc.

ISBN 0-914446-03-7

All orders must be sent in writing to:
Forum Coordinator
Sigma Xi, The Scientific Research Society
P.O. Box 13975
Research Triangle Park, NC 27709
Orders for single copies must be accompanied with prepayment of $18.50 plus $2.00 for shipping and handling.

Printed in the United States of America by Edwards Brothers, Inc.

94-0436 War

Contents

iv

Preface *by Rita R. Colwell, Sigma Xi President*

Sigma Xi, The Scientific Research Society has undertaken annual forums to promote public debate, stimulate research, and foster enlightened action on critical issues facing science and society in the decades ahead. In keeping with the renewal of its primary mission and expanding its horizons for the Second Century, topics with broad implications for the human family in the 21st century and beyond are addressed. Global change, and its ramifications on the human prospect, is clearly such an issue. The 1991 Sigma Xi Forum on *Global Change and the Human Prospect: Issues in Population, Science, Technology, and Equity* involves the sum of human activities — social, political, cultural, economic, and scientific.

The Forum proved a success from all measures, with 650 attendees, including leaders from around the world in academia, business, industry, and government. A series of plenary and break-out sessions were held. The participants explored the global change issues from the perspective of three important questions: What kind of world do we have? What kind of world do we want? What must we do to get there?

The Forum organizers and participants chose not to focus on the symptoms of global change, such as ozone depletion, pollution, global warming, or endangered species and habitats, since these have been addressed in detail at many other conferences and symposia in recent years. It was the intention to address the driving forces behind these and related problems in order to address their root causes.

The Forum was structured to include break-out groups, each of which developed recommendations for the scientific and engineering community, with respect to recommended actions and/or responses to global change. There was unanimity in the view that the decade of the 1990s provides extraordinary opportunities for making those decisions that will ensure a bright prospect for humankind.

Sustainable development, defined by David Pearce in this volume, is "economic and social change which gives rise to a sustained rising per capita level of well-being for people over time," i.e., in the language of the economist, it is "non-declining utility." To achieve sustainable development, the global trends in fertility and mortality, described by Dean T. Jamison and W.

Henry Mosley, need to be addressed. The population-environment debate requires delving deeper into the complexity of the issues, rather than trying to use mechanistic, predictive models to generate, at best, probable scenarios, as enunciated by Lourdes Arizpe and Margarita Velazquez. A new framework for the debate on population and environment must expand definitions of the issues and focus not only on population size, density, rate of increase, age distribution, sex ratios, but also on access to resources, livelihoods, social dimensions of gender, and structures of power.

As eloquently stated by Adnan Badran, UNESCO has a scientific contribution to make, as do UNEP, ICSU, and the entire family of international organizations. The United Nations Conference on Environment and Development (UNCED) is the first full-fledged United Nations conference on these topics at the summit level. It may, in fact, turn out to be the conference of the century.

The 1991 Sigma Xi Forum was intended to support and deepen the discussion at the June 1992 UNCED in Rio de Janeiro, Brazil. Individual members of Sigma Xi and the five organizations that co-sponsored the Forum: the American Association for the Advancement of Science (AAAS), the American Association of Engineering Societies (AAES), the Consortium of Social Science Associations (COSSA), the Council of Scientific Society Presidents (CSSP), and the Social Science Research Council (SSRC), shared the objective of initiating sustained consideration of the global change issues from the fullest perspective possible. More than 25 other professional societies also participated.

The success of the symposium is measured by the criteria given above, but also, significantly, by the thoughtful writings found in this volume. Discussion within the scientific and engineering community should be provoked, as well as among the many groups, both public and private, whose involvement at the organizational and individual levels is fundamentally important in finding solutions to the problems inherent in global change. It is hoped that all who read the chapters of this volume will, themselves, find new perspectives and renewed challenge to participate in what may prove to be the ultimate challenge to all humankind — producing a socially and economically sustainable world. Although tomorrow cannot be known, we can purposefully move to build a sustainable global society.

Foreword *by Thomas F. Malone, Steering Committee Chair*

At the Forum on Global Change and the Human Prospect, the community of natural, social and engineering sciences probed deeply into the forces underlying global changes that are now engaging worldwide attention. Many of these forces have improved the human condition. Apocalypse is *not* impending. An attractive human prospect *is* within reach. However, in several respects the world is embarked on a trajectory that *could* lead to severe problems. The task for our generation is to change the forces determining that trajectory so that its terminus is that attractive human prospect.

The 1990s constitute a window of opportunity. It can be described as *The Decade for Decisions*. The next century will be held hostage to decisions made and actions taken, or not taken, during this decade.

The scholarly community has, in the words of Derek Bok, a special opportunity to serve as "society's scouts," signaling impending problems and opportunities before they are generally perceived. Followed by actions, individually and collectively, these deliberations can be effective in constructively modifying the trajectory of human progress and provide robustness to cope with the inevitable "surprises."

The Forum gave a powerful message to its own community and to society by seeking the answers to three basic questions:

What kind of a world do we have?
What kind of a world do we want?
What must we do to get there?

WE HAVE

We have a world approaching a crossroads. The possibility exists that it could move forward in an unsustainable and inequitable mode.

The global population is doubling every few decades. It is likely to reach 10 billion by 2030. The energy- and technology-driven world economy that transforms natural resources into goods and services to meet human needs and wants is also doubling every few decades. It is expected to more than triple by 2030. More people every year, each making greater demands on planet Earth's life-support system, is *unsustainable* in the long run.

World Bank statistics tell us that for every person born in industrialized regions, 15 to 20 are born in developing regions where the population is already five times that in the industrialized part of the world. On the other hand, for every dollar added to each person's income in the developing countries, 15 to 20 dollars are added to the per-person income in the industrialized regions, where the income per person is already more than twenty times greater than in developing regions. Continuation or exacerbation of these disparities would lead to an increasingly *inequitable* world.

Environmental degradation, resource depletion and poverty plague the poor regions, with implications for the continued habitability of planet Earth. The methods of industrialization that built the economy in the richer regions leave residues that threaten the global environment. Thus, we have a disparate and divided world at just the time when common problems are signaling the onset of an era of greatly increased global interdependence, generating a need for greater international cooperation in the new *Age of Global Responsibility.*

But we also have a rapidly expanding knowledge base about our natural world and how to establish our place in it. The world storehouse of knowledge more than doubles each decade. It is already sufficient to enable us to influence human destiny. It has demonstrated a capability to improve the human condition. Data assembled by the UN Development Programme show that over the last three decades life expectancy has increased by 12 years for the world at large, and by 16 years in developing countries. The under-five mortality rate has been halved in most regions. Daily calory supply and adult literacy have improved everywhere except in Sub-Saharan Africa. World economic output per capita increased two and a half times for both the world as a whole and in all developing countries.

The power of deploying this knowledge in the human interest is becoming evident at a moment in history when the will to act on it is being fostered by the spread — sometimes haltingly, but inexorably — of individual freedom and responsibility, human rights and equality, democratic institutions and the emergence of a dynamic and increasingly sensitive system of private enterprise. What is now needed is a sustained series of modest but wise and imaginative actions constructed on this knowledge base, taken cooperatively, and motivated by the new vista of opportunities opening before us.

WE WANT

We want an equitable society in a sustainable environment. This is a world in which the needs and aspirations of the present generation are met without foreclosing options for future generations. This means both *intra*generational and *inter*generational equity. It is a world that accepts and welcomes diversity in cultures among societies and in accomplishments among individuals. It is one that discriminates sensitively between equity and complete equality. It welcomes constructive competition and imaginative entrepreneurship as stimuli to progress. It reconciles technological developments and quality of the environment.

It is a world that distinguishes between growth that seeks more of everything and human development that creates an environment enabling people, individually and collectively, to develop their full potential with a reasonable chance of leading productive and creative lives in accord with their needs, interests and talents. We want a world in which people live in harmony with each other and with nature. It is a world that pursues assiduously the elimination of absolute poverty wherever it occurs, assures human rights and freedom while emphasizing individual obligations to society. It is a world that recognizes that *economic* development must be fostered in ways that avoid the problems of the past while supporting *human* development.

WE MUST

To achieve a sustainable and equitable world, we must pursue deliberately, purposefully and simultaneously three objectives. We need:

To transform the energy- and technology-driven economy into one that is compatible with the assimilative capacity of the biosphere. Properly directed, technology is a powerful tool to influence constructively global change and human development;

To reconcile population growth with local, regional and global environmental limits; and

To reduce the growing disparity in the quality of life among parts of the world at different stages of economic development with conscious efforts directed toward the elimination of poverty.

Transformation of the goods- and services-producing system into one that is "environmentally benign" requires technological innovation in the flow of materials and energy in the industrial and agricultural processes, adequate information on potential environmental impacts, and proper accounting for those impacts on the total cost of production. These challenges are now being addressed. They require a synergistic interaction among the sectors of private business and industry, the research community and government. A critical issue from the standpoint of sustainability and equity is the long-term sources for energy. This is especially important in the Asian subcontinent.

Reconciliation of population growth with environmental limits can be achieved only if other actions are taken: economic development, improved infant and child mortality, responsible parenthood, and provision of services such as family planning, so that prospective parents have greater assurance that their children will survive and have meaningful educational and occupational opportunities. The issues of local, regional and global environmental limits need to be ascertained. A critical step in much of the world would be to assure women an equal role with men in societal affairs.

Reduction in the disparities in the quality of life among regions requires a judicious balance among a complex array of measures that include:

Improvement in the identification of indices that determine the quality of life;

Internal social and political renewal;

Equality for women;

Economic sufficiency through development of environmentally benign technological systems;

Continued reduction in fertility where the environmental stress from a large and growing population is high;

Restraint in consumer demands on natural resources where industrialization is highly advanced;

Revitalization of the instrumentalities for economic and technological interaction between industrialized and industrializing countries; and

Innovation in the array of institutions dedicated to developing and utilizing knowledge.

THE KNOWLEDGE POTENTIAL

The overarching need is to bring to bear on these problems the expanding storehouse of knowledge about the world in which we live and our role in that world. This requires a balance among the tasks of extending, integrating, disseminating and applying this knowledge.

We need to extend and deepen our understanding of human development — and not just the admittedly important economic part — that measures progress toward an attractive human prospect. The objective of human development is to expand individual capacity to influence human destiny by providing access to income and employment opportunities, education, health, a clean and safe physical environment and political freedom.

The issue of global equity will demand new ways of thinking about growth, and involve a value- and ethics-laden distinction between economic development and human development. The concept of "limits to growth" needs to be reexamined with regard to the robustness of the biosphere and photosynthetic productivity, rather than simply in relation to the stock of mineral resources.

We need to understand the dynamics of population growth and distribution and the consequent increased demands on the life-support capacity of the biosphere. The task of understanding reproductive biology and applying that knowledge to the stabilization of world population in a manner compatible with evolving individual mores is a formidable challenge. It will require the cooperation of every field of intellectual enquiry.

We also need to know much more about the flow of energy and materials in the expanding technological systems that convert renewable and nonrenewable resources into goods and services and the impact of by-products of these systems on both local and global environments. We must to be able to anticipate and assess anthropogenic perturbations in the biosphere such as (a) the appropriation of biomass for human use, (b) global greenhouse-gas warming, (c) depletion of stratospheric ozone, (d) degradation of natural ecosystems, and (e) species extinction. We need to develop ways to incorporate the true costs to society of environmental deterioration and the drawdown of renewable resources and what this means to future generations. We must be able to assess realistically the cost and benefits of energy alternatives.

We must know more about the interaction among disparate demographic and economic growth rates in different parts of the world, and their implications for social instability and international security.

These knowledge requirements underscore the imperative of addressing the integration of knowledge. The contributions of individual investigators in extending the frontiers of knowledge need to be augmented by new modes of interdisciplinary cooperation among natural scientists, social scientists, engineers, humanists and scholars in values and ethics, and decision makers in the public and the private sectors. Institutional renewal and innovation will be necessary.

If it is to the storehouse of knowledge that we must turn in order to assure an attractive human prospect, dissemination of that knowledge through formal and informal education are matters of vital concern. This topic has many strands. An ubiquitous task is to integrate the findings and culture of science into the intellectual development of students at all levels of the educational system. The boundaries among traditional categories of subject matter need to be softened and the several topics in science, mathematics and technology must be related to each other and to the social and ethical domains. A prerequisite for alleviating the problems associated with poverty in the least-developed countries is a strong and effective educational system. These countries where the knowledge needs are greatest have less than six percent of the world's research community.

The final task is the application of knowledge. Deferring all decisions until the edifice of knowledge has been completed will not correct the flawed trajectory of human progress. The art of decision making under uncertainty has a long history; the science of that activity is still in a rudimentary stage and deserves imaginative thought. We must not be driven to poor choices by emotional convictions. But we must not be deferred from action by rigid ideological beliefs.

Preoccupied for centuries with the ebb and flow of economic and military power, the world has not yet addressed the potential of knowledge — its extension, integration, application and dissemination — as a vital contributor to enhancement of the human prospect.

INSTITUTIONAL INNOVATION

A particular urgency exists for institutional innovation to link industrialized and industrializing countries in the task of bringing knowledge to bear on assuring equity in the access to the life-supporting resources of planet Earth. The case was set forth persuasively by the World Commission on Environment and Development in the report *Our Common Future* in these words: "A major reorientation is needed in many policies and institutional arrangements at the international as well as national levels because the rate of (global) change is outstripping the ability of scientific disciplines and our current capabilities to assess and advise. A new international programme for cooperation among largely nongovernmental organizations, scientific bodies, and industry groups should therefore be established for this purpose."

A pressing need exists during *The Decade for Decisions* to forge new partnerships of effort among (a) governments charged with attending to the commonweal, (b) business and industry responsible for the production of goods and services, and with special interest in technological innovation and (c) universities and research institutions which serve as generators and custodians of knowledge.

The Scientific Committee for the International Geosphere-Biosphere Programme of the International Council of Scientific Unions has set in motion a process to establish a global system of regional networks dedicated to analysis, research and training on issues of global change. Identified by the acronym **START** (SysTem, Analysis, Research, Training), the network undergirds an ambitious program to describe and understand the interactive physical, chemical, biological and social processes that determine the unique environment for life on planet Earth and the changes that are occurring in the total Earth system as a result of human activity. It has the potential of bringing together the physical, biological, social and engineering sciences with participation from the public and private sectors to develop policy options.

In essence, the view is emerging that a habitable planet Earth will be the aggregate of an array of perhaps a dozen or so diverse but closely linked habitable regions. The entire array would be pursuing the common objective of an equitable society and a sustainable environment. In a world in which confrontation and conflict are moving from a bipolar mode to decentralized regional levels, the need for unifying themes in pursuit of a common regional vision in the global context would have a salutary effect.

Some tasks would be best carried out as internationalized endeavors. The effective utilization of the enormous power of remote sensing from space to understand and anticipate changes in the physical characteristics of the earth will require an internationalization of space programs which will challenge the organizational and political capacity of sovereign nations. That could well be one important heritage of the International Space Year in 1992.

Other activities will be shared responsibilities. The ultimate transition to a post-fossil-fuel society will require combining diverse regional studies and an international effort of an unprecedented dimension to develop and articulate a world energy strategy. To reconcile world energy needs with sound environmental practices in a world undergoing nearly daily political change will require an effort in technological innovation that could serve as a unifying activity to replace preoccupation with competing interests.

It is time to put in place the institutional arrangements to realize the potential of an attractive human prospect that an expanding knowledge base has brought within reach. This needs to be done nationally and internationally. It is timely for the community of natural, social and engineering sciences to address this matter. The complex issues of global change require a profound change in our way of thinking — *metanoia*. The *Age of Global Responsibility* emerging from new dimensions of global interdependence will require a unifying global ethic as the basis for a sustainable and equitable world.

The Forum is one discrete step toward changing our way of thinking. The Earth Summit in Brazil in June 1992, the UN Conference on Environment and Development, will be another. In each instance, it will be the subsequent — and specific — actions of individuals working in concert through their associations and professional societies that will be critical in changing the trajectory of human progress.

INDIVIDUAL RESPONSE

The three basic questions posed at the forum provide a framework for reflection by each individual on their personal role in extending, integrating, applying and disseminating knowledge. The impact of individuals is leveraged through associations and professional societies. The recommendations developed at the forum provide an agenda deserving continuing attention during *The Decade for Decisions*. Each organization can best determine its own mode of response. There is great strength in diversity. Cultivation of interdisciplinary efforts and innovation in new modalities of interaction with other sectors of society can take many forms. of central importance is the suggestion at the forum that each scientist "tithe" his or her time and devote this segment to becoming informed and active on this paramount issue of our generation.

The chapters and clubs of Sigma Xi have a special opportunity and responsibility by virtue of their unique geographic outreach into every sector of society. Sigma Xi culminated its centennial observance with a commitment to enlarging its mission to embrace the challenge of fostering, world-wide, a dynamic and creative interaction among science, technology and society.

In 1987, chapters and clubs became familiar at their annual meeting with the International Geosphere-Biosphere Program, *A Study of Global Change*. In 1988, science literacy was the theme. In 1989, science education and participation with AAAS, the

Smithsonian Institution and the National Academies in the *Forum on Global Change* and *Our Common Future* engaged their attention.

A new dynamism is emerging in the Society with the relocation of its headquarters to the stimulating environment of the Research Triangle Park and the planning for the Sigma Xi Center to widen and deepen the discussions at this Forum. The outlines of the *New Agenda* that was the hallmark of the centennial observance is emerging and will be reflected in the agendas of chapter and club meetings during this decade.

A number of signs suggest that the social contract forged more than four decades ago between the research community and society is up for renewal. Some of the terms are becoming clear. They are of interest to us all. They will involve summoning our individual and collective wisdom and will to influence global change in the interests of the human prospect. The dimensions of the challenge are matched only by the magnitude of the opportunities.

Two centuries ago, Immanuel Kant framed another set of questions: What *can* I know? What *ought* I do? What *may* I hope? These questions have a special relevance to the response of individuals to the challenge of *Global Change and the Human Prospect.*

Section I

What Kind of World Do We Have?

Global Trends in Fertility and Mortality: Implications for Policy Formulation

Dean T. Jamison and W. Henry Mosley

I. INTRODUCTION

The policy debate in international health has often been polarized around conflicting viewpoints on such issues as preventive versus curative services, selective versus comprehensive primary health care, or integrated versus vertical programs. As we approach the 21st century, it is becoming clear that framing the issues in these terms will not enlighten the policy process, primarily because it limits the options largely to actions that can be carried out directly by ministries of health. Profound social and economic transformations are projected to impact on health in the developing countries in the 1990s and beyond; implications for the epidemiological profiles of these countries will be dramatic.[2,3,4] Our purpose in this paper is to provide an overview of these changes. This leads to the arguments that a more comprehensive analytical approach is required to formulate population and health policies that will not only respond to, but actually guide, the development process to maximize its health gains, minimize its potential adverse consequences, and deal cost-effectively with the emerging quantitative importance of noncommunicable diseases.

Over the next decade, there will indeed remain perhaps thirty to forty countries in the lowest income bracket where the health problems will be dominated by the infectious and parasitic diseases of childhood, along with under nutrition and high fertility.[5] Most of these are in Sub-Saharan Africa and South Asia, and intervention strategies must continue to focus on establishing

Dean Jamison is former Senior Economist for the World Bank and Professor of Public Health at the University of California at Los Angeles.

Henry Mosley is Professor and Chairman of the Department of Population Dynamics at the Johns Hopkins University School of Hygiene and Public Health.

basic infrastructures and delivering established, low-cost technologies.[6] At the same time, however, there will be a larger group of countries, predominantly in Latin America and East Asia, that are newly emerging into the middle income category. Most of these countries are not free of the infectious diseases, yet at the same time are beginning to face a new set of health problems related to rapid urbanization and industrialization.[3,7,8] These include injuries, occupational diseases and, increasingly, preventable chronic diseases among an aging population.[9] Such a growing epidemiological diversity among and within countries in the developing world demands a flexible approach to international health policy formulation. Before further discussing epidemiological trends, we set the context by delineating the tasks required for health policy formulation.

II. POLICY DEVELOPMENT

It is useful to consider health policy development as involving three complementary tasks: <u>first</u>, identifying the major disease problems, assessing their social and economic consequences, and evaluating the costs and effectiveness of alternative intervention strategies; <u>second</u>, designing health care delivery systems including establishing the human and physical infrastructures, providing for drugs and logistical support, and developing managerial capacities and funding mechanisms; and <u>third</u>, defining and choosing what governments can do through the full range of policy instruments that are at their disposal in the areas of persuasion, taxation, regulation and the provision of services.

Like a three-legged stool, coherent health policies require a solid foundation of technical analysis in all three areas in order to identify effective strategies and establish sustainable programs. Through the 1960s and 1970s, the second task, designing institution-based delivery systems (generally following a Western medical model), was the dominant theme in health policy formulation for the developing world. It was in this period that the policy debates centered around the relative allocation of resources for preventive versus curative services and, when disease eradication programs were being implemented, vertical versus integrated programs. The Alma Ata Conference on Primary Health Care in

1978 introduced the principle of "Health For All."[10] Conceptually this encompassed all health problems in the population, was community-based, and involved all sectors of government. Given the resource constraints in the health sector, many health professionals and donors narrowed the agenda, limiting consideration to childhood communicable diseases.[11] This led to selective primary health care programs, focusing largely on population-based technical interventions, such as oral rehydration therapy and immunizations for child survival,[12] which, in turn, led to policy debates about the relative merits of selective versus comprehensive primary health care interventions.[13]

The third task, assessing the full array of government instruments available, particularly those outside the traditional purview of ministries of health (such as regulation and taxation) to protect and promote the health of populations, is not well established in much of the developing world. The full range of instruments is, however, fully entering the public debate on policy in a number of industrialized countries. For example, in the United States the process was initiated with the publication of "Healthy People: The Surgeon General's Report on Health Promotion and Disease" in 1979, which defined a set of health goals for 1990 for infants, children, adolescents, adults and the aged.[14] To achieve these goals, fifteen priority areas for intervention were identified and grouped under three strategic approaches: preventive health services, health protection, and health promotion.[15] Preventive health services included primary preventive interventions, such as immunizations and family planning, secondary prevention for conditions like high blood pressure, as well as curative services for such conditions as sexually transmitted diseases. Health protection encompassed areas where regulation and taxation would be important, including toxic agent control, occupational safety, accident prevention, and fluoridation. The health promotion strategies involving behavioral changes related to smoking, alcohol and drug abuse, diet and exercise required government interventions, not only in education, but also through regulation and taxation.

Three factors have been key to the successful mobilization of public and professional interest and debate in the U.S.[16] First, there was a clear definition of the health problems of concern and their social and economic, as well as medical, determinants. Second, the fifteen priority areas selected for health improvement were further subdivided into 227 health promotion objectives for the 1980s.[17] These detailed objectives represented precise, quantifiable management strategies which were realistic in terms of resource constraints and time frame for implementation, yet demanding enough to push the system to new levels of capability. Third, the process of problem identification and health policy formulation involved the broadest participation of all segments of society.[18] On the one hand, a considerable breadth of expertise was drawn from the fields of epidemiology, management sciences, economics, behavioral sciences and communications to define the problems and issues to be addressed and propose strategic alternatives. On the other hand, there was broad political and public participation in devising solutions. The necessity of this third step (which is rare in developing countries) cannot be overemphasized: the policy formulation process should be an educational experience about the health problems for all concerned, since it will be necessary to reach a wide national consensus on issues, policies and implementation strategies which will cut across many sectors, including finance, trade, agriculture, transportation, industry, education, and others. It must also be stressed that successful mobilization of debate and concern is far from sufficient, as the example of the U.S. also, unfortunately, attests. Where the political will for public action is lacking and resources are unallocated, health outcome indicators, such as infant mortality rates among minority groups, can remain shamefully high.

A first task in a comprehensive analysis of the health sector requires an estimation of the burden of disease in the population. It is the extraordinary pace of change in the composition of disease burden — induced by changes in the levels of fertility and mortality — that we review in this paper. The pace of change does, of course, differ enormously across developing countries; hence it is unrealistic and, indeed, inappropriate to come up with global policies. Rather, what is presented here is a conceptual and analytical approach with illustrations of the range of factors which must be considered in any particular setting. This approach takes into account that there will be a continuing evolution of disease control priorities, based on the social and economic transformations countries are undergoing with their accompanying demographic and epidemiologic transitions.[19]

III. THE CHANGING DETERMINANTS OF DISEASE

A first determinant of the changing health picture developing countries will be experiencing is the demographic transition, largely driven by the rate of fertility decline. This will produce major changes in the age structure of populations, which will have a large impact on the health picture.[20] Figure 1 illustrates the mechanisms through which fertility decline is both determined and, in turn, influences age structure; the set of relationships depicted has come to be known as the 'health transition'. Table 1, taken from World Bank projections for the period 1985 to 2015, illustrates the changing demographic and health picture for developing countries worldwide.[21] Figures 2 and 3 illustrate these trends with data and projections from the United Nations (Figure 2 on trends in fertility) and the DHS Surveys (Figure 3 on trends in under-5 mortality rates). Overall, slower growth of the childhood population, coupled with declining death rates, are projected to reduce health problems for all age groups. But this is more than counterbalanced by the rapid increase in the adult and aging population.

Regionally, the picture is much more diverse. The population of children under five in Latin America and Asia will increase by only 2% to 5%, respectively, in size. By contrast, this age group is projected to grow 38% in the Middle East and 70% in Sub-Saharan Africa from 1985 to 2015. Clearly, the future requirements for maternal and child health services will be quite different across these regions. At the other end of the age spectrum, a very different picture emerges. In all of these regions the populations over age 65 will be dramatically growing in size, with projected increases ranging from 134% to 164%. This continuing growth in the older age groups is due to a phenomenon called the "momentum" of population growth. It is a consequence of the large numbers of children born in the past, when fertility was high, who advance through older age groups over time. The result is that essentially all developing countries will have to provide for the health needs of a rapidly increasing adult and aged population for many years into the future.[4] A broad assessment of how to meet these needs may be found in Feachem, et al. (forthcoming).[22] At the same time, in those countries where the fertility transition is barely underway (largely in Sub-Saharan Africa), policymakers must simultaneously plan to continue to rapidly expand maternal and child health services.

A second determinant of the changing health picture is the major social and economic trends which are transforming the risk factors themselves.[23] The most obvious indicator of these trends is the shift from rural to urban living. In 1985, barely over 30% of the population of the less developed regions lived in urban areas, but this pattern is changing rapidly.[24] The urban population will reach 40% by the year 2000, and surpass 50% by the year 2015. Already seven of the world's twelve megacities (population 10-million or more) are in developing countries. By the year 2000 the developing world will add six more cities to this number.

A shift from a rural subsistence economy to an urban market-oriented industrial economy is generally associated with reductions in risks to communicable diseases because of better sanitation in urban areas. At the same time, however, economic growth brings with it new health problems.[25] Very high rates of injuries related to motor vehicles, industrial accidents, and toxic chemicals (e.g. pesticides) are usually seen in developing countries because of a lack of resources and institutions to establish and enforce safety measures.[26] Undernutrition may diminish because of improved markets, only to be replaced by overnutrition with rising risks of death due to obesity, hypertension, atherosclerosis, and diabetes.[27] Rising incomes also bring changes in lifestyle, including increases in smoking, alcohol use, and substance abuse, all of which are expected to increase the risk for chronic diseases.

An analysis of the tobacco-related diseases provides an excellent illustration of how a disease-oriented approach can inform health policy.[28] In the United States, it is now well established that tobacco use is responsible for more than 30% of all cancer deaths, as well as being among the strongest risk factors for chronic obstructive pulmonary disease and ischemic heart disease.[29,30] In recent years, rising rates of lung cancer associated with cigarette consumption have been observed in Japan, Singapore, and Shanghai.[31] A recent analysis by the World Bank has documented a direct relationship between tobacco consumption and higher levels of national income among developing countries.[32] This relationship is not coincidental. Rather, it is driven by promotion, pricing, tax policies, and even international trade relations. The impact of the latter is best attested by the rapid increases in cigarette consumption among young people in several east Asian countries where multinational tobacco corporations have recently opened new markets, assisted in some cases by aggressive (even coercive) trade policies of the United States government.[33]

Taking China as an example, Peto projects that, if current smoking trends continue due to a failure to introduce the array of policies necessary to reduce tobacco consumption in the next several years, an estimated two million Chinese men will die annually from tobacco-related health problems by the year 2025.[34] Cumulatively, one may anticipate fifty million tobacco-related deaths among the 500 million Chinese now under the age of twenty. National policies to protect populations from tobacco-related diseases clearly must move beyond the usual realm of the health sector into areas of regulation and taxation of the industrial enterprise related to the manufacture and distribution of tobacco products and, in many countries, including the United States, ultimately into a restructuring of rural economies where tobacco is produced.[35,36,37]

The AIDS epidemic provides another illustration of some of the links between economic development and disease transmission. In assessing the situation in Sub-Saharan Africa, Over and Piot document a strong correlation between the rate of HIV infection in 18 cities, a high ratio of males to females in urban centers and a low level of female education.[38] The implications of these findings are that AIDS transmission is facilitated by development strategies which favor males for urban employment. This generates a high demand for prostitutes; prostitution, in turn, is facilitated by low levels of female education, so that women have few alternative economic opportunities open to them. An AIDS-control program must go beyond promoting the use of condoms and treating STDs and consider broader social policies relating to female education and labor force participation.

IV. EPIDEMIOLOGIC POLARIZATION

The epidemiologic transition in the developing world is neither a steady nor a uniform process. The great variations in life expectancy between countries attests to this. As of 1988, a dozen Sub-Saharan African countries still had life expectancies under 50 years, while an equal number of countries in Latin America and Asia (including China) had life expectancies of 70 years or greater.[39] Figure 4 illustrates both this great regional disparity in life expectancy and, importantly, the generally very favorable trends that were already indicated (in Figure 3) for under-5 mortality rates. Additionally, within developing countries (and developed countries as well) wide disparities in health conditions across different social classes or different regions are not uncommon. Frenk and colleagues have referred to these disparities as "epidemiologic polarization" and "epidemiological stagnation".[3,40] These disparities are not limited to the infectious diseases of infants and children, but include the chronic diseases of adults as well.[7,22] A centrally important conclusion for health policy is that in most developing countries pre- and post-epidemiological transition problems will co-exist.[40] As Foege and Henderson have observed, the developing countries "...will not have the luxury of dealing with two kinds of problems sequentially. For the remainder of this century they will be dealing with both simultaneously."[41]

The increasing burden of chronic disease is initially likely to affect the relatively more affluent and politically vocal older groups, who are growing in numbers. This being the case, governments will need to take great care to assure that the infectious diseases which predominantly affect children and the poor are not neglected in the face of resource demands placed in large measure by the relatively better off. The challenge is to develop equitable policies and strategies to meet these unprecedented conditions in the developing world.

V. ASSESSING DISEASE CONTROL PRIORITIES

The World Bank, as a part of an exercise to assess the cost and effectiveness of alternative intervention strategies for over two dozen acute and chronic diseases of adults and children, commissioned a series of analytical studies, each co-authored by individuals combining economic, epidemiological, and clinical expertise. The motivation for this exercise was to initiate development of a policy response to the epidemiologic changes that have just been described. Cost effectiveness was expressed in terms of dollar cost per discounted healthy life years gained (DHLY). The details of these studies are reported elsewhere.[42] Several general conclusions which emerged from this undertaking will be described here in terms of their implications for the process of policy development in developing countries.

First, while child survival interventions (immunizations, provision of antenatal and delivery care, vitamin A supplementation, improvements in domestic hygiene, oral rehydration therapy (ORT) for diarrheal diseases in high mortality environments, and antibiotic therapy for acute respiratory infections) appear to be highly cost effective ($5-50 per DHLY), there were a range of adult health interventions which were estimated to be equally cost-effective. Among the most prominent are: anti-smoking campaigns plus tobacco taxes, passive case finding and short-course chemotherapy for tuberculosis, the targeted management of sexually transmitted diseases, cataract surgery, the use of condoms to prevent HIV transmission, and hepatitis B immunization to prevent liver cancer and cirrhosis. At the other extreme, the cost per DHLY for a number of adult diseases is so high (greater than $1000) that public policy should probably discourage their use in settings where health resources are severely constrained. Among these are coronary bypass surgery, mitral valve replacement for rheumatic heart disease, medical management for hypertension, and tertiary management of lung, liver, esophageal, and stomach cancer. With reference to cancer, it should be noted that cancer pain control appears to be a relatively cost-effective intervention for adults ($150 per DHLY) reaching the same level as: maternity care services for maternal mortality; public preventive campaigns to prevent cardiovascular disease; medical management of angina; and insulin management of insulin-dependent diabetes melitis.

This analytical approach revealed a number of neglected and emerging health problems which should be accorded far higher priority. Topping the list of emerging problems are the tobacco-related diseases which, interestingly enough, were not even mentioned in the 1980 World Bank Health Sector Report.[43] Tuberculosis appears to be the greatest "neglected" disease.[44] In 1990 there will be an estimated 8.4 million new cases and 2.7 million deaths, over two-thirds of which will be among productive adults (ages 15-59), primarily the poor. Significantly, this disease alone accounts for about 37% of an estimated 7 million avoidable adult deaths in the developing world.

Some findings challenge the current international donor commitment to global priority setting. Provision of ORT in low mortality environments (at $200 per DHLY) is estimated to be about 20 times less cost effective than tuberculosis control (using passive case detection and short course chemotherapy) or leprosy rehabilitation. Even cervical cancer screening (Papanicolaou smears) are estimated to be an equally good buy for the money. In high mortality environments, in contrast, ORT can be quite cost-effective, underscoring the need for analysis at the country or even district level.

A major observation from the World Bank exercise is the paucity of empirical data from a majority of the developing countries about most of the major chronic diseases of adults.[22,45] Considering that, on a global level, more than half the world's deaths due to cancers and cardiovascular diseases, three-fourth of the injury deaths, and 85% of the chronic obstructive pulmonary disease deaths occur in developing countries, the virtual absence of any information about the levels, trends and determinants of these conditions for the majority of the world's population is truly tragic. Given this lack of developing country data, most of the estimates of the cost-effectiveness of interventions for the World Bank study had to be derived from research carried out in the industrialized world. While these estimates are probably reasonable in grossly illustrating the relative cost-effectiveness of alternative interventions, the actual cost-effectiveness of a particular intervention could easily vary by two- to tenfold or more in any given situation, depending on a host of local factors. For example, with interventions, like immunizations, that require total population coverage, cost-effectiveness is strongly conditioned by the underlying level of disease incidence and case fatality rates. For therapeutic interventions, cost-effectiveness is not only determined by the institutional costs of reaching the target group and then making the correct diagnosis, but also by the probability that appropriate therapy will be prescribed by the caregiver and that the patient will actually comply with the treatment regimen.[46,47,48,49] Similarly, the costs of monitoring and enforcing regulatory approaches depend upon the reach and capability of the governmental infrastructure.

VI. IMPLICATIONS FOR NATIONAL GOVERNMENTS

It should be clear that there is an urgent need to reassess health sector priorities in developing countries. National health policy assessment can be usefully informed with a consideration of global trends and findings such as presented above, but it must quickly evolve to a critical analysis of the local epidemiological picture cast in its social-cultural, administrative, economic, and political context. Such an approach to policy formulation must begin by assessing the full range of health problems in a society; examining broadly their demographic, social, and economic determinants; and identifying alternative courses of action in all of these areas which could improve the situation. This last step must take into consideration the costs and effectiveness of all possible instruments of government intervention, including taxation and regulation as well as persuasion and the direct provision of services.[4]

Many governments will need to create new institutions and reconfigure old ones to build the capacities required for policy analysis and implementation. Among the analytical and technical capacities required are the following:

Demographic analysis — These capabilities provide the fundamental underpinnings for a population-based health system. Demographic data provide the basis for designing intervention strategies as well as for assessing the impact of the disease burden on the population.

Epidemiological surveillance — While some epidemiological surveillance is carried out in most developing countries, it is usually limited to selected infectious diseases. These capacities will need to be greatly strengthened as health program strategies move more toward interventions involving regulation, taxation, subsidies, and information programs, in order to reduce acute and chronic disease risks by changing behaviors and improving environmental conditions.

Economic and financial analysis — These capabilities will be essential to measure the cost-effectiveness of alternative intervention strategies, as well as to assess the overall claim of the health sector on scarce development resources.

Health technology assessment and control — Institutional capabilities in this area must include not only the assessment of the effectiveness of new drugs, vaccines or treatments, but also their costs and benefits when introduced into the health system.

Environmental monitoring and control — In most developing countries, capabilities in this area must be greatly expanded beyond the traditional water and sanitation activities to monitor and control (through taxation as well as regulation) a much broader range of environmental risks, including air pollution, toxic wastes, traffic hazards, and other injury risks.

Occupational safety — Rapid urbanization and industrialization in developing countries is often associated with risks of work-related injury five to ten times higher than in developed countries. There is a major need to develop the capacity to monitor and control occupational health risks.

While many of these institutional capacities exist in some measure in health ministries, their functions are limited for a variety of reasons, including lack of professionally qualified personnel, limited resources and, particularly, lack of enforceable statutory authority. If health systems are to be transformed to meet the challenges of the future, a high priority must be given to empowering health ministries to carry out the monitoring and regulatory tasks needed to effectively function in new areas. In addition, mechanisms need to be established that will give them an appropriate voice in tax policy. Ultimately these capacities will need to be developed at regional and local levels within countries, as well as at the national level.

VII. IMPLICATIONS FOR INTERNATIONAL AID

Official development financing for health by bilateral and multilateral donors in 1986 amounted to $3.7 billion, with the U.S. contribution accounting for 16% of the total.[50] While external support represents only a small fraction of the total public and private sector health expenditures in developing countries, in fact, because much of the donor assistance is directed toward the poorest countries, its proportional impact in influencing health policies and program strategies is relatively large. This is particularly true when it promotes policies which lead to a reallocation of national resources. The impact of the donor driven child survival initiative in promoting immunizations and oral rehydration therapy worldwide is an excellent illustration of this.[51]

In looking to the future, it is useful to categorize international aid on the basis of whether its objective is to: 1) support the provision of services; 2) influence the policy environment; or 3) support research. Table 2 divides approaches to meeting these three objectives into two modalities of assistance: program implementation and capacity strengthening. Program implementation is largely oriented toward short-term results, while capacity strengthening generally requires long-term investments in institutional development. Traditionally, the dominant role of international assistance has been to provide services and related commodities where they were unavailable or inadequate; most donor support to child survival programs falls in this category. Recently, more attention is being given to structuring aid to change the policy environment, either directly, for example, by channeling more support to private and non-profit NGO sectors, or indirectly, by attaching conditions to aid packages, for example, by requiring cost recovery or extension of services to underserved populations. Presently only a small fraction of aid is directed toward research, much of which, in fact, is in specialized programs such as the Tropical Disease Research Programme or in a few institutions like the International Center for Diarrheal Disease Research, Bangladesh.[52]

The earlier discussion has highlighted the fact that developing countries are now moving through the epidemiologic transition at very different paces and often incompletely. As a result, there is a great diversity both in health conditions and in institutional capacities among and within countries.[2] This creates a far more diffuse planning environment than existed when most of these countries were still in a pre-transitional stage two or three decades earlier. No longer can a few strategic objectives command central importance for health policy. Rather, a much broader range of relatively less prominent health conditions and associated interventions will compete for resources and attention. In light of this, and given the fact that extremely little is known about the levels, trends, and determinants of the majority of diseases afflicting populations in the developing world, the conclusion is inescapable that, as far as donor assistance is concerned, far higher priority should be given to research, both building research capacity and conducting research to strengthen the formulation of health policy. This, in fact, is the conclusion reached by the Commission on Health Research for Development in its recent report.[52] The Commission specifically placed a high priority on local epidemiological and operational analyses, which they labeled as "Essential National Health Research" (ENHR).

Broadening the array of diseases for consideration to encompass all ages and expanding the arena of policy options to include the full range of instruments for government intervention will demand a diversity of analytical skills. National governments will require broad technical competence, not only in the biomedical and clinical sciences, including epidemiology, but also in economics, sociology, anthropology, the management sciences, and communication. In most countries, new institutions may need to be developed. The international donor community generally, and the United States in particular, could most effectively use its limited resources in the areas of education, training, research, and technical assistance, where it has strong comparative advantage.[53] Furthermore, because most of the major disease problems are actually of global concern (e.g. tobacco-related diseases, substance abuse, AIDS, injuries, occupational diseases, cardiovascular disease, cancer, malnutrition), much could be gained through international collaborative endeavors in these disease control efforts.

VIII. CONCLUSION

For over a decade the international public health community has given a priority to the communicable childhood diseases. This has been appropriate. The problems are major, the technological and epidemiological tools have become powerful, and the payoff for adapting and applying what is known is high. While the implementation strategy for selective primary health care as originally proposed by Walsh and Warren may have been oversimplified and too narrowly concerned with infectious diseases, the problem-oriented, population-based conceptual approach is fundamentally correct.[11,54] Furthermore, as more and more governments have seriously addressed the problem of child survival, the range of interventions has broadened.[55] For example, diarrhea control programs have moved from simply relying on packets of oral rehydration salts to the use of homemade fluids, the dietary management of diarrhea, the promotion of personal hygiene, and use of soap. More importantly, policy recommendations supporting child survival have now expanded widely, encompassing such issues as female education and the status of women.

The rapid demographic transition that many developing countries are undergoing is now producing great epidemiological diversity among developing countries; this demands that health policymakers consider a broader range of options. Over the next twenty-five years, it is not unreasonable to project a 50% to 60% decline in the number of deaths among infants and children, related to advances in child health coupled with rapidly declining birth rates, which will stabilize the numbers of newborns from year to year over much of the world. Overall, however, there will be a rise in the total number of deaths as the population evolves toward an older age structure. The epidemiological transition is not occurring uniformly, however, and most countries will have a large lingering burden of communicable diseases among children, particularly in Sub-Saharan Africa where the fertility transition has hardly begun. This situation will impose the greatest challenge on health systems operating under constrained resources to select the most effective and efficient means of disease prevention, case management, and rehabilitation.

It must be stressed that extending the range of choices means not only choosing to implement new initiatives but also choosing to reduce investments of public funds in health care activities that are clearly not cost-effective. While this may be difficult, given the traditions of Western medical practice, the fundamental issues of equity as well as efficiency are involved. Efficient resource allocation is desirable in every sector. In the health sector, however, in a very direct way, unnecessary death, disability, and illness occur if resources are committed to one intervention when another has higher health gains per unit of expenditure. The human cost of uneconomic resource allocation is very real and very large. Perhaps even more than in other sectors, then, the imperative exists for policymakers in the health sector to undertake constant assessment of intervention cost-effectiveness.

Probably the most important advance in policy formulation that could come from a disease-control strategic approach is a willingness to consider a range of options available to governments beyond the direct provision of health services. Particularly important as countries are moving through an accelerated process of economic development is the judicious use of regulation, legislation, taxation and subsidies to promote or discourage enterprises, activities, or behaviors which may have health consequences. Also, the importance of mass communication for social mobilization to promote health cannot be over-emphasized. A high priority problem demanding such multi-faceted policy intervention and global cooperation is tobacco consumption.

It is universally recognized that improved health in the broadest sense is a fundamental indicator of the development process. As the Nobel Laureate T. W. Schultz observed, "...the wealth of nations (has) come to be predominantly the acquired abilities of people -- their education, experience, skills, and health".[56] The task of health policy is to define clear, realistic, and measurable objectives which can guide the development process toward effectively and efficiently producing good health for all. In doing so, health policy needs integration, as we have stressed, into a broader range of environmental and economic policies; in this sense, integration of thinking about health into the recently proposed "START" initiative would provide an attractive approach.[57]

Table 1: Health Problems of Different Age Groups

Age Group	Population in Developing Countries, millions		Deaths in Developing Countries, millions		Important Health Problems	
					Problems on the Unfinished Agenda	Emerging Problems
	1985	2015	1985	2015		
Young children (0 - 4 years)	490	626	14.6	7.5	Diarrheal disease ARI Measles, tetanus, polio PEM Malaria Micronutrient deficiencies	Injury Learning disability
School-age children (5 - 14 years)	885	1196	1.6	1.3	Schistosomiasis Geohelminth infection Micronutrient deficiencies	Learning disability
Young adults (15 - 44 years)	1667	2918	5.0	6.0	Maternal mortality Malaria Tuberculosis Excess fertility	Injury AIDS STDs Mental Illness
Middle-aged (45 - 64 years)	474	1131	5.9	10.4		Cardiovascular disease Cancers Diabetes COPD
Elderly (65+ years)	153	358	11.0	22.5		Disability Depression Cataract
TOTALS	3669	6229	37.9	47.7		

<u>Source</u>: See Jamison and Mosley[1].

<u>Note</u>: Many of the conditions for older age groups manifest themselves clinically long after the processes leading to the clinical condition have been initiated; preventive intervention will, therefore, need to be directed to younger ages.

Table 2: Instruments of Aid

Objective	Modality of Assistance	
	Program Implementation	**Capacity Strengthening**
1. Service Delivery	Supports acquisition of drugs, equipment, and technical assistance for delivery of EPI, vector control programs, hospital services, etc.	Invests in institutional development and staff training to improve efficacy of service delivery -- e.g. through improved logistics and supply systems.
2. Policy Improvement	Identifies specific areas of policy improvement (e.g. tobacco advertising bans or introduction of cost-recovery mechanisms) and includes them (usually with conditionality) as part of an assistance package.	Invests in development of policy and planning departments in ministries or universities; invests in staff training and advanced education.
3. Undertaking Research (including epidemiologic, evaluational and economic analyses)	Conducts (perhaps with involvement of aid agency or expatriate staff) research or analyses to strengthen formulation of policy or delivery of service.	Invests in national (and international) capacity for undertaking research relevant to epidemiological and economic conditions of developing countries. This capacity strengthening involves both institutional and human resource development.

Source: Jamison and Mosley[1].

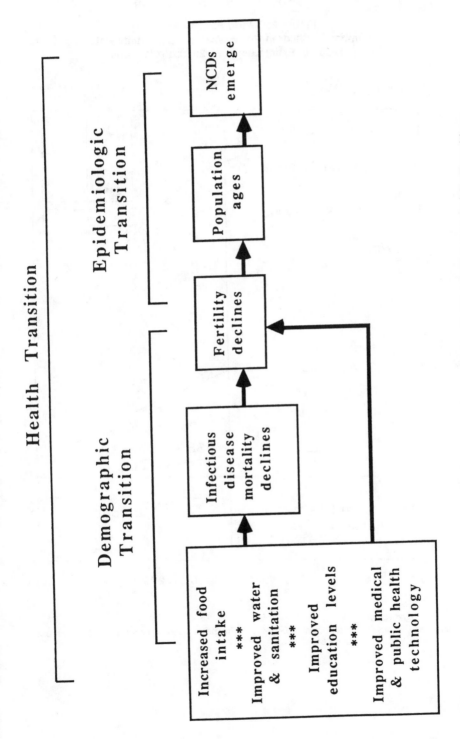

Figure 1: Relations Among the Demographic, Epidemiologic and Health Transitions

Figure 2: World Fertility Trends.
Number of Children Per Woman (Total Fertility Rate);
1950-85: Estimates; 1985-2020: Projections

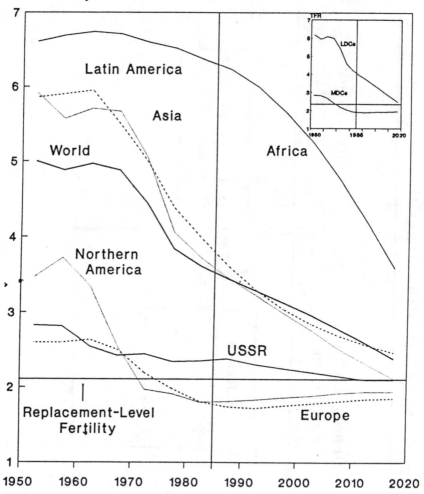

Total Fertility Rate

Source: United Nations 1989.
Reference: Demeny P. World Population Growth and Prospects. Working paper No. 4. Research Division.
         New York: Population Council, 1989.

Figure 3: Under-five Mortality Rates for the Periods 1-4 and 10-14 Years Prior to the Survey
Demographic and Health Surveys 1986-1990

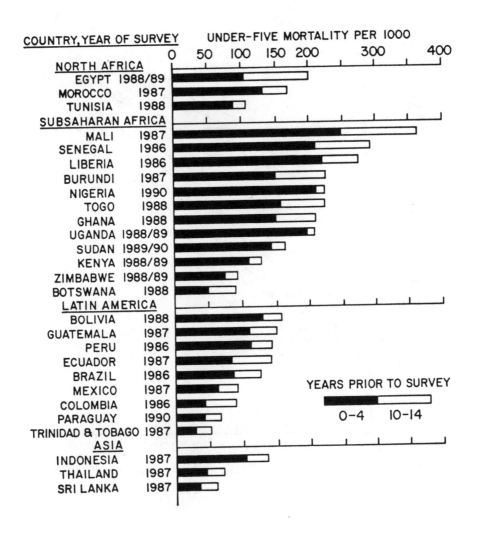

Source: Sullivan JM. The pace of decline under-five mortality: evidence from the DHS Surveys. Paper presented at the Demographic and Health Surveys (DHS) World Conference, August 5-7, 1991, Washington, D.C., 1991.

**Figure 4: Estimates and Projections in Life Expectancy
by Major Regions of the World
1950 - 2020**

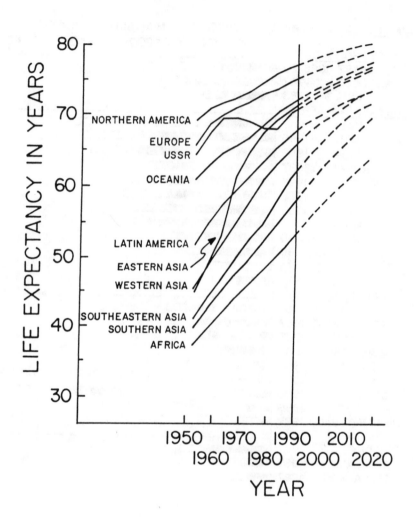

Source: United Nations. *World Population Prospects.* Population Studies No. 120. Department of International Economic and Social Affairs. New York: United Nations, 1991.

ACKNOWLEDGEMENTS

This paper draws in part on an earlier paper by the same authors[1]; it is based on work undertaken for the Population, Health, and Nutrition Division of the World Bank. The authors are indebted to Drs. J.L. Bobadilla, R. Feachem, D. A. Henderson and A. R. Measham for valuable comments. The views expressed in the paper are those of the authors and are not necessarily those of the World Bank.

REFERENCES

1. Jamison DT, Mosley WH. Disease control priorities in developing countries: health policy responses to epidemiological change. *American Journal of Public Health 81*:15-21, 1991.

2. United Nations Development Program. *Human Development Report 1990*. New York, Toronto: Oxford University Press, 1990.

3. Frenk J, Bobadilla JL, Sepulveda J, Cervantes ML. Health transition in middle-income countries: new challenges for health care. *Health Policy and Planning 4* :29-39, 1989.

4. Mosley WH, Jamison DT, Henderson DA. The health sector in developing countries: prospects for the 1990s and beyond. Pp 335-358 in L Breslow et al. (eds) *Annual Review of Public Health, Volume 11*. Palo Alto, CA: Annual Reviews Press, 1990.

5. World Health Organization. *Global Estimates for Health Situation Assessment and Projections, 1990*, Geneva: WHO, 1990.

6. Feachem RGA, Jamison DT, Bos ER. Changing patterns of disease and mortality in Sub-Saharan Africa. Pages 3-28 in Feachem and Jamison (eds) *Disease and Mortality in Sub-Saharan Africa*. Oxford: Oxford University Press for the World Bank, 1991.

7. Briscoe J, et al. Adult health in Brazil: Adjusting to new challenges. Report No. 7807-BR. Washington, D.C.: The World Bank, 1989.

8. Jamison DT, Evans JR, King T, Porter I, Prescott N, Prost A. *China: The Health Sector*. A World Bank country study. Washington, D.C.: The World Bank, 1984.

9. Murray CJL, Feachem RG. Adult mortality in developing countries. *Transactions of the Royal Society of Tropical Medicine and Hygiene 84*:1-2,1990.

10. WHO/UNICEF: *Primary Health Care.* Geneva: WHO, 1978.

11. Walsh JA, Warren KS. Selective primary health care -- An interim strategy for disease control in developing countries. *New England Journal of Medicine 301*:18-28, 1979.

12. Grant JP. *The State of the World's Children 1982-83.* United Kingdom: Oxford University Press for UNICEF, 1982.

13. Editorial. The debate on selective or comprehensive primary health care. *Social Sciences and Medicine 26*:877-878, 1988.

14. US Department of Health, Education, and Welfare/Public Health Service. *Healthy people: The surgeon general's report on health promotion and disease prevention.* Washington, D.C.: US Government Printing Office DHEW publication no. (PHS) 79-55071, 1979.

15. Breslow L. Setting objectives for public health. *Annual Review of Public Health, Volume 8*:289-307. Palo Alto, CA: Annual Reviews Press, 1987.

16. McGinnis J. Setting objectives for public health in the 1990s: experience and prospects. *Annual Review of Public Health, Volume 11*:231-249. Palo Alto, CA: Annual Reviews Press, 1990.

17. US Department of Health and Human Services/Public Health Service. *Promoting Health/Preventing Disease: Objectives for the Nation.* Washington, D.C: US Government Printing Office, 1980.

18. US Department of Health and Human Services/Public Health Service. *Prospects for a Healthier America: Achieving the Nation's Health Promotion Objectives.* Proceedings of a two-day meeting February 6-7, 1984, Washington, D.C: Office of Disease Prevention and Health Promotion, November 1984.

19. Omran AR. The epidemiological transition: a theory of the epidemiology of population change. *Milbank Memorial Fund Quarterly 49*:509-538, 1971.

20. Kinsella K. *Aging in the Third World*. International Population Reports Series P-95, No. 79, Washington, D.C.: US Department of Commerce, Bureau of the Census, September 1988.

21. Bulatao RA, Stephens PW. Demographic estimates and projections, by region, 1970-2015. Chapter 2 in Jamison and Mosley (eds) *Disease Control Priorities in Developing Countries*. Oxford and New York: Oxford University Press for the World Bank, forthcoming.

22. Feachem RGA, Kjellstrom T, Murray CJL, Over M, Phillips MA (eds). *The Health of Adults in the Developing World*. Oxford: Oxford University Press for The World Bank, forthcoming.

23. Roemer MI and Roemer R. Global health, national development, and the role of government. *American Journal of Public Health* 80:1188-92, 1990.

24. United Nations. *Global estimates and projections of population by sex and age: the 1988 revision*, Department of International Economic and Social Affairs. New York: United Nations, 1989.

25. Susser M. Industrialization, urbanization and health: an epidemiological view. *International Population Conference, Manila, 1981*, Vol. 2:273-303. Liege, Belgium: IUSSP, 1981.

26. Stansfield SK, Smith GS, McGreevey W. Injury. Chapter 24 in Jamison and Mosley (eds) *Disease Control Priorities in Developing Countries*. Oxford and New York: Oxford University Press for the World Bank, forthcoming.

27. Pearson TA, Jamison DT, Trejo-Gutierrez J. Cardiovascular diseases. Chapter 22 in Jamison and Mosley (eds) *Disease Control Priorities in Developing Countries*. Oxford and New York: Oxford University Press for the World Bank, forthcoming.

28. Zaridze DG, Peto R (eds). *Tobacco: A Major International Hazard*. World Health Organization/IARC Scientific Publication No. 74. New York: Oxford University Press, 1986.

29. Ernster VL. Trends in smoking, cancer risk, and cigarette promotion. *Cancer* 62:1702-1712, 1988.

30. Bumgarner JR, Speizer FE. Chronic obstructive pulmonary disease. Chapter 23 in Jamison and Mosley (eds) *Disease Control Priorities in Developing Countries*. Oxford and New York: Oxford University Press for the World Bank, forthcoming.

31. Lee HP, Duffy SW, Day NE, Shanmugarathnam K. Recent trends in cancer incidence among Singapore Chinese. *International Journal of Cancer* 42:159-166, 1988.

32. Barnum H, Greenberg R. Cancers. Chapter 19 in Jamison and Mosley (eds) *Disease Control Priorities in Developing Countries*. Oxford and New York: Oxford University Press for the World Bank, forthcoming.

33. Chen TTL, Winder AI. (commentary) The opium wars revisited as US forces tobacco exports in Asia. *American Journal of Public Health* 80:659-662, 1990.

34. Peto R. Tobacco related deaths in China. *Lancet* 2:211, 1987.

35. Warner KE. Health and economic implications of a tobacco-free society. *Journal of the American Medical Association* 258:2080-2086, 1987.

36. Warner KE. (editorial) Tobacco taxation as health policy in the third world. *American Journal of Public Health* 80:529-531, 1990.

37. Yu JJ, Mattson MF, Boyd GM, Mueller MD, Shopland DR, Pechacek TF, Cullen JW. A comparison of smoking patterns in the People's Republic of China with the United States. *Journal of the American Medical Association* 264:1575-1570, 1990.

38. Over M, Piot P. HIV infection and other sexually transmitted diseases. Chapter 10 in Jamison and Mosley (eds). *Disease Control Priorities in Developing Countries*. Oxford and New York: Oxford University Press for the World Bank, forthcoming.

39. World Bank. *World Development Report 1990*. New York: Oxford University Press, 1990.

40. Bobadilla JL, Frenk J, Frejka R, Lozano R, Stern C. The epidemiological transition and health priorities. Chapter 3 in Jamison and Mosley (eds) *Disease Control Priorities in Developing Countries*. Oxford and New York: Oxford University Press for the World Bank, forthcoming.

41. Foege WH, Henderson DA. Management priorities in primary health care. Pp 313-321 in Walsh JA, Warren KS (eds) *Strategies for Primary Health Care.* Chicago and London: University of Chicago Press, 1986.

42. Jamison DT, Mosley WH (eds). *Disease Control Priorities in Developing Countries.* Oxford and New York: Oxford University Press for the World Bank, forthcoming.

43. World Bank. *Health Sector Policy Paper.* Washington, D.C.: The World Bank, 1980.

44. Murray CJL, Styblo K, Rouillon A. Tuberculosis. Chapter 11 in Jamison and Mosley (eds) *Disease Control Priorities in Developing Countries.* Oxford and New York: Oxford University Press for the World Bank, forthcoming.

45. Lopez AD. Causes of death in the industrialized and the developing countries: Estimates for 1985. Chapter 3 in Jamison and Mosley WH (eds). *Disease Control Priorities in Developing Countries.* Oxford and New York: Oxford University Press for the World Bank, forthcoming.

46. Daulaire NMP. Practical issues of ARI program implementation. Pp 91-104 in Gadomski A (ed) *Acute Lower Respiratory Infection and Child Survival in Developing Countries: Understanding the Current Status and Directions for the 1990s.* Proceedings of a workshop held in Washington, D.C. August 2-3, 1989. Baltimore, MD: The Johns Hopkins University Institute for International Programs, 1990.

47. Stansfield S. Potential savings through reduction of inappropriate use of pharmaceuticals in the treatment of ARI. Pp 193-200 in Gadomski A (ed) *Acute Lower Respiratory Infection and Child Survival in Developing Countries: Understanding the Current Status and Directions for the 1990s.* Proceedings of a workshop held in Washington, D.C. August 2-3, 1989. Baltimore, MD: The Johns Hopkins University Institute for International Programs, 1990.

48. Mosley WH. Interactions of technology with household production of health. In *Towards More Efficacy in Child Survival Strategies: Understanding the Social and Private Constraints and Responsibilities.* Baltimore, MD: The Johns Hopkins University School of Hygiene and Public Health, 1989.

49. Leslie J. Women's time: a factor in the use of child survival technologies? *Health Policy and Planning* 4:1-16, 1989.

50. Organization for Economic Cooperation and Development (OECD). *Strengthening development cooperation for primary health care: A DAC concern.* Paris: OECD, 1989.

51. Grant JP. *State of the World's Children 1990.* United Kingdom: Oxford University Press for UNICEF, 1990.

52. Commission on Health Research for Development. *Health Research: Essential Link to Equity in Development.* Oxford: Oxford University Press, 1990.

53. Committee on Foreign Affairs. *Report of the Task Force on Foreign Assistance to the Committee on Foreign Affairs, US House of Representatives.* Washington, D.C.: US Government Printing Office, 1989.

54. Mosley WH. Is there a middle way? Categorical programs for PHC. *Social Science and Medicine* 26:907-908, 1988.

55. Warren KS. The evaluation of selective primary health care. *Social Science and Medicine* 26:891-898, 1988.

56. Schultz TW. *Investing in People: The Economics of Population Quality.* Berkeley, CA: University of California Press, 1981.

57. Eddy JA, Malone TF, McCarthy JJ, Rosswall T (eds). *Global Change System for Analysis, Research and Teaching (START):* Report of a meeting at Bellagio, December 3-7, 1990. Boulder, Colorado: International Geosphere-Biosphere Programme: A Study of Global Change (IGBP), Report No. 15, 1991.

Population and Societies

Lourdes Arizpe and Margarita Velazquez

I. INTRODUCTION

The technological wonders of modern society seemed to have left behind humanity's immemorial fear of extinction. How ironic that one of humanity's greatest achievements has, in its turn, created yet another threat of extinction, this time at a higher level of magnitude. At a global level, the new challenge is our inability to harmonize population growth and human expectations with the rate at which the planet's natural resources are being used or polluted.

A page of history is turning now, and human control of the environment is being overridden by unexpected new phenomena — the greenhouse effect (leading to climate change) ozone depletion — or by the cumulative effects of old phenomena — desertification, loss of biological and cultural diversity, soil erosion, among others. So we are back at square one: humans are vulnerable now to natural and human-made hazards of a different order and with three aggravating factors.

Firstly, due to the scale of such phenomena, the number of people which may be affected by global change is historically unprecedented. Secondly, it is worth noting that ecological mismanagement by societies has occurred in the past; as a result, they moved to other places. This time, however, there is no other place to go. Thirdly, nature's inequities in the geographical distribution of resources have been further aggravated by the concentration of human-made capital in industrialized nations and in elite circles of less developed countries.

A challenge such as this, of a higher magnitude and complexity than humanity has had to face in the past, requires thinking and

Lourdes Arizpe is Director of the Institute of Anthropological Research at the National University of Mexico.

Margarita Velazquez is a junior researcher on gender, population and environmental issues.

31

planning at another level of magnitude and complexity. And this is what we still don't have. Since we lack appropriate scientific and political frameworks to think in this way, issues tend to be constructed and dealt with around single factor explanations and ensuing simplistic actions. A case in point is the popular rendering of the population debate, which is seen as two-sided, while the complexity of the issues involved actually require a debate on the political and economic planning for a global world.

This paper contends that the population-environment debate has become deadlocked because it has become a question of taking sides, instead of delving deeper into the complexity of the issues, and of trying to use mechanistic, predictive models, when the most we can come up with now are probable scenarios. Population issues have been decontextualized from actual social environments as well as from the broader and more profound issues concerning the new, emerging economic and political structure of the world and its relationship to the resource base of the planet.

It may be thought that engaging in the analysis of such broad issues may distract from the urgent need to act on population problems. On the contrary, policy solutions focussed exclusively on deterring population growth have been shown to be ineffective, while more encompassing economic and social reforms achieve better results. The most urgent task, then, is to establish a hierarchy of goals — economic, ecological, social and cultural — to provide a sense of meaning and direction to the already existing potential for action.

At present, the disarray in the debate on population and resource use has been attributed to a lack of reliable data and the uncertainty of predictions. But it is also associated with the failure to analyze population trends in their relationships to other processes. Accordingly, this paper contends that all demographic transitions have been embedded in broader socio-economic transitions; that population growth is not a driving force but an accelerating force, except under rare circumstances where all other conditions remain static; and that population growth can only be understood by analyzing it in relation to rates of growth in the consumption of natural and human-made resources.

As to solutions, it is argued that curbing population growth, as many authors have repeatedly stated, must be linked to solutions for **sustainable** development at a national, regional and global scale (Ehrlich, 1989 and 1991; Keyfitz, 1991; Costanza, 1991; Leff,E., 1990; Keyfitz, 1991; Little and Horowitz, 1987; Toledo,1990; Maihold and Urquidi, 1990).

II. POPULATION TRENDS AT THE THRESHOLD OF THE NEW MILLENNIUM

The demographic transitions in North America and Western Europe at the end of the 19th century were linked to improved medical services and nutrition levels, which led to a decline in mortality due to infectious diseases (Demeny, 1990; Lutz and Prinz, 1991). But these were made possible by the shift from an agricultural to an urban-industrial society and by associated changes in family composition, age at marriage, education, and the rule of law, which ensured personal security and the rise of a culture of possessive individualism.

In contrast, mortality decline in less developed countries in the second half of the 20th century has come about mainly as a result of improved medical and health care services, in many cases without the accompanying social, economic and political transformations. Since these socio-economic transitions have occurred unevenly, frequently inequitably, and sometimes have even been reversed, the demographic transitions in such countries have not been completed, especially in Africa.

Some authors believe a general demographic transition is already underway, e.g. Julian Simons (1991), who argues that fertility rates have decreased in countries all over the world, while others reject this optimistic view or believe that such transitions are occurring too slowly (Ehrlich, 1989 and 1991; Grant and Tanton, 1981). Recent figures, in fact, show that world-wide, the crude birth rate decreased from 33.9 (1950-70) to 27.1 (1985-90), while the total fertility rate fell from 5.9 to 3.3 during that same period (World Resources Institute, 1990:256) (Figure 1).

Lutz and Prinz state that projections for the next 30 years are actually rather reliable, since they are insensitive to minor changes in mortality, migration and fertility (Lutz and Prinz, 1991). Figure 2 by Wolgang Lutz summarizes projections according to different scenarios. It is estimated that world population will reach around

Figure 1

FERTILITY   TRENDS   IN   THE
DEVELOPING   WORLD

Y E A R	AVERAGE NO. BIRTHS/WOMEN
1950–55	6.1
1955–60	6.0
1960–65	6.1
1965–70	6.0
1970–75	5.4
1975–80	4.5
1980–85	4.2

SOURCE: BONGAARTS, MAULDIN AND PHILLIPS, 1990.

<u>Figure 2</u>

Total projected world population 1990-2100 according to scenario

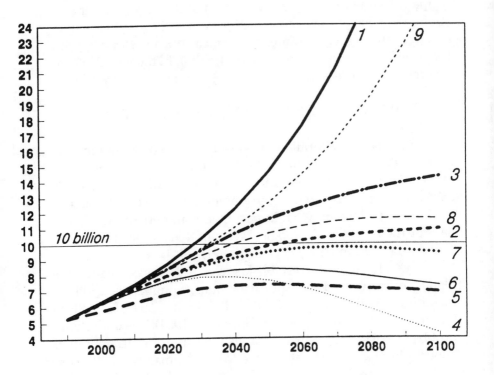

Scenario 1: Constant Rates; constant 1985-1990 fertility and mortality rates
Scenario 2: UN Medium Variant; strong fertility and mortality decline until 2025, then constant
Scenario 3: Slow Fertility Decline; UN fertility decline 25 years delayed, UN medium mortality
Scenario 4: Rapid Fertility Decline; TFR = 1.4 all over the world in 2025, UN medium mortality
Scenario 5: Immediate Replacement Fertility; assumed TFR = 2.1 in 1990, UN medium mortality
Scenario 6: Constant Mortality; TFR = 2.1 all over the world in 2025, constant mortality
Scenario 7: Slow Mortality Decline; UN mortality decline 25 years delayed, TFR = 2.1 in 2025
Scenario 8: Rapid Mortality Decline; life expectancy of 80/85 years and TFR = 2.1 in 2025
Scenario 9: Third World Crisis; constant fertility and 10% increase in mortality in Africa and
Southern Asia; TFR = 2.1 in 2025 and UN mortality for the rest of the world

Note: "TFR" is the Total Fertility Rate (= average number of children per woman)

Source: Lutz, 1991

8 billion by the year 2010 (UNFPA, 1991:3 & 48; U.N. Population Prospects, 1989; Demeny, 1990:41; Sanchez, 1989:16; UNDP, 1990:166).

As Lutz emphasizes, the <u>momentum</u> of population growth has to be taken into account, that is, the fact that the age structure of a fast growing population is so young that <u>even if fertility per woman declined to a very low level, the increasing number of young women entering reproductive ages will cause the population to grow further for quite some time</u> (Lutz and Prinz, <u>op.cit.</u>). Projections begin to vary from 8 to 14 billion in the year 2050 and diverge even more widely for the next century after that (<u>Ibid.</u>).

III. WHAT DO POPULATION NUMBERS MEAN?

The concept of population as a summation of the numbers of human bodies is of very limited use for understanding the future of societies in a global context. It is what these bodies do, what they extract and give back to the environment, what use they make of land, trees, water, and what impact their commerce and industry have on their social and ecological systems that is crucial (Demeny, 1988:217; Harrison, 1990; Durning, 1991).

An early attempt to establish such a link was estimating the planet's carrying capacity. Approximations, though, varied widely, including 7.5 billion (Gilland, 1983), 12 billion (Clark, C.,1958), 40 billion (Revelle, 1976), 50 billion (Brown, H. 1954). The underlying problem is, of course, how to establish the appropriate amount of kilocalories that are to be attributed to each human being (Blaxter, 1986). "For humans, a physical definition of needs may be irrelevant. Human needs and aspirations are culturally determined: they can and do grow so as to encompass an increasing amount of 'goods,' well beyond what is necessary for mere survival" (Demeny, 1988:215-6).

Other authors point out that the concept of carrying capacity and self-regulating mechanisms applied to animal populations should not be extrapolated to human populations (Sanchez, 1989:26), and argue that socioeconomic, technological or environmental changes are so decisive in altering this carrying capacity that the concept itself is of little use (Blaikie and Brookfield, 1987). A more appropriate exercise, then, should be to try and develop global accounting systems that relate population, per capita resource use and wealth distribution.

A different approach is taken by those trying to forecast the socio-economic and environmental impacts of population projections. Gordon and Suzuki, in their 1991 assessment of environmental change, present a harsh scenario for the year 2040: overpopulation, unbreathable air, high temperatures, desertification, loss of land due to soil erosion and rising seas, food rioting in the Third World, and so on. They insist that the "sacred truths," that the earth is infinite and progress is possible, must be discarded (Gordon and Suzuki, 1991).

A different issue, in which population overlaps with political interests, is the differential demographic growth of regions and of diverse ethnic and religious groups within countries. Figure 3 shows the difference in the proportion of population between the North and the South based on U.N. "medium" growth assumptions (UNDP, 1990). By the year 2010, 6 out of every 7 people will live, or will have been born, in less developed countries of the South (FAO, Vital World Statistics, 1990) (Figure 4). Such differential growth is being seen increasingly as a potential threat to countries in the North (Grant and Tanton, 1981).

Importantly, in the last few years, population growth has increasingly been considered the driving force in environmental degradation, increased pollution, and in fostering international conflicts, for example, over water in the Middle East (Myers,1987). It is interesting to note that, in linking population growth to environmental depletion, the disparities in the natural resource base and in the distribution of goods and services in different societies are frequently left out of the picture. It would seem, in fact, that population growth, in some cases, is used to compensate such existing disparities and inequities. To understand this, population numbers must be analyzed according to human development indicators.

IV. POPULATION AND HUMAN DEVELOPMENT

Notable progress made during this century and in recent decades in human development makes it even more difficult to accept our present predicament. On a world scale, life expectancy

Figure 3

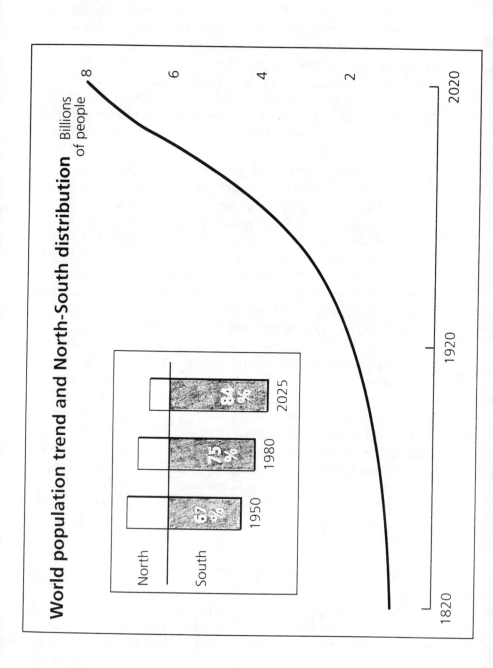

Figure 4

POPULATION INDICATORS FOR MAJOR
REGIONS OF THE WORLD

REGION	Population millions 1990	Av. Rate Growth % 1990-95	IMR* per 1,000 1990	% Urban 1990	Urban growth % 1990-95
WORLD	5,292.2	1.7	63	45	3.0
"NORTH"	1,206.6	0.5	12	73	0.8
"SOUTH"	4,084.6	2.1	70	37	4.2
AFRICA	642.1	3.0	94	34	4.9
NORTH AMERICA	275.9	0.7	8	75	1.0
LATIN AMERICA	448.1	1.9	48	72	2.6
ASIA	3,112.7	1.8	64	34	4.2
EUROPE	498.4	0.2	11	73	0.7
OCEANIA	26.5	1.4	23	71	1.4
USSR	288.6	0.7	20	66	0.9

* INFANT MORTALITY RATE

SOURCE: SAGE, 1991

has risen from 54.9 years (1950-70) to 61.5 (1985-90) (World Resources Institute, 1990:256). In developing countries, average infant mortality decreased from nearly 200 deaths per 1,000 live births to about 80 in about four decades (1950-88), "...a feat that took the industrial countries nearly a century to accomplish" (UNDP,1990:2). Primary health care was extended to 61% of the population, and safe drinking water to 55% and, despite the addition of 2 billion people in developing countries, the rise in food production exceeded the rise in population by about 20% (Ibid.).

In spite of the above progress, in 1985 more than a billion people in developing countries were trapped in absolute poverty, with some groups living in poverty also in developed nations (UNDP, 1990:22-23). In 12 of the 23 developing countries where such a comparison is available, the income of the richest groups was 15 times or more than that of the poorest group, particularly in Latin America (Ibid.). FAO estimates that about 30 million agricultural households have no land and about 138 million are almost landless, two-thirds of them in Asia (Ibid.). Looking at deprivation, a major conclusion of research is that some 500 million to one billion poor rural women in developing countries suffer the greatest deprivation; "for them, there has been little progress over the past 30 years" (Ibid.: 33) (Figure 5).

Importantly, inequities in the distribution of financial and human capital did not decrease but actually grew in the 1980s, both within and between nations. This is illustrated in Figure 6, which shows the financial flows from developing to developed countries in the 1980s. What recommendations have been given to solve this reversal in the fragile progress of human development? The authors of UNDP's 1990 Report on Human Development conclude that "resumed economic growth is thus essential to allow the expansion of incomes, employment and government spending needed for human development in the long run. Without some end to the continuing debt and foreign exchange crisis in much of Africa and Latin America, the impressive human achievements recorded so far may soon be lost" (UNDP, 1990:36).

The above shows that the range of variables impinging on the population question is much more diverse than is usually taken into account in what has been called the "population debate" in the United States and Europe.

Figure 5

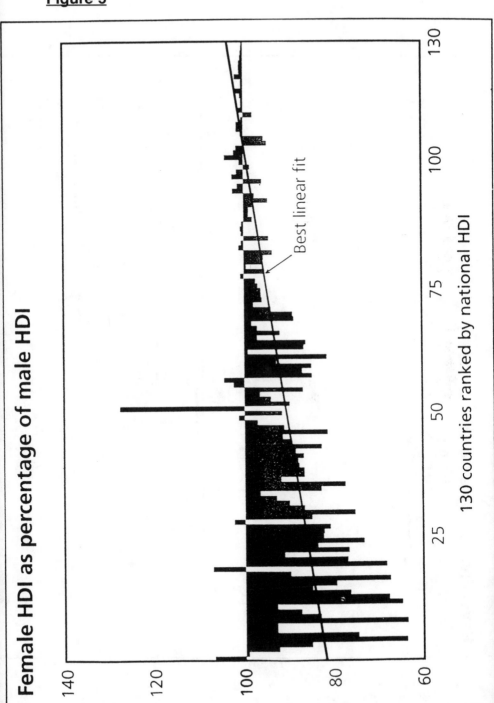

Female HDI as percentage of male HDI

130 countries ranked by national HDI

Best linear fit

Figure 6

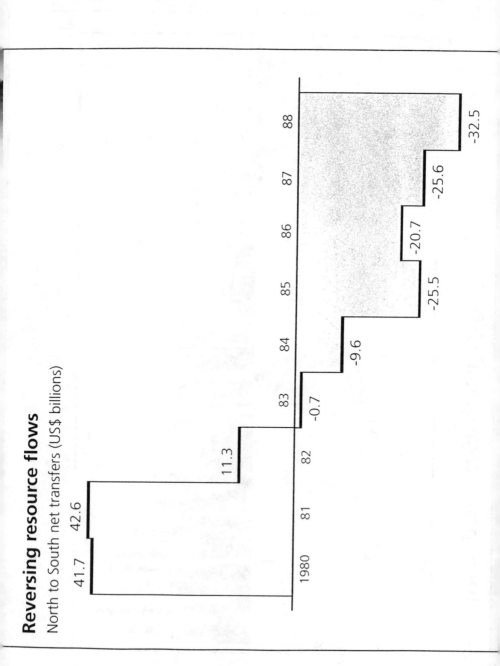

Reversing resource flows

North to South net transfers (US$ billions)

41.7 42.6 11.3 -0.7 -9.6 -25.5 -20.7 -25.6 -32.5

1980 81 82 83 84 85 86 87 88

V. THE POPULATION DEBATE

The debate on population has polarized into two major positions. One position holds that an increasing population is the principal driving force that threatens the planet's finite resources. Paul Ehrlich mentions that overconsumption, increasing dependence on ecologically unsound technologies to supply that consumption, and unequal access to resources and poverty, play a major role in environmental crises (Ehrlich, et al., 1991). He concludes that "the key to understanding overpopulation is not population density but the number of people in an area relative to its resources and the capacity of the environment to sustain human activities" (Ehrlich, 1991:38-39).

Much more extreme positions have likened human population expansion to a cancerous growth bound to kill its hospitable planet (Hern, 1990:30) or to a jar of yeast: the yeast makes alcohol which eventually kills it (Grant and Tanton,1981).

However, case studies have been reported indicating that "there is no linear relation between growing population and density, and such pressures (towards land degradation and desertification)" (Caldwell, 1984). In fact, one study found that land degradation can occur under rising pressure of population on resources (PPR), under declining PPR and without PPR (Blaikie and Brookfield, 1987). Therefore, the scientific agenda must look towards more complex, systemic models where the effects of population pressures can be analyzed in relationship to other factors (Garcia, 1990). This would allow us to differentiate population as a "proximate" cause of environmental degradation, from the concatenation of effects of population with other factors as the "ultimate" cause of such degradation (Asian Development Bank Paper, 1990). Also concerned about population growth, other authors such as Eckholm give greater emphasis to improving humanity's lot (Eckholm, 1982).

The other position holds that population growth can be dealt with through technological solutions that infinite human creativity will continue to find (Simon, 1990; Kasun, 1988). An even more optimistic view, originally put forth by Hirschman and Boserup, saw high rates of population growth as stimulating economic development through inducing technological and organizational changes (Hirschman, 1958; Boserup, 1965).

Such positions, though, ignore the dangers of environmental depletion implicit in unchecked economic growth: consumption increases and rapidly-growing populations that can put a very real burden upon the resources of the earth and bring about social and political strife for control of such resources. This position also assumes that technological creativity will have the same outcomes in the South as in the North, a questionable assumption. Finally, it heavily discounts the importance of the loss of biodiversity, a loss which is irreversible and whose human consequences are as yet unknown (SSRC/ISSC/DAWN, 1991). Neither position, according to other authors, represents the state of the art of scientific understanding (Johnson and Lee, 1987; Repetto, 1987).

In contrast, other authors state that "population is not a relevant variable" in terms of resource depletion and stress income inequality, that is, poverty, as a more important factor (Gallopin, 1990; Leff, E. 1990). More specifically, resource consumption, particularly overconsumption by the affluent, is considered by many authors as the key factor to environmental depletion (Hardoy and Satterthwatte, 1991; Harrison, 1990; Durning, 1991). OECD countries represent only 16% of the world population and 24% of the land area; but their economies account for about 72% of world gross product, 78% of road vehicles, 50% of global energy use. They generate about 76% of world trade, 73% of chemical product exports, and 73% of forest product imports (OECD, 1991). The main policy instrument, in this case, the short term, is to reduce consumption.

Finally, a "revisionist" position states that "neither alarmism nor total complacency about population growth can be supported by the current evidence" (Kelley, 1986). This author cites Kuznets' summary judgment: "...we have not tested, or even approximated, empirical coefficients, with which to weigh the various positive and negative aspects of population growth. While we may be able to distinguish the advantages and disadvantages, we rarely know the character of the function that relates them to different magnitudes of population growth" (Kuznets, 1960:339).

Importantly, historical demographic studies have demonstrated that no simple correlations can be established between population and environmental transformations. In the study *Earth Transformed*, researchers found that the time scale of population variability is asynchronous with given environmental transformations and recovery (Whitmore et al., 1990:37). Consistently, the authors stress "the need for caution in using population as a simple surrogate for environmental transformation" (Ibid.).

They also found evidence of divergence between global and regional population trends, and concluded that "if the experience of past regional population changes and their accompanying environmental transformations has relevance for the future, the projected global scale population 'leveling out' need not diminish the scale and profundity of global environmental change. This is particularly true on the regional or local scale, where global zero population growth (of population or transformation) need not be accompanied by local or regional equilibrium" (Ibid.:37). Furthermore, they warn that "regional population declines are possible, potentially brutal, and even likely, accompaniments to zero population growth on a global scale" (Ibid.)

VI. EXPLORING NEW RESEARCH METHODS

As mentioned previously, it is necessary to focus research not on population as an isolated variable but on the relationship between population and the use of natural and human-made resources (Demeny, 1988:217; Harrison, 1990; Durning, 1991; Arizpe, Costanza and Lutz, 1991).

Research priorities must begin by exploring methods for more precisely estimating the relationship between population and resource use. William Clark (1991) suggests that the "Ehrlich identity" (Pollution/Area = People/Area X Economic Production/People X Pollution/Economic Production), can be operationalized as (CO_2 Emissions/Km^2 = Population/Km^2 X GNP/Population X CO_2 Emissions/GNP). Clark and his colleagues examined data for 12 countries from 1925 to 1985 and concluded that the same loading of pollution on the environment can come from radically different combinations of population size, consumption, and production. Thus no single factor dominates the changing patterns of environmental loadings across time.

This points to the need for local studies of causal relations in systemic combinations of population, consumption and production, noting that these local studies need to aim for a general theory that will account for the great variety of local experience.

Another research priority is to look at the effect that adding a new person has on resources, according to consumption levels, and the effect that efficiency has on rising levels of consumption. Barbara Torrey and Gretchen Kolsrud (1991) examined population growth and energy efficiency in several countries and concluded that the very small population growth forecast for developed countries over the next forty years will add a burden of CO_2 emissions that will be <u>equal</u> to that added by the much larger population growth forecast for the less developed countries. Improving energy efficiency in developed countries could dramatically decrease CO_2 emissions globally (if consumption per person remains constant). It is only under a scenario of severe constraints on emissions in the developed countries that population growth in less developed countries plays a major global role in emissions. If energy efficiency could be improved in the latter as well as the former, then population increase would play a much smaller role. Jose Goldemberg has pointed out that enabling developing countries to "leap-frog" in adopting new energy efficiency technologies could accomplish this goal.

VII. POPULATION, MIGRATION AND URBANIZATION

Another major concern over the effects of population growth is the expansion of migration and urbanization trends. The demise of agrarian societies the world over, coupled with population increase, has contributed to creating massive migratory movements in the last few decades. In the early 1980s, the number of economic migrants was estimated at around 20 million; adding a similar count for illegal migrants, perhaps 40 to 50 million people had moved in hope of a bigger share in the world development benefits (UNDP, 1990:28).

In the first decades of the next century, such movements will increase and diversify, adding to their contingents ecological refugees which will be principally moving from South to North, although also from South to South. (<u>Ibid.</u>).

The classic pattern of rural outmigration linked to price changes that led to the breakup of the Central and Western European peasant economies — which sent out 52 million migrants overseas in Europe from 1848 to 1912 (Brinley, 1961) — still continues to be the main driving force in outmigration in many developing countries. At present, it is associated to (1) the fall in the price of agricultural products in the world market, and (2) the structure of prices of agricultural products (subsidies in the European Economic Community to protect their own farmers in the 1980s and 90s have intensified conditions that increase the rural exodus in many countries of the South). Or it may push them into environmentally unsound activities: deforestation, mono-culture, crop intensification, overuse of fertilizers or pesticides, all of which means depletion of natural resources. Population growth may increase the rate at which such activities are carried out, but the structures that drive such activities are economic and financial, not demographic. If this were not the case, Europe would not have sent out as many migrants overseas last century.

The important question here is what will happen as market forces continue to integrate agrarian societies into a globalized market, thus continuing pressures for rural outmigration. Measures to protect farmers from the market have failed in most countries. They have either transferred the problem to other countries, as has already been mentioned for the EEC, so that a local Western European solution to an economic and political problem has fueled local problems of impoverishment, outmigration and resource depletion in many countries of the South, which in turn, as in the case of deforestation, is intensifying yet another global problem. Or, the clientelistic-corporatist relationship between farmers and the government has turned into a political or economic morass, as in the case of Mexico.

The other two solutions to the economic crisis of agrarian societies all over the world are population control and migration strategies. The former will be dealt with later on in this paper, so discussion will now concentrate on migration strategies.

Agrarian societies have been fighting back through a myriad of strategies, from increased self-exploitation in work and malnourishment, especially among poor rural women, to intensification and diversification of income-generating activities, to

permanent or recurrent, "swallow" migration as we call it in
Mexico, outmigration (Arizpe, 1982; Arizpe, 1986; Arizpe, 1989).

In terms of this paper, the question is whether having more
children survive has been used by farmers in this unequal struggle
to adapt to a global market. And the answer is "yes," in many
ways, but I will focus only on those related to migration strategies.

Since farmers are not having <u>more</u> offspring but are finding
that more of them survive, what is being asked of them is that they
change a millennium-old pattern of reproduction. This requires
not only a strong economic incentive which, in the case of the more
than one billion rural poor in countries of the South is not there, but
a cultural and political change whereby rural people will feel they
have a stake in the new global society that is being created.

For small agricultural family producers, children do have an
economic value in farm labor; but, additionally, in recent decades,
they are being helpful to their families in relay migration, by
sending remittances back to offset the family economic deficit
(Arizpe, 1982). Such a strategy, though, is possible only when
cities offer unlimited opportunities for economic gain, which
increasingly is not the case in many mega-cities in developing
countries.

Thus, adaptive strategies to disappearing rural livelihoods,
given present market conditions, are limited, so it may be assumed
that rural outmigration will continue to increase and be directed
towards mega-cities and to international destinations.

Rural-urban disparities continue to increase the attraction of
cities: in most countries, urban incomes per person run 50% to
100% higher than rural incomes (UNDP,1990:30). In Nigeria, the
average urban family income in 1978-79 was 4.6 times the rural; in
Mexico, urban per capita income was 2.6 times that of the rural
(<u>Ibid.</u>).

Urbanization, then, will become the dominant social process
in the next 50 years and most mega-cities will be in low latitudes
in tropical regions, as can be seen in Table 7 (Douglas, 1991),
although some authors believe the rate of urbanization in the Third
World will not be as high as United Nations figures suggest
(Hardoy and Satterthwatte, 1991).

Such a trend must create great concern, since "in the places
where man's activities are most densely concentrated — his
settlements — the environmental impact is greatest and the risks

Table 7

Projected increases in urban population in major world regions, 1985-2000

Region	Urban population (millions)		Absolute increase (millions)	Percentage increase
	1985	2000		
Africa	174	361	187	108
Asia	700	1,187	487	70
Latin America	279	417	138	49
Oceania	1.3	2.3	1	77
Developing countries	1,154	1,967	813	70
Industrial countries	844	950	106	13
World	1,998	2,917	919	46

of environmental damage are most acute" (United Nations, 1974). Indeed, since the United Nations pointed this out in 1974, urbanization has continued at a rapid pace. Globally, it has been forecast that 24 million hectares of cropland will be transformed to urban-industrial uses by the year 2000; this is only 2 per cent of the world total, but it is equivalent to the present-day food supply of some 84 million people (Douglas, 1991:8). The loss of agricultural land to urbanization is most severe in the developing countries, where more than 476,000 hectares of land a year will become built up in the remaining years of the 20th century (World Resources Institute, 1988 cited in Douglas, op.cit.).

While in previous decades cities in developing countries were able to absorb, even under dire poverty conditions, migrants from their rural hinterland, this is no longer the case in the nineties. Migrants from Eastern Europe and Africa are overflowing into Western Europe, and Peruvians and Bolivians are now joining Mexicans and Central Americans in migrating to the United States (Grant and Tanton, 1981). No doubt the numbers of economic and ecological migrants knocking at the North's door would be lower if population growth in the South were decreased, but the trend would still be there. Why? Because, if capital investments do not flow where the people are, then the people will flow to where capital investments are. One example will suffice: in California alone, it is estimated that seven million jobs will be created in the 1990s, most of them low-paying, non-skilled jobs which Americans will not be able to fill (Cornelius, 1989). Consequently, with both push factors in the South and pull factors in the U.S. at work, the flow of Latin American migrants, with the acquiescence of potential employers, will overwhelm any border patrol programs that try to stop them. It is rarely pointed out that migration flows from developing to developed countries also constitute a loss of resources for the former: migrants are housed, fed and nurtured in poor rural households in the Philippines, Peru or Jamaica; or trained and educated in developing countries at great cost.

VIII. POPULATION AND RESOURCE USE IN SOCIAL CONTEXTS

The gradual decline in human mortality since the end of last century must be considered one of the greatest achievements of

Western civilization, both on scientific and on human management grounds. Rarely in history has such a unanimous, concerted action been successfully undertaken by such a large number of human agents: scientists, doctors, firms producing medicines, voluntary groups, pharmaceutical companies and governments, even if the latter two may be also guided by their own economic or political interests.

The Hippocratic oath defending human lives over and above any other consideration gave philosophical sustenance to these activities. Many other cultures, though, do not give such preeminence to the struggle against death; for some it means coming closer to spiritual liberation, or an opportunity for the soul to transmigrate into other realms or beings. Importantly for our discussion, many traditional cultures, especially those living in inclement natural habitats, did subordinate individual human life to the survival of the group. A vast array of fertility control and abortive practices were, and in some cases still are, present in many traditional cultures. The point is that, for centuries, many societies had evolved some kind of accounting system whereby the number of people in their group, and their age structure, were thought of in relation to available natural resources. This was especially true in hunting and gathering, pastoralist and horticultural societies; less so in agrarian societies where food cultivation could be expanded and more people fed. Other, more aggressive societies, obtained the resources needed to sustain their populations through warfare.

These built-in social and ecological accounting systems in many indigenous cultures placed the responsibility for managing socio-demographic processes on the societies themselves. This, in my view, has been greatly undermined as a result of four driving forces. Firstly, the centralization of power that led to the subordination of rural societies to the needs of the urban systems. Secondly, the loss of cultural diversity, which eroded cohesive social mechanisms as traditional societies were pulled into market economies and subjected to uninformed educational and media systems. Thirdly, the spread of the urban culture, in which people are no longer in direct contact with the natural sources of the things they eat, use or play with and so lose all their bearings as to the depletion of natural stocks. Indeed, the steel and concrete urban environment gives the impression that goods appear purely out of thin air through technological manipulation. Urbanites, however, are becoming keenly aware of the piling up of human bodies in cities, thereby reinforcing their view that the problem is the number of human <u>bodies</u> occupying space and competing for goods, rather than the overall <u>relationship</u> of the urban pattern of consumption of natural resources and planetary stocks. Fourthly, scientific models have tended to leave out the cultural and social matrices in which population processes are embedded, and thus undermined local and meso-level capabilities of organizing their own socio-demographic processes.

The point is that such socially operated cultural accounting systems, which foster local and regional social management, must be allowed to be revitalized in societies around the world. In developing regions, this would allow communities and local peoples to adjust their reproductive behavior to real expectations of sustainable livelihoods, natural resource availability and locally defined measures of quality of life. Adapting growth in developing countries to the environmental limits, however, need not entail accepting the economic limits imposed by continuing subsidies for the wasteful, polluting affluent life style of some sectors in industrialized countries of the North.

X. CURBING GROWTH IN POPULATION AND IN RESOURCE USE

A global perspective of the population-resource use issue means that a reduction in population growth in underconsuming nations must go hand in hand with reducing consumption among affluent groups and nations. This can only be achieved by lowering birth and death rates, alleviating poverty, reducing pressures on resources, and improving women's opportunities, employment-generating policies and health care (Repetto, 1986). At present the debate in the North deals more with population policies to implement in the South rather than with curbing overconsumption in the North (WorldWatch Institute, 1988).

Population control is known to be insufficient: it has repeatedly been shown that it is not easily achieved in and of itself, and that, in addition, important social and economic transformations must accompany it, such as reduction of poverty.

"Population can only be expected to fall when livelihoods (of the poor) are secure, for only then does it become rational for poor people to limit family size" (Chambers, 1988; DAWN, 1988). According to a World Bank study of 64 countries, when the income of the poor rises by 1%, general fertility rates drop by 3% (Lappe and Schurman, 1988). Although reduction of poverty may be a necessary condition for decreasing fertility, it is not, however, a sufficient condition, as the cases of Kerala, Sri Lanka and other regions demonstrate (Gordon and Suzuki, 1991). Nor do lower population growth rates translate immediately into improved environmental conditions; even in those cases where population growth has been successfully controlled, as in China, the welfare of the people has not necessarily improved and the environment is not necessarily exposed to lower rates of hazard.

To reduce pressures on resources, research priorities should look at situations where demand, either subsistent or commercial, becomes large relative to the maximum sustainable yield of the resource; or where the regenerative capacity of the resource is relatively low; or where the incentives and restraints facing the exploiters of the resource are such as to induce them to value present gains much more highly than future gains (Repetto and Holmes, 1983).

Natural resource scarcity studies indicate that a transition will have to be made during the next century from cheap, plentiful use of oil, to inherently less desirable sources of energy (Mackellar and Vining, 1987), although other authors are more optimistic about unlimited availability of energy (Gilland, 1986). As to the problem of food, prudent optimism largely prevails as to the possibilities of increasing agricultural productivity to feed the increase in population through the year 2000 (Srinivasan, 1987; Mackellar and Vining, 1987). Some authors, however, are not as optimistic (Brown, 1983). To analyze such possibilities, the real problem of production of more food must be separated from the economic and political problem of hunger, that is, of food distribution: the food vs. feed issue. Biotechnology provides grounds for optimism, although it seems that its commercial applications will not have effects until around the year 2010.

Deforestation, on the other hand, presents a rather more pessimistic picture, although different sources cannot agree on the rates of deforestation (Mackellar and Vining, 1987; FAO, 1990; Williams, M., 1991). In 1950, industrialized countries imported 4.2 million square meters of tropical woods; in 1980, they imported 66 million (Myers, R., 1981). The outcome will depend on whether consumption of tropical woods and population pressures on the fringes of tropical rain-forests can be decreased.

X. TOWARD A GLOBAL SOCIETY

It would seem contradictory to argue in this paper that one of the driving forces behind the population "bomb" was that population, as a variable, was abstracted from actual societies with highly disparate natural resource and income distribution bases, and yet emphasize that a "global society," another abstract construction, must be built. Indeed, I do agree with the Brundtland Commission that there will be no future if we are unable to build one <u>world</u>. To be more precise, I would say that a global society must begin to be <u>interpreted as such</u>, so that it can be <u>seen as such</u>, and therefore, <u>built</u> (Arizpe, in press).

But the answer is that such a global society must be built in the same way that the nation-states have been built: almost without exception, they are internally plural in ethnic and religious identities, per capita income, economic regionalism, demographic growth rates and so on, yet juridically and politically they function as a unit. In other words, almost without exception, the unity of nation-states is not an empirical reality, yet the transactions of national and international life are undertaken on the basis of this unity.

In the same way, one can posit that a global society has become a juridical, political and even cultural necessity, yet the global empirical reality will always be made up of nations and societies, themselves made up of a plurality of trends, some converging, others diverging, that are still not fully understood, nor are they susceptible to being totally controlled. They can, however, through negotiations, be successfully managed and pointed in the right direction. That is, if a direction can be agreed upon. Thus, abstracting population as a single factor in models purporting to represent complex empirical reality is inappropriate, but dealing with population as one of the main issues in building a global society is not only appropriate but necessary.

The deeper issue here, one which underlies debates all the way from the Lacandon rain-forest in Mexico to the Preparatory Committee for UNCED, is this: <u>who</u> is going to build this new economic and accounting system for the world? This is, indeed, a political issue at the international level. Since nations are still trying to enhance their own "wealth of nations," never having left the berth of classical economics, each will try to build a system which, minimally, will keep their own interests untouched, or maximally, will increase their benefits.

At a more local level, the question of who is creating the new rules of a global society is perceived in more immediate terms as: who is going to bear the cost, in actual or potential benefits, of the preventing or adapting to new conditions? Whether the debate engages rain-forest cattle ranchers and indigenous peoples on deforestation, or poor urban dwellers and rich urbanites on urban pollution, or corporations and ecologists on economic development, or the North and the South on the future of the world, what is at stake is the capacity of human beings to negotiate a common future. And for this purpose, the concept of humanity, that is, of human beings with a capacity for discernment, seems more germane than that of populations, which refers to human bodies which consume.

XI. CONCLUSIONS

A new framework for the debate on population and environment should expand definitions of issues and focus not only on population size, density, rate of increase, age distribution, sex ratios, but also on access to resources, livelihoods, social dimensions of gender, and structures of power. New models have to be explored in which population control is not simply a question of family planning but of social and political planning (United Nations, 1990: 202-216; Jacobson, 1988: 152-54); in which the wasteful use of resources is not simply a question of finding new substitutes but of reshaping affluent lifestyles (Sack, 1990; Meadows, 1988; Repetto, 1987); and in which pollution control is not simply a matter of "polluter pays" but also of emission controls, which in turn are associated with political and social processes; and in which sustainability is seen not only as a global aggregate process but one having to do with sustainable livelihoods for a majority of local peoples.[1]

Models analyzing population growth must be relational and contextualized, aimed at understanding how a certain pattern of growth is embedded in complex systems linking livelihoods, per capita income, gender roles and educational levels. Special attention should be given to how people belonging to different social and ethnic groups have access to, and capacities for exchanging, natural and human-made capital resources.

However, analysis is not enough. A different intellectual endeavor must be undertaken at the same time, namely, a hierarchy of goals must be set for global management. Previous goals of increased GNP, unlimited and free use and waste of natural resources, and incentives for infinite bloating of consumerism must be discarded. Our primary goal must be sustainability. Not, however, related uniquely to conserving and managing natural resources and preventing global climatic change. Social sustainability is just as important, and this has equity and democracy as its preconditions. In other words, the new forms governability of a global reality take will determine the social sustainability of a society and this, in turn, will harmonize population growth to social goals.

Cultural sustainability is another matter: basic principles of human rights must be ensured across cultures, yet freedom to believe and express a plurality of value systems must also be conserved and managed.

Finally, as mentioned in the text, it is essential that we go beyond the analysis of what is happening today and projecting it in a most uncertain way towards the future. Tomorrow cannot be known, but it can be built purposefully. Our priority must be

---

[1] Many of the ideas expressed in this section were discussed at meetings of the Social Science Research Council, International Social Science Council, Development Alternatives for Women in a New Era project on Population and Environment, funded by the MacArthur Foundation and other foundations. My thanks to Richard Rockwell, Gita Sen, William Clark, Rosina Wiltshire and Alberto Palloni.

sustainability and human development. Priority must be given to establishing a hierarchy of goals for a global society; one based on the existing realities of the "wealth of nations," but with a mandate to enhance the "wealth of humanity."

ACKNOWLEDGEMENTS

The authors benefitted from previous collaboration with Robert Costanza and Wolfgang Lutz. Bibliographic research work for the project was carried out by Christine Halvorson, Veronica Behn and Alan Scholefield.

REFERENCES

Alba, F. and Potter, J.. "Population and Development in Mexico since 1940: An Interpretation". In <u>Population and Development Review</u>, vol. 12, No. 1, March 1986. pp. 47-75.

Arizpe, L. "Problemas teóricos en el estudio de la migración de pequeños grupos: el caso de migrantes campesinos a la Ciudad de México", en: <u>Cahiers des Ameriques Latines</u>, 12, 2nd. semester, 1975. pp. 201-222.

---------. <u>Migración, etnicismo y cambio económico.</u> México: El Colegio de México, 1978.

---------. "The Rural Exodus in Mexico and Mexican Migration to the United States". In: <u>International Migration Review</u>, Vol. XV, No. 4, Winter, 1981. pp. 626-650.

---------. "Relay Migration and the Survival of the Peasant Household". In: <u>Why People Move</u>, J. Balan, ed., Paris, UNESCO, 1982.

---------. "On the Social and Cultural Sustainability of World Development". In: <u>One World or Several?</u> Emmerij, L., ed., Paris: OECD Development Center, 1989. pp. 207-219.

---------. <u>La mujer en el desarrollo de México y de América Latina.</u> México:UNAM/Juan Pablos, 1990.

---------. "The Global Cube: Social Models in a Global Context" in International Social Science Journal. In press.

---------, Costanza, R. and Lutz, W. "Primary Factors Affecting Natural Resource Use." Paper prepared for the International Council of Scientific Unions, ASCEND 21, 1991.

Asian Development Bank. "Population Pressure and Natural Resource Management: Key Issues and Possible Actions." Paper No. 6. 1990.

Blaikie, M. and Brookfield, B. "Land Degradation and Society." Methuen, London, 1987.

Blaxter, Kenneth F.R.S. People, Food and Resources. Cambridge University Press, 1986.

Boserup, Esther. The Conditions of Agricultural Growth: The Economics of Agrarian Change Under Population Pressure. Chicago: Aldine, 1965.

Brinley, Thomas. International Migration and Economic Development. UNESCO, 1961.

Brown, Harrison. The Challenge of Man's Future. New York: The Viking Press, 1954.

Brown, Lester. "Global Food Prospects: Shadow of Malthus." In: Glassner, Global Resources. New York: Praeger, 1983.

-------------. "La Ilusion de Progreso"; in: El Mundo: Medio Ambiente 1990. Fundacion Universo Veintiuno, S.C. Mexico, 1990. pp. 1-24.

Caldwell, John. "Desertification: Demographic Evidence, 1973-83." Australian National University, Occasional Paper No. 37, 1984.

Clark, Collin. "Population Growth and Living Standards" in The Economics of Underdevelopment, ed. A.N. Agarwal and S.P.Singh. London: Oxford University Press, 1958. pp. 32-53.

Clark, William. Paper presented at the Annual Meeting of the American Association for the Advancement of Science, Washington, D.C., February, 1991.

Conroy and Litvinoff. The Greening of Aid. Earthscan, 1988.

Costanza, R. (ed.). Ecological Economics. The Science and Management of Sustainability. New York: Columbia University Press, 1991.

Chambers, R. Sustainable Livelihoods, Environment and Development: Putting Poor People First. Brighton, U.K.: Institute of Development Studies, University of Sussex, 1988.

DAWN. Development, Crises and Alternative Visions: Third World Women's Perspectives. 1988.

Demeny, Paul. "Demography and the Limits of Growth"; in: Population and Development Review Supplement. Vol. 14, 1988, pp. 213-244.

-------------. "Population" in Turner, B.L. et al., The Earth Transformed by Human Action. Global and Regional Changes in the Biosphere over the Past 300 Years. New York: Cambridge University Press with Clark University, 1990. pp. 41-54.

Douglas, Ian. "Human Settlements." Paper presented at the Office for Interdisciplinary Earth Studies Workshop on Global Change held on July 28 - August 10, 1991, Snowmass, Colorado.

Durning, Alan. "Asking How Much is Enough"; in: Brown, L.R., et al. State of the World 1991. A WorldWatch Institute Report on Progress Toward a Sustainable Development. 1991. pp. 153-169.

Ehrlich, Paul, et al. "Global Change and Carrying Capacity: Implications for Life on Earth" in Ruth DeFries and Thomas Malone (eds.) Global Change and Our Common Future: Papers from a Forum. Washington: National Academy Press, 1989. pp. 19-27.

Ehrlich, Paul R. and Anne H. Ehrlich, The Population Explosion. Touchstone, Simon & Schuster Inc., New York, 1991.

Eckholm, R. Down to Earth: Environmental and Human Needs. New York: Norton, 1982.

FAO. Vital World Statistics. Rome: FAO, 1990.

Gallopin, Gilberto C. "Global Impoverishment, Sustainable Development and the Environment." Ecological Analysis Group, 1990.

60   *Lourdes Arizpe and Margarita Velazquez*

7310.

Gilland, Bernard. "Considerations on World Population and Food Supply"; in: Population and Development Review, Vol. 9, No. 2, 1983. pp. 203-211.

----------------. "On Resources and Economic Development"; in: Population and Development Review, Vol. 12, No. 2, 1986. pp. 295-305.

Goeller, H. E., and Alvin M. Weinberg. "The Age of Substitutability: What do we do when the mercury runs out?" Science, 191. 1976. pp.683-689.

Gordon and Suzuki. It's a Matter of Survival. Cambridge: Harvard University Press, 1991.

Grant and Tanton. "Immigration and the American Conscience" in Progress as if Survival Mattered, Nash (Friends of the Earth) ed. 1981.

Hardoy, E and W. Satterthwatte. "Environmental Problems of the Third World Cities: A Global Issue Ignored?" in: Public Administration and Development, Vol. 11, 1991.

Harrison, Paul. "Too Much Life on Earth?" New Scientist. May 19, 1990.

Hern, Warren M. "Why Are There So Many of Us? Description and Diagnosis of a Planetary Ecopathological Process" in Population and Environment: A Journal of Interdisciplinary Studies. Volume 12, Number 1, Fall, 1990.

Hirsh, Fred. Social Limits to Growth. Cambridge, Mass.: Harvard University Press, 1976.

Hirschman, Albert. The Strategy of Economic Development. New Haven, Conn.: Yale University Press, 1958.

Jacobson, Jodi. "Planning the Global Family"; in: Brown, L.R., et al. State of the World 1988. A WorldWatch Institute Report on Progress Toward a Sustainable Development. 1988. pp. 151-169.

Johnson, D. Gale and Lee, D. Ronald (eds.). Population Growth and Economic Development: Issues and Evidence. Madison: University of

Wisconsin Press, 1987. A Publication of the National Research Council Committee on Population.

Kasun. The War Against Population. San Francisco: Ignatius Press, 1988.

Kelley, Allen. "Review of the National Research Council Report Population Growth and Economic Development: Policy Questions" in Population and Development Review, 12, 3, September, 1986: 563-567.

Keyfitz, Nathan. "Need we Have Confusion on Population and Environment?" International Institute for Applied Systems Analysis, Laxenburg, Austria. August, 1991.

---------------. "From Malthus to Sustainable Growth". International Institute for Applied Systems Analysis, Laxenburg, Austria. July, 1991.

Lappe and Schurman. Taking Population Seriously. New York: Earthscan, 1988.

Leff, Enrique. "Población y medio ambiente. Es urgente detener la degradación ambiental." In: DEMOS. Carta demográfica sobre México. México, 1990.

Little, P. and Horowitz, M. with A. Endre Nyerges (eds.). Lands at Risk in the Third World: Local-Level Perspectives. Westview Press, 1987.

Lutz, W. and Prinz, C. "Scenarios for the World Population in the Next Century: Excessive Growth or Extreme Aging." WP-91-22. International Institute for Applied Systems Analysis, Laxenburg, Austria, 1991.

Mackellar, F.L. and Vining Jr., D. R. "Natural Resource Scarcity" in Population Growth and Economic Development, Johnson and Lee, eds. Madison: University of Wisconsin Press, 1987.

Maihold, Gunter and Urquidi, Victor. Compiladores. Diálogo con nuestro futuro común. Perspectivas latinoamericanas del Informe Brundtland. Fundación Frederich Ebert, México. Venezuela: Editorial Nueva Sociedad, 1990.

Meadows, Donella. "Quality of Life." In: Earth's 88: Changing Geographic Perspectives. National Geographic Society. Washington, D.C., 1988. pp.332-349.

Myers, N. Not Far Afield: US Interests and the Global Environment. Washington, D.C.: World Resources Institute, 1987.

Myers, R. "Deforestation in the tropics: who gains, who loses?" in Where have all the Flowers Gone? Studies in Third World Societies, ed. Williamsburg, 1981.

Organization of Economic Co-operation and Development (OECD). The State of the Environment. Paris: OECD, 1991.

Repetto, Robert. World Enough and Time. New Haven: Yale University Press, 1986.

--------------. Population, Resources, Environment: An Uncertain Future. Washington: Population Reference Bureau, 1987.

--------------, and Holmes, Thomas. "The Role of Population in Resource Depletion in Developing Countries"; in: Population and Development Review, Vol. 9, No. 4, December, 1983.

Revelle, Roger. "The Resources Available for Agriculture." Scientific American, September, 1976. pp. 165-178.

Sánchez, Vicente, Margarita Castillejos y Leonora Rojas. Población, recursos y medio ambiente en México. Fundación Universo Veintiuno, A.C. México, 1989.

Simon, Julian. Population Matters: People, Resource, Environment and Immigration. New Brunswick: Transaction Publishers. 1990.

SSRC/ISSC/DAWN. "Recasting the Population-Environment Debate: A Proposal for a Research Program," 1991.

Srinivasan. "Population and Food." In: Population Growth and Economic Development. Johnson and Lee, eds. Madison, University of Wisconsin Press, 1987.

Swaminathan, M. S. "Global Agriculture at the Crossroads." in Earth's 88: Changing Geographic Perspectives. Washington, D.C.: National Geographic Society, 1988. pp.316-331.

Toledo, Víctor Manuel. "Modernidad y ecologia. La nueva crisis planetaria." Document, April, 1991. México.

Torrey, Barbara and Gretchen Kolsrud. Paper presented at the Annual Meeting of the American Association for the Advancement of Science, Washington, D.C. February, 1991.

Turner II, B.L., et al., The Earth Transformed by Human Action. Global and Regional Changes in the Biosphere over the Past 300 Years. New York: Cambridge University Press with Clark University, 1990.

United Nations. Human Settlements: the Environmental Challenge London: MacMillan, 1974.

United Nations Department of International Economic and Social Affairs. World Population Prospects 1988. New York, 1989.

United Nations Development Programme. Human Development Report 1990. New York: Oxford University Press, 1990.

United Nations Population Fund. The State of the World Population 1991. New York: Oxford University Press, 1991.

United Nations. Global Outlook 2000. An Economic, Social and Environmental Perspective. United Nations Publications, 1990.

Whitmore, Thomas M., et al. "Long-Term Population Change" in Turner, B.L. et al. The Earth Transformed by Human Action. Global and Regional Changes in the Biosphere over the Past 300 Years. New York: Cambridge University Press with Clark University, 1990. pp. 25-39.

Williams, Michael. "Forest and Tree Cover." Paper presented at the Office for Interdisciplinary Earth Studies Workshop on Global Change held on July 28 - August 10, 1991, Snowmass, Colorado.

World Resources Institute. World Resources 1990-91. A Guide to the Global Environment. New York: Oxford University Press, 1990.

WorldWatch Institute. State of the World 1988. A WorldWatch Institute Report on Progress Toward a Sustainable Society. New York, 1988.

WorldWatch Institute. State of the World 1990. A WorldWatch Institute Report on Progress Toward a Sustainable Society. New York, 1990.

WorldWatch Institute. State of the World 1991. A WorldWatch Institute Report on Progress Toward a Sustainable Society. New York, 1991.

An Economic Perspective

David Pearce

I. WHERE WE ARE NOW

In its *Human Development Report*, the United Nations Development Programme has provided a convenient snapshot of the state of the world in 1991 [UNDP, 1991]. Figure 1 indicates the advances and setbacks in the past few decades in the industrialized and developing world. The distinction between rich and developing countries is familiar to everyone, but we still need reminding that 77% of the world's population earns 15% of the world's income. The North's average income of $12,500 is 18 times that of the South ($700). Figure 1 shows that the developing countries have made great strides in the past 30 years: life expectancy has improved by 30%, two thirds of the people now have access to some form of health service; literacy rates have improved; real per capita incomes grew by over 4% per annum. By focussing on the problems that remain, we often tend to overlook the fact that most developing countries truly are developing, they are not regressing. But the task ahead is truly daunting nonetheless. Some 24 million young people die each year from preventable causes; half a million women die from causes related to pregnancy and childbirth; 20% of the population still goes hungry each day; real per capita incomes have fallen in the 1980s in Latin America and Sub-Saharan Africa. And if we look ahead, what progress we have made threatens to be swamped by the sheer growth in numbers: a projected 60% rise in population between now and 2025 in the world as a whole; an 80% increase in the low income countries [World Bank, 1991]. Without doubt, population growth is the greatest challenge to the prospects for a sustainable world.

David Pearce is a Professor at The University College of London's Centre for Social and Economic Research on the Global Environment.

Figure 1

Balance sheet of human development — developing countries

PROGRESS   DEPRIVATION

Life Expectancy

PROGRESS	DEPRIVATION
· Average life expectancy increased by over one-third between 1960 and 1990 — and is now 63 years.	· Ten million older children and young adults and 14 million young children die each year — most from preventable causes.

Health

PROGRESS	DEPRIVATION
· The proportion of people with access to health services has risen to 63%.	· 1.5 billion people still lack basic health care. · Over 1.5 billion people do not have safe water, and over 2 billion lack safe sanitation.

Food and Nutrition

PROGRESS	DEPRIVATION
· Average calorie supplies as a percentage of requirements increased between 1965 and 1985 from 90% to 107%.	· One-fifth of the population still goes hungry every day.

Education

PROGRESS	DEPRIVATION
· Adult literacy rates increased between 1970 and 1985, from 46% to 60%.	· Over 1 billion adults are still illiterate. · 300 million children are not in primary or secondary school.

Income

PROGRESS	DEPRIVATION
· Income per head grew annually in the 1980s by almost 4% — and 9% in East Asia. · More than one person in four in the 1980s lived in countries with growth rates above 5%.	· More than 1 billion people still live in absolute poverty. · Income per head has declined over the last decade in Latin America and Sub-Saharan Africa.

Children

PROGRESS	DEPRIVATION
· Under five mortality rates were halved over the last three decades. · Immunization coverage for one-year-olds increased dramatically during the 1980s, saving an estimated 1.5 million lives annually.	· Over 14 million children die each year before reaching their fifth birthday. · 180 million children under five suffer from serious malnutrition.

Women

PROGRESS	DEPRIVATION
· Primary school enrollment for girls increased between 1960 and 1988 from 79% to 87%. · Women's enrollment in tertiary education has increased almost everywhere — and achieved near equality with men in Latin America and the Caribbean.	· Half the rural women over age 15 are illiterate. · Women are often denied the right to decide whether or when to have children. Half a million women die each year from causes related to pregnancy and childbirth. · Women are often legally (or effectively) denied the right to own, inherit or control property.

Rural and Urban Areas

PROGRESS	DEPRIVATION
· The proportion of people living in rural areas with access to adequate sanitation has doubled over the past decade. · 88% of urban dwellers have access to health care, and 81% have access to safe water.	· Only 44% of the rural population have access to basic health care. · There are 2.4 people per habitable room, three times the average in the North. One urban dweller in five lives in the nation's largest city.

Balance sheet of human development — industrial countries

PROGRESS	DEPRIVATION
Life Expectancy & Health	
· Average life expectancy is 75 years. · Virtually all births are attended by health personnel, and the maternal mortality rate is only 24 per 100,000 live births. · Two-thirds of the population is covered by public health insurance. · On average, 8.3% of GNP is spent on health care.	· Adults on average smoke 1,800 cigarettes per year and consume 4 liters of pure alcohol. · More than half the people born today are likely to die of circulatory and respiratory diseases, many of which will be closely linked to sedentary lifestyles, fat-rich diets, alcohol consumption and cigarette smoking. · The US alone reported 137,000 cases of AIDS in 1989.
Education	
· Governments provide on average nine years of full-time compulsory education. · Over one-third of all graduates are science students. · On average, 6% of GNP is spent on education.	· Almost four persons in ten lack any upper secondary school education. · Only 15% of the youth in the age group 20-24 enroll for full-time tertiary education.
Income & Employment	
· GNP per capita has increased between 1976 and 1988 from $4,850 to $12,510. · Industrial countries produce 85% of the global wealth every year.	· The wealthiest 20% of the population receive almost seven times as much income as the poorest 20%. · About 6.5% of the total labor force is unemployed, one-third of it for more than 12 months.
Social Security	
· Social welfare expenditures now account on average for 11% of GDP.	· About 100 million people lived below the poverty level in 1990 (200 million if the USSR and Eastern Europe are included).
Women	
· As many women as men are now enrolled in secondary and tertiary education. · Females above the age of 25 have already received, on average, 9 years of schooling. · One-fourth of the female graduates are science students.	· Women's wages are still only two-thirds of men's wages. · There are 50 reported rapes per 100,000 females aged 15-59. · Only one-fifth of the parliamentary representatives are women.
Social Fabric	
· People have the opportunity to be informed and connected with one another: there is one radio for every person, one TV set and telephone for every two people. · The average family owns a car. · Every third person purchases a daily newspaper. · There are six library books per person.	· Many industrial countries are experiencing a fast change in their social fabric. Most striking examples: Finland, the highest proportion of single parent homes (10%); Sweden, the highest illegitimacy ratio (42%); USA, the highest divorce rate (8%). · About 433 persons out of every 100,000 are seriously injured every year in road accidents.
Population & Environment	
· The current annual population growth rate is around 0.5%. · Almost the entire population has access to safe water and sanitation facilities.	· The dependency ratio is as high as 50%. · Annual emission of traditional air pollutants is 42 kilograms per 100 people. · The greenhouse index had already reached 3.5 by 1989.

II. ECONOMY AND ENVIRONMENT

Figure 1 is fairly silent about the environment. Many see environmental degradation as the gravest threat to a viable future. The link to population is obvious. As population expands, the pressure on urban areas increases, both from natural increase within those areas and from rural-urban migrants. In the high income countries, more than three-quarters of the population live in towns and cities; in middle income countries, the proportion is roughly 60%; in low income countries, around 36%. In each income type, the proportion has increased: moderately in the high income countries, by around 40% in the middle income countries, and by over 100% in the low income countries. There are 30,000 people per square kilometer in Cairo, 45,000 in Manila, 88,000 in Calcutta. The result is, all too often, urban squalor, excessive noise and pollution, congestion, water and sanitation problems. In rural areas in the developing world, around 1% of the forest area is converted each year, mainly for low productivity agriculture, sometimes for hardwood exports, sometimes for fuelwood. In Nepal, that percentage is 4%, in Cote d'Ivoire, 5%, and in Costa Rica, it is 7% per annum. The result is not just the "mining" of an essentially renewable resource, but the gradual build up of long-run damage to watersheds through loss of the forests' ecological functions.

The environment matters not just because it is our natural life support system, not just because of its scientific value, not just because of aesthetics and moral concern, but because damaging it impairs our chances of sustainable development. Bluntly put, the world is losing good old-fashioned gross national product (GNP) because of pollution and resource degradation. Figure 2 brings together some estimates of such losses. By looking at the relationship between, for example, soil erosion and crop productivity, it is possible to gain some idea of what output would have been had the erosion not occurred. What is being lost is potential GNP. The numbers are large. Burkina Faso can ill afford to forgo 9% of its GNP or Nigeria 17%. The loss of 4% of German GNP is some $50 billion; 2% of United States GNP is $100 billion.

Although environmental economists have shown very clearly the links between the economy and environment, our politicians,

FIGURE 2: Summary National Environmental Damage Estimates

Country	Form of Environmental Damage	Year	%GNP
Burkina Faso	Crop, livestock and fuelwood losses due to land degradation	1988	8.8
Ethiopia	Effects of deforestation on fuelwood supply and crop output	1983	6.0- 9.0
Madagascar	Land burning and erosion	1988	5.0-15.0
Malawi	Soil erosion	1988	0.5- 3.1
Mali	On site soil erosion losses	1988	0.4
Nigeria	Soil degradation, deforestation, water pollution, other erosion	1989	17.4
Indonesia	Soil erosion and deforestation	1984	4.0
Hungary	Pollution damage	late 80s	5.0
Poland	Pollution damage	1987	4.4- 7.7
Germany*	Pollution damage	1990	1.7- 4.2
Netherlands	Some pollution damage	1986	0.5- 0.8
USA**	Air pollution control Water pollution control	1981 1985	0.8- 2.1 0.4

----

* pre-unification
** benefits of environmental policy, i.e. avoided damages rather than actual
   damages

Sources: Burkina Faso: D.Lallement, Burkina Faso: Economic Issues in Renewable Natural Resource Management, Agriculture Operations, Sahelian Dept., Africa Region, World Bank, June 1990; Ethiopia: K.Newcombe, 'An Economic Justification for Rural Afforestation: the Case of Ethiopia,' in G.Schramm and J.Warford, Environmental Management and Economic Development, Johns Hopkins University Press, Baltimore, 1989; Madagascar: World Bank, Madagascar - Environmental Action Plan, July 1988; Malawi: J.Bishop, The Cost of Soil Erosion in Malawi, Report to Malawi Country Operations Department, World Bank, November 1990; Mali: J.Bishop and J.Allen, The On-Site Costs of Soil Erosion in Mali, World Bank, Environment Department Working Paper No.21, November 1989; Nigeria: World Bank, Towards the Development of an Environmental Action Plan for Nigeria, World Bank, Dec.18, 1990; Indonesia: R.Repetto, Wasting Assets - Natural Resources in the National Income Accounts, World Resources Institute, Washington, 1989, and W.McGrath and P.Arens, The Costs of Soil Erosion on Java: a Natural Resource Accounting Approach, World Bank, Environment Department Working Paper 15, Washington, August 1989; Hungary: World Bank, Hungary - Environmental Issues, Washington DC, November 1990; Poland: D.W.Pearce and J.Warford, Environment and Economic Development: Managing Natural Resources in the Developing World, forthcoming 1992; Germany: D.W.Pearce, 'German Studies of Environmental Damage,' CSERGE, London, 1991, mimeo; Netherlands: J.Opschoor, 'A Review of Monetary Estimates of Benefits of Environmental Improvement in the Netherlands,' OECD, Paris, October 1986; USA: P.Portney, 'Air Pollution Policy,' in P.Portney (ed), Public Policies for Environmental Protection, Resources for the Future, Washington DC, 1990, and A.Freeman, 'Water Pollution Policy,' in Portney, op.cit.

industrialists and all of us as citizens still persist in treating the environment as some kind of addendum to the economy, something to be attended to when things get really bad, and only then if we think we can afford it. Yet the fundamental fact is that <u>all</u> economic decisions affect the environment and all environmental change has an economic dimension. There is, of course, nothing sacrosanct about the current state of the environment, and nothing sacrosanct about environments past that we may remember as children or that we cull from our history books. What matters is that, when we make economic decisions, we take into account that we have necessarily made environmental decisions too. Environmental impacts have to be integrated into economic decision-making, not just when we build roads or houses, but when we decide the budget deficit, change interest rates and reduce tariff barriers. We have begun to do this in a modest way. In Europe, for example, we at least asked the question 'What are the environmental implications of creating a Single Market in 1992 ?' [European Commission, 1989]. But there is a long way to go.

Figure 3 shows the essential links between economy and environment. Economic activity involves taking matter and energy and converting its form to produce the goods and services we consume. Yet, by the laws of thermodynamics, we cannot destroy that matter/energy. It must reappear in the overall system somewhere, unless it is locked into very long lasting capital assets. It reappears as waste. Thus there is a materials balance: what we take from the environment, we discharge back into the environment [Boulding, 1966; Ayres and Kneese, 1969]. The more people there are and the greater the amount of economic activity, the greater the flow of materials and energy through the economic system, and hence, the greater the amount of waste. The more waste there is, the more shocks and stress we impose on ecological systems, and the more vulnerable we make our life support systems to further shocks and stress. If we understood fully how ecological systems work, this process of 'eating away' at them might be manageable and sustainable. But we do not understand how they work and it is an arrogant pretense to suggest that we can fully judge the consequences of our economic actions. We cannot.

The challenge posed by the economy and environment link goes deeper than the issue of policy design. There is a challenge to

Figure 3

The Materials Balance View of Economy-Environment Linkage

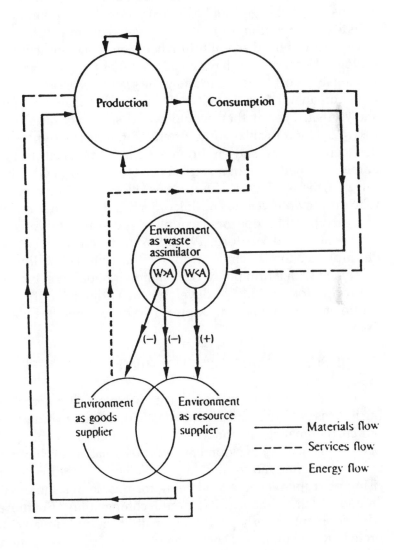

economic and ecological science too. Both sciences deal with the concept of <u>equilibrium</u>, and economists certainly spend a good deal of time trying to determine whether equilibria exist. But what has not been investigated properly is the equilibrium relationship between economies and environments, i.e. just what kind of economy is consistent with the set of life-support systems we have, and just what changes can be made in those life-support systems so as to ensure equilibrium with any given economic system. Some have observed the disequilibrium between economic activity and ecological systems and have concluded that the only chance of a sustainable world lies in curtailing the <u>scale</u> of economic activity - both human numbers and GNP [Daly, 1991]. A glance at Figure 3 shows that, even if they would work, such measures are not <u>necessary</u> for a livable world, provided the thermodynamic link between economy and environment can be reduced. If, for example, the coefficient of materials used to each $1 of GNP can be lowered, then each year's GNP can be at lower environmental cost than the previous year's. The link can never be broken completely, of course, but the scope for 'decoupling' is enormous [Pearce <u>et al.</u>, 1989; Pearce and Warford, 1992]. Strong financial incentives to decouple economic activity from its effect on the environment, combined with a firm policy on containing population growth, is the recipe for sustainable development without sacrificing the legitimate aspirations of people to improve their standard of living.

III. SUSTAINABLE DEVELOPMENT

It is perhaps time to define sustainable development. Defining it turns out to be far less problematic than finding out whether our current management of the world economy is keeping us on or off a sustainable development path. Sustainable development is simply economic and social change which gives rise to a sustained rising per capita level of well-being for people over time. In the language of the economist, it is 'non-declining utility.' But the term "development" is perhaps wider than utility as traditionally interpreted by economists. Development embraces some notion of equity between the members of a generation, some notion of basic freedoms and human rights, some notion of mental and spiritual welfare.

Finding a <u>measure</u> of development is problematic. Perhaps the closest we have come is the <u>human development index</u> produced by a team of experts working for the United Nations Development Programme. Their idea was to combine, in an ingenious way, a country's achievement with respect to literacy, life expectancy (a surrogate for health) and gross income (net income being very difficult to estimate for many countries). Figure 4 shows a table of the top countries' rankings according to the human development index, compared to their rankings by gross national income.

Whatever the virtues of the development index, it does at least serve to remind us that economic growth, as many have said, is not a reliable indicator of human progress. Interestingly, the early economists were concerned with income as a measure of well-being. The actual process of <u>measuring</u> a nation's income has, however, become more concerned with income as a measure of economic activity, of the 'busyness' of the economy. The pendulum has swung back, and now we are once again concerned to get some measure of our sustainable well-being.

An index of human development enables us to define sustainable development fairly simply. We could say that a nation is developing sustainably if its human development index rises systematically over time, allowing, perhaps, for a limited number of short-term deviations. In terms of Figure 5, path A would be sustainable development, path B would probably qualify, and path C would be unsustainable development.

But how do we know if we are on path A rather than C, if our position in time is point T on the graph? Simple extrapolation of past trends is illicit, since path C would not be foreseen by such a procedure. The answer lies in looking at the capital base of society. All of us are familiar with the idea of living off capital, and with the caution that we can do so only temporarily. If we are to <u>sustain</u> our livelihoods, we have to put income aside to cover the depreciation on the assets upon which we rely for our income. Nations are no different. In calculating the nation's wealth and income, we do indeed make some estimate of the depreciation of our infrastructure, machinery and factories. What we should always look at is

FIGURE 4

Country Rankings by Human Development Index and Gross National Income

	HDI	GNP capita
Japan	1	13
Canada	2	3
Iceland	3	5
Sweden	4	6
Switzerland	5	4
Norway	6	12
U.S.A	7	2
Netherlands	8	20
Australia	9	8
France	10	15
U.K	11	17
Denmark	12	14
Finland	13	11
Germany	14	16
New Zealand	15	23
Belgium	16	18
Austria	17	21
Italy	18	19
Luxembourg	19	9
Spain	20	-
United Arab Republic	56	1
Brunei	42	7
Hong Kong	25	10

Source: UNDP [1991].

FIGURE 5

Picturing Sustainable Development

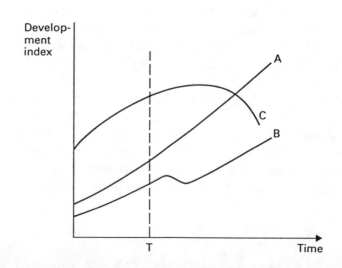

net income, not gross income. The difference between gross and net income provides us with our first clue for conditions that need to be fulfilled in order to achieve sustainable development. No nation can say its economic activity is sustainable if it fails to replace the capital that depreciates. Similarly, no nation will expand its future income unless it invests in new capital. The first requirement for sustainable development, therefore, is that a nation must invest enough both to replace depreciated capital and to create new capital. Of course, the picture is complicated by technological progress which makes future capital more productive. But it is useful to note that population growth may serve to offset much technological progress.

We need to think of the components of a human development index as reflecting different types of capital. The capital which supports and generates income is of course man-made capital: machines and roads, factories and vehicles. Let us call this K_M. Human health and education are features of what the economist calls human capital (K_H). We need to think of the skills and capabilities of individuals as a form of capital, just like machinery. We need to invest in that capital through education and through health care and preventive medicine. If K_M and K_H begin to decline we are not on a sustainable development path. The result is none too surprising and is in accord with the layman's perception that we can ill-afford to run down our education, research and health sectors, nor our technology and man-made capital. We must keep our capital intact and, if we are to develop, we must increase it. To find out if we are on a sustainable development path, we need to assess the state of our capital resources and their rate of change.

IV. SUSTAINABILITY AND THE ENVIRONMENT

Nearly all the popular discussion about sustainable development makes it clear that sustainability involves looking after the environment. We can build that idea into the discussion by observing that environmental assets are another form of capital. We can call them natural capital (K_N). They are capital because they yield flows of goods and services. Think of a tropical rain forest. It produces commodities such as timber, minor forest products such as latex, nuts, rattan, honey, fruits, and so on. The forest protects the watershed system, controlling floods, preventing landslides and erosion, cleaning the water. The forest scrubs pollutants from the air and stores carbon dioxide. It helps manage the local climate and perhaps the regional and even the global climate. It is the home of indigenous peoples and the habitat for some of the world's richest biological diversity. The tropical forest is a piece of capital. Suitably protected and managed, it can provide this flow of services indefinitely. Destroyed for logging, cleared for agricultural land, pillaged for its minerals, the tropical forest becomes capital that is consumed.

What is true of tropical forests is true of ozone layers and global carbon cycles, of soil fertility and natural rivers, mangroves and coral reefs. To our panoply of capital, therefore, we must add natural capital (Figure 6).

Our rule for securing sustainable development now tells us to keep all forms of capital intact: man-made, human and natural [Pearce, et al., 1990]. But we have a problem. It is perfectly possible to keep the aggregate of these forms of capital intact while allowing any one of them to depreciate. We can allow the Amazon forest to be destroyed if, in the process, we are building up some other type of capital. That, indeed, is how many economists would characterize sustainable development. That is, as a process of continuous development which is achieved by keeping capital intact, but with due allowance being made for the inherent substitutability of types of capital.

FIGURE 6

THE CAPITAL BASE OF SUSTAINABLE DEVELOPMENT

'Maintaining capital intact' means maintaining the three types of capital:

MAN-MADE CAPITAL K_M e.g.   machinery, roads

HUMAN CAPITAL K_H e.g.   knowledge, health

NATURAL CAPITAL K_N e.g.   species, tropical forests, ozone layer

Notice, however, that, even in this argument, it is only legitimate to degrade natural environments if the proceeds are reinvested in other forms of capital. Frequently that is not how environmental degradation happens. Rather, the proceeds of despoliation are <u>consumed</u> rather than invested. Figure 7 shows this for Indonesia, a country rich in natural resources. The graph shows the effect of deducting from the official figures for capital investment (GDI) the depreciation on oil stocks, forests and soil. The apparent growth of investment through time is seen to be illusory. Net investment generally fell throughout the 1970s and was even negative in 1979 and 1980. Indonesia was consuming the proceeds of its natural wealth. Figure 8 shows some partial results of adjusting the national accounts in a rich country, the United Kingdom. Notice that the adjustments are not always negative. In this case, the modified sectoral GNP rises when environmental adjustments are made.

Adjusting the national income accounts in this way is important, but it will not by itself generate sustainable development. For that we need the <u>incentives</u> to decouple economic activity and environmental impact. The two ways of achieving that are through traditional 'command-and-control' regulations, setting environmental standards and regulating to ensure they are complied with, and 'market based instruments' (the use of fiscal incentives to reduce pollution and resource degradation). Economists tend to prefer the latter for reasons that have been explored extensively elsewhere [Pearce, <u>et al.</u>, 1989; Stavins, 1991]. The general conclusion of the debate over the form of market intervention is that there is enormous scope for correcting market signals to improve the environment. Moreover, a number of countries are already developing these policies. The prospects are that, in the future, we shall see more of our public revenues raised through pollution taxes and less through direct taxes on effort and enterprise (Pearce, 1991).

If, as is said, the meaning of words is best discovered through their use, then it is odd to equate sustainable development with a situation in which we allow natural resources to be degraded. That is simply not how the phrase has entered into the language of global resource management. Part of the problem arises because economists tend to <u>assume</u> substitutability. It makes life a lot easier and allows the application of continuous mathematical

FIGURE 7

Consuming Natural Resource Proceeds in Indonesia

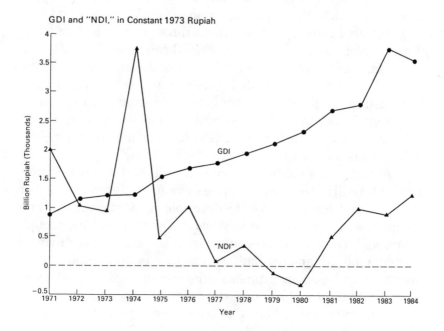

GDI and "NDI," in Constant 1973 Rupiah

FIGURE 8

MODIFIED NATIONAL ACCOUNTS: AGRICULTURE AND FORESTRY IN THE UNITED KINGDOM

Provisional but non-official adjustments have been made to one sector of the UK's national accounts: agriculture and forestry. In line with the requirement that positive environmental effects (benefits) be added to GNP for this sector and that negative effects are deducted, the following adjustments can be made:

Pounds-UK, million (1988)

Final marketed output	11,161
- Inputs	- 5,663
= <u>Gross product</u>	= <u>5,498</u>
- Depreciation	- 1,470
= <u>Net Product</u>	= <u>4,028</u>
+ Environmental services	
biodiversity	+ 94
amenity: green belt	+ 642
amenity: nat.parks	+ 152
- Govt expenditure to maintain	- 58
landscape and conserved	
areas, clean-up pollution	
- Household defensive exp.	- n.a.
- Depreciation (D_n)	
carbon fixing	+ 146
water	- 11
= <u>Sustainable Net Product</u>	= <u>≤4993</u>

To make the adjustments to net product, estimates were made of the per hectare recreational and amenity values obtained from sample valuation studies. These were then applied to the whole area under conservation designations of one form or another. Willingness-to-pay to avoid damage was not estimated directly. The defensive expenditure approach was used, omitting companies' expenditure and including government anti-pollution expenditures. No estimates were available for household expenditures. Natural capital depreciation involved estimates for the net accretion or release of carbon dioxide and the valuation of water pollution. Because this sector has a net fixation rate of CO_2, this item appears positive in the adjustments. If household expenditures can be ignored, then the sector's accounts show an upwards revaluation by 24%, a significant adjustment.

Source: Adger and Whitby [1991]

techniques. Yet, in real life, we protest vigorously if the health of the population declines, or if educational standards fall. We do not, in other words, tolerate reductions in human capital. I suspect we would greet any decline in the man-made stock of capital in the same way. We have to learn to treat natural capital in the same way, perhaps not all of it, and certainly not each and every part of it. But the aggregate of natural capital needs to be conserved, unless we can show that the gains to human well-being from its conversion into other forms of capital, or even its conversion into pure consumption, are very high. This is akin to what economists call the 'safe minimum standards' approach. The presumption should be in favor of conservation, unless we can show that the gains from not conserving are very high [Ciriacy-Wantrup, 1952; Bishop, 1978; Randall, 1988].

V. CONCLUDING REMARKS: ARE WE ON A SUSTAINABLE DEVELOPMENT PATH?

It is too early to determine yet if any one country, or the world as a whole, is on a sustainable development path. Determining that must await more empirical work on the measurement of sustainable income, i.e. 'green GNP.' The alternative to using sustainable income indicators is to look at the underlying conditions for sustainable development. If they are not being fulfilled, then we are unlikely to be on a sustainable path. But it turns out that determining whether the conditions are met or not requires the same kinds of measurement as for sustainable income: some measure of capital stocks and their rate of depreciation. Some preliminary evidence has been provided here. Interpreting that evidence is not straightforward, but we might hazard the idea that the condition for sustainability is that an economy's savings rate should exceed the depreciation on both man-made capital and natural capital combined [Proops and Pearce, forthcoming]. In the United Kingdom, the savings-to-GNP ratio is 20%; depreciation on man-made capital is 13%. If, therefore, depreciation on natural capital is running at 7% or more, we might argue that the UK is not on a sustainable development path. My guess is that the UK is very much like Germany in respect of environmental degradation, and Figure 1 shows that degradation may be running as high as 4% of

GNP there. If the UK is the same, then, the UK just makes it, with a savings ratio of 20% against an overall depreciation ratio of 17%. A similar back-of-the-envelope calculation for Burkina Faso tells a different story. Gross domestic savings there currently run at only 2% of GNP, compared to the 9% depreciation on natural capital shown in Figure 1. Burkina Faso is on an unsustainable path even without bothering to account for depreciation on man-made capital. This result is unsurprising given the poverty of Burkina Faso, but other countries are less obviously unsustainable. Nigeria's savings rate is high at around 21%. However, if we allow a nominal 10% for man-made capital depreciation and add it to the 17% natural capital depreciation shown in Figure 1, then Nigeria is on an unsustainable path. In short, while we cannot be certain yet, economic analysis is beginning to point the way towards an answer to the question: where are we now? We are, I believe, perilously close to unsustainable development in many parts of the world.

ACKNOWLEDGEMENTS

The first discussion of 'sustainable development' in fairly popular terms was The World Conservation Strategy produced by the International Union for the Conservation of Nature in 1980 (Gland, Switzerland). The widest dissemination of the concept came with the World Commission on Environment and Development's, Our Common Future (Oxford University Press, oxford, 1987) - the 'Brundtland Commission'.

REFERENCES

Adger,N and Whitby,M [1991], 'National Accounting for the Externalities of Agriculture and Forestry,' Countryside Change Unit, University of Newcastle-upon-Tyne, Working Paper 16, April.

Ayres,R and Kneese,A [1969], 'Production, Consumption and Externality,' American Economic Review, Vol.LIX, June.

Bishop,R [1978], 'Endangered Species and Uncertainty: The Economics of a Safe Minimum Standard,' American Journal of Agricultural Economics, February.

Boulding,K [1966], 'The Economics of the Coming Spaceship Earth,' in H. Jarrett (ed), Environmental Quality in a Growing Economy, Johns Hopkins University Press, Baltimore.

Ciriacy-Wantrup,SV [1952], Resource Conservation: Economics and Policies, University of California Press, Berkeley.

Daly,H [1991], Steady State Economics, Island Press, Washington, D.C.

European Commission [1989]. Task Force Report on the Environment and the Internal Market, European Commission, Brussels.

Pearce,DW [1991], 'New Environmental Policies: The Recent Experience of OECD Countries and Its Relevance to the Developing World,' in D.Eröcal (ed), Environmental Management in Developing Countries, Organisation for Economic Cooperation and Development, Paris.

Pearce,DW , Markandya,A and Barbier,E [1989], Blueprint for a Green Economy, Earthscan, London.

Pearce,DW, Barbier,E and Markandya,A [1990], Sustainable Development: Economics and Environment in the Third World, Earthscan, London.

Pearce,DW and Warford,J [1992], Environment and Economic Development: Managing Natural Resources in the Developing World, forthcoming.

Proops,J and Pearce,DW [forthcoming], 'Is the Planetary Economy Sustainable ?' Centre for Social and Economic Research on the Global Environment, University College London.

Randall,A [1988], 'What Mainstream Economists Have to Say About the Value of Biodiversity,' in E.O.Wilson (ed.), Biodiversity, National Academy Press, Washington, D.C.

Repetto,R, McGrath,W, Wells,M, Beer,C, and Rossini,F [1989], Wasting Assets: Natural Resources in the National Income Accounts, World Resources Institute, Washington, D.C., 1989.

Stavins,R [1991], <u>Project 88 - Round II: Incentives for Action: Designing Market-Based Environmental Strategies</u>, U.S. Congress, Washington, D.C.

United Nations Development Programme [1991], <u>Human Development Report 1991</u>, Oxford University Press, Oxford and New York.

World Bank [1991], <u>World Development Report 1991</u>, Oxford University Press, Oxford and New York.

An Environmental Perspective

David A. Munro

I. INTRODUCTION

This paper briefly describes the changes that are occurring in the human environment in 1991, giving particular attention to their causes and impacts and to the ways in which they are perceived. It is not intended as a definitive description of the state of the environment in 1991. For that sort of treatment reference can be made to many other sources[1], notably the reports published by World Resources Institute and others and the State of the Environment report to be published by UNEP in 1992. This paper draws heavily on information assembled for the forthcoming UNEP report, and the author would like to express his gratitude for the opportunity to review it in its draft form.

The environment is not something apart from other matters of human concern; it provides the context within which all our activities take place and its condition is central to our future. It affects all our activities and is affected by them.

Our environment, or to use another term, the biosphere, is an interdependent system. Disturbing one part of it can affect another part or the whole. The ecological processes that keep the planet fit for life — that shape climate, cleanse air and water, regulate water flow, recycle essential nutrients, create and regenerate soil and enable ecosystems to renew themselves — are linked by the flows of water and air and the activities of animals. As the activities of humans have become more pervasive and significant, they have affected many of these processes and linkages.

Human dependence upon the products of nature has always been clear. So too has the fact that people can have a significant impact on local environments; for example, forest clearing in Europe and irrigation in China, Egypt and the Middle East are among the practices that precede written history. Despite these changes, until recently the activities of people had no effect on the

David Munro is Project Director for Caring for the World and a former Director General of the World Conservation Union.

global environment and the place of human beings within it was not significantly unlike that of any other species.

The profound and complex revolution in human activities that began over 200 years ago has fundamentally changed the relationship between people and their environment, with implications that are still being revealed. In its simplest terms, the most significant aspect of that revolution was the symbiotic growth of science and technology, which enabled a dramatic increase in the rate of human survival and unprecedented growth in the production of goods and the supply of services. Application of the new technologies was driven by the requirements of an increasing population within a system that seemed to have only temporary, technical constraints and no ultimate limits. Key elements in the use of the new technologies were the use of vastly increased amounts of energy and chemicals, including many synthetics — the characteristics of which were, and are still, imperfectly understood.

Environmental issues are closely related to problems of human health and welfare, and to a wide range of social and economic issues, including the quality of life and the sustainability of economic enterprises. Environmental questions impinge on those of science policy, notably whether policy should be modified to support increased attention to ecology and other environmentally related subjects.

While other papers in this proceedings deal more directly with certain social and economic issues, it is necessary at least to touch on some of them here as well. It is hoped that this paper will provide a useful introduction to those in the second and third sections of this volume, which define the sort of world we want and the steps we must take to reach it.

II. CHARACTERISTICS OF ENVIRONMENTAL CHANGE

Environmental change is continual and pervasive. The erosion of rock and the transport of soil, for example, must have occurred as far into the past as we can imagine and are likely to go on occurring indefinitely. The records of geological strata and the fossils embedded in them testify to changes in the extent of the seas, the form of the land and the identity and abundance of the plants and animals that populated the earth. Most such change is believed to have taken place slowly, but there may also have been sudden, cataclysmic changes. There is also clear evidence of changes in climate, but the rates at which they took place are not known.

Changes in the environment and their effects may be discerned locally or regionally, close to the point of their cause or far from it. Direct causes of environmental change, such as the emission of pollutants or the destruction of vegetation, are inevitably local. Throughout most of human history the effects of such changes were also of limited extent. But as the points where changes originate become more numerous and widespread and the causes of change themselves change — increases in the quantity and toxicity of pollutants, and in the extent and rapidity of destruction of forests, for example — their effects may become regional or global, although not necessarily in a uniform fashion.

The indirect effects of environmental change may be felt over a much greater area than are direct effects because the physical well-being of people, or other forms of life, in an area not directly affected by an environmental change may depend upon goods or ecological services supplied by another area which is affected by such change. For example, an industry in one location may have to shut down because a distant source of raw materials has been exhausted. A water supply may become less reliable because its source lies in an area where the natural storage capacity has been reduced by wetland drainage or deforestation. The social and economic effects of such change can be very important. The indirect effects of environmental change need not be just those that have an impact on material well-being: they may also be the perception of loss experienced as a consequence of damage to a valued but distant landscape or biota.

The significance of environmental change may be felt well beyond the areas of direct or indirect impact. Thus, people may be concerned about and respond to the plight of those far away who suffer from the effects of drought, flood and other disasters associated with environmental change.

It is apparent that classification of environmental changes in terms of their extent is difficult and that the term "global change" may therefore not mean exactly what it seems. In this paper, global change is used to refer not only to phenomena such as the depletion of the ozone layer and the enhancement of the greenhouse effect, which may have some sort of direct impact on all parts of the world, but also to changes such as soil degradation and the loss of biological diversity, which have direct impacts that are scattered but widespread and may have indirect impacts that are even more extended.

Five categories of change in the human environment will be considered, namely, those in the atmosphere (and relating to climate), those in marine and fresh waters, those on the land, those in the status of living resources or biota and those in human settlements and transport. Changes in one category are frequently, if not always in an obvious way, linked to changes in one or more others.

III. CHANGES IN THE ATMOSPHERE

Most atmospheric changes are caused by pollution — from industry, agriculture or the domestic use of fossil fuels — or by changes in the stores of carbon, such as are caused by deforestation. Deforestation also affects levels of atmospheric water vapor and consequently precipitation. Volcanic eruptions can create major impacts on the atmosphere, sometimes lasting for a long time. The effects of changes in the atmosphere are of three types.

The first consists of qualitative changes caused by pollution of the lower atmosphere that may affect the health of plants and animals as a result of direct contact, or indirectly through impacts on the quality of water and soil. These changes are caused by emissions resulting from human activities, both industrial and domestic, principally of sulphur, nitrogen and carbon oxides, chlorinated hydrocarbons and particulates, including lead.

The effects of air pollution on human well-being, particularly in cities, have been known for centuries. Severe episodes, involving primarily sulphur dioxide and particulates and which resulted in illness and death, were one of the causes of the public concern about the environment which characterized recent decades. In many developed countries, there has been considerable progress in reducing emissions of sulphur dioxide and particulate matter, but this is by no means the case in large parts of eastern Europe, the Soviet Union and China.

Air pollution described as photochemical smog, which is formed by reactions among nitrogen oxides and reactive hydrocarbons, is a hazard to human health and causes damage to vegetation and buildings. It is a problem that is spreading and becoming more acute, largely because of the world-wide increase in the numbers and use of motor vehicles. There is not a major city in the world that does not now suffer from it to some degree, but it is most acute where local topography and weather cause frequent temperature inversions and where controls on automobile emissions are inadequate.

The phenomenon of acid deposition, largely a result of the long range transport of oxides of sulphur and nitrogen released by the combustion of fossil fuels, has been shown to cause the reduction and extinction of populations of fresh water fish and invertebrates and to contribute to forest dieback in Europe and North America. Rates of acid deposition have decreased in those regions, but not enough to eliminate its adverse effects. Acid deposition is an increasing threat in many developing countries.

While the atmospheric changes just mentioned are not global in the sense of having a direct impact in every part of the world, they may, because of what has been called the "measles effect," be considered of global significance. They are widely recognized, and public concern about their effects continues to grow. Emission control regulations are becoming progressively more stringent in many countries. The Geneva Convention on Long Range Transboundary Air Pollution (1979) and its Helsinki (1985) and Sofia (1988) protocols control transboundary effects among countries of the ECE region. The many instances of transboundary air pollution in other regions remain uncontrolled.

The second type of atmospheric change is the depletion of the stratospheric ozone layer as a result of chemical reactions involving chlorofluorocarbons (CFCs), methane, nitrous oxides, and halons. Certain amounts of some of these substances (not, however, the CFCs nor Halon 1301) are emitted as a result of natural processes; but the critical fraction of the aggregate is provided by anthropogenic emissions. By allowing an increase in ultra-violet B radiation, depletion of the ozone layer results in an increase in skin cancer and increased damage to the eyes. Increased UVB radiation also damages animal immune systems and adversely affects plant growth and production on land and in the sea. Studies of the extent of effects on plants and animals are not complete, but it is likely that the indirect effects of substantial ozone layer depletion on human welfare through disruption of food chains would be significant.[2]

Depletion of the stratospheric ozone layer by CFCs was first hypothesized less than 20 years ago.[3] The existence of a hole in the ozone layer over Antarctica in the southern springtime was discovered ten years later.[4] It has grown in extent since then. In 1989, parallel, though less extreme, conditions were reported for the northern hemisphere.[5]

Evidence of the depletion of ozone was followed by an impressive advance in scientific understanding of its dynamics and unusually prompt international and national regulatory action. The first international meeting of experts to consider the implications of ozone depletion was convened by UNEP in 1977. International legal instruments are the Vienna Convention for the Protection of the Ozone Layer (1985), the Montreal Protocol on Substances that Deplete the Ozone Layer (1987) and its London Amendments (1990). By May, 1991, 78 nations had ratified the Vienna Convention; 71, the Montreal protocol; and 3, the London Amendments. This is a relatively rapid reaction in the field of international affairs, but even if the most effective controls were instituted right away, the damage to the ozone layer may not be repaired for almost 100 years, because the critical reactants are so persistent. In fact, there is as yet no assurance that effective controls will be put in place throughout the world.

The third change related to the atmosphere is that which may be taking place in the earth's climate, namely, an increase in global mean temperature as a result of an enhanced greenhouse effect resulting from increased emissions of carbon dioxide, methane, CFCs, nitrous oxide, ozone and water vapor. There is a chance that this change, of which there is already some evidence, will not materialize, but only a few scientists now challenge the view that the threat of greenhouse warming is real. The consensus is that the atmosphere will warm on average by between 1.5 and 4.5 deg. C. during the next 50 years.

In the meantime, the atmospheric concentrations of the most important greenhouse gases continue to increase. Current rates of increase per year are 0.4% for carbon dioxide, 1.0% for methane, 5.0% for each of CFC 11 and CFC 12 and 0.2% for nitrous oxide.[1d] The main source of carbon dioxide which is susceptible to control is the use of fossil fuels. Nitrous oxides are released from the same processes and also as a result of microbial action. Methane is released by the action of anaerobic bacteria occurring in natural wetlands, rice paddies and the digestive tracts of a large number of animals that consume cellulose. CFCs are emitted as a result of the use of various propellants, solvents and coolants.

While there is much uncertainty about the likely manifestations of climate change in terms of local temperatures, precipitation, winds, etc., there is no doubt that the effects will differ from region to region. The effects will relate to the growth of forests and agricultural crops, the distribution and abundance of wild fauna and flora, the supply of water and the level of the seas, among other things. All these changes will require significant and in some instances uncomfortable adaptations by people.

The rise in sea levels that is considered likely will clearly require difficult adaptations in the uses of the world's coastal zones. These are the areas between the outer edges of the continental shelves and the inland limits of the coastal plains. These are the regions of greatest biological productivity in the world. They are the home of 60% of the world's population. Adaptation to sea level rise will involve deciding which areas should be protected from inundation and which should be allowed to be flooded. These will be difficult judgments, requiring consideration of not only the value of existing infrastructures and of land as space but also the biological productivity of the threatened land, its freedom from contamination etc.

Changes in the ozone layer and climate change due to the enhancement of the greenhouse effect are clearly global in that the effects that they cause can be felt everywhere. Both types of change have received a lot of attention from the media and are becoming widely known, but while there has, as noted above, been significant reaction to the threat of the depleted ozone layer, little has been done to diminish the likelihood of global warming. One may speculate that there are two reasons for this; one is that the evidence for the depletion of the ozone layer is more compelling; the other is that the sacrifices that people must make to reduce damage to the ozone layer are much less significant than those that would be required to diminish the speed and amplitude of global warming.

IV. CHANGES IN FRESH AND MARINE WATERS

Fresh water is a requirement of all life. People cannot live without it nor can they live without the food that they derive from the plants and animals that similarly depend upon it.

Increasing numbers of people using ever greater quantities of water, particularly in developed countries where luxury uses are commonly encouraged by improper pricing policies, are placing a stress upon water supplies that may soon be out of hand. Global water withdrawals have increased 35 times during the past three centuries.[1d] Access to water for domestic use and for irrigation is a crucial factor in the sustainability of arid land societies. Irrigated agriculture accounts for about 70% of water withdrawals throughout the world. If present trends of use continue, water withdrawals will increase by as much as 35% by 2000. The increase in water withdrawals cannot go on forever. Already ground water resources are being severely depleted in many areas, including the American west, by "mining" at rates in excess of their rates of replenishment. It will not be possible to sustain current patterns of freshwater use if human populations reach their projected total of 10 billion by 2050. Competition for water is already a reality in several of the more arid parts of the world and threatens to become a severely destabilizing factor in some regions.

Apart from problems related to the actual quantity of water available for use, many people in developing countries must spend considerable time and effort to obtain it. In 1989, 1,550 million people were without ready access to potable water.[6] This was a decline of 500 million over the preceding decade, a slight improvement that would have been much greater if the human population had not increased so much.

Rivers, lakes and wetlands, and ground water as well as coastal waters may be polluted by industrial and agricultural effluents. Contamination by pesticides and fertilizers seems to be increasing and is considered increasingly important. Treated and especially untreated domestic wastes and the sediments yielded by accelerated erosion are also important pollutants. Provision of sanitation in developing countries is falling behind the rate of population increase. The pathogens found in polluted waters are the biggest cause of illness and death in developing countries. Salinization, acidification, and toxic contamination of fresh waters are widespread. All the factors which cause a decline in water quality significantly reduce the value of water to people, change the characteristics of aquatic ecosystems and may threaten the survival of aquatic plant and animal life.

Changes in the quality of both fresh and marine waters can occur as a result of deposition from the atmosphere or by direct contamination from shipping, shoreline discharges, and river outfalls. More than three quarters of marine pollution comes from land-based sources. Much pollution, including major oil spills, is the result of carelessness or unavoidable accident. But despite both global and regional conventions that regulate the process, some wastes are still deliberately dumped. Most of the adverse effects of marine pollution, whether by heavy metals and other toxins or hydrocarbons, are on plant and animal life; corals and mangroves, being immobile, are particularly vulnerable. Pollution caused by the deposition of sediments is widespread and serious[7] and is a particularly significant threat to corals. The presence of persistent plastic debris, largely a result of carelessness in the fishing industry, is a nuisance to tourists and also a threat to marine life.

International action to deal with pollution of the seas began almost 40 years ago with the conclusion of the Convention for the Prevention of the Pollution of the Sea by Oil (1954). A broader and more effective instrument, the International Convention for the Prevention of Pollution from Ships was concluded in 1973. During the preparations for the Stockholm Conference, negotiation began on a Convention to control dumping of wastes at sea, adopted in 1972 as the London Dumping Convention, while pollution from land-based sources of the marine environment of the North Sea and the Northeast Atlantic was covered by the Paris Convention of 1974. Effective action aimed at the control of pollution in the so-called regional seas, such as the Mediterranean and the Caribbean, where problems of the transboundary flow of pollutants were particularly troublesome, began in the late 1970s when UNEP got its Regional Seas Programme under way.

Action to manage fresh waters that cross international boundaries has been limited. The Boundary Waters Convention of 1909 (Canada and the United States) and the agreements of 1963 and 1976 covering the waters of the Rhine River are the most important. Beginnings have been made in negotiating several other agreements for the management of international inland waters, for example, the Nile, the Zambezi and Lake Chad, but much more remains to be done.

V. CHANGES IN THE LAND

The land is changed when it is converted from one use to another or degraded because of misuse. Practically all changes, except some of those resulting from fire and natural erosion, are caused by people. Changes in the land occurred before our history was recorded; they continue and intensify as a consequence of mounting human numbers and increasing per capita demand (particularly in developed countries) for some of the products of the land. The use of new technologies, such as the application of fertilizers and pesticides; the employment of heavy equipment for tilling the soil, harvesting crops, cutting trees and moving logs; and new methods of irrigation also change the land by affecting plant cover and microfauna as well as the tilth, inherent fertility and stability of the soil.

We have changed the land and continue to do so to secure much of the food, fibre and special products that we need or want. In doing so, the 5.3 billion people now on earth use 40% of the energy of the sun that is made available by green plants on land.[8] We also use land as space for settlements, infrastructure and industries. In a number of countries, these sorts of uses have taken over a significant extent of valuable agricultural land.

Considered along with air, water and biota as one of the elements of ecosystems, land also provides a wide range of valuable ecological services. As ecosystems are degraded, the extent and quality of those services diminishes and it becomes necessary to compensate for the loss by artificial and often costly means.

Global data on land use, and on the extent of land degradation and desertification, are incomplete and difficult to compare from year to year or region to region. It is nevertheless clear that land degradation is increasingly severe and widespread. The extent and productivity of arable, pastoral and forest land continues to decline because of poor agricultural, pastoral and forestry practices. Of the earth's total land surface of just over 13,076 million hectares, 15%, (almost 2,000 million hectares) is affected by human-induced soil degradation. The total extent of the world's croplands is 1,473 million hectares; of this, 4 to 5% (some 6 to 7 million hectares) is made unproductive each year by erosion. Of the 220 million hectares of irrigated land, 30% is affected by secondary salinization. Urbanization claims almost 1 million hectares a year, much of it prime farmland. Data on global rates of desertification are unsatisfactory but various national examples indicate that annual rates of desertification of up to 4% are not uncommon and can reach 10%.[9] The overall result is that the world inventory of agriculturally productive land is diminishing quite rapidly in both quality and quantity.

While the land has many uses, its use for food production is the most vital from the human standpoint. Despite substantial increases in productivity in developed countries and in countries where Green Revolution techniques have been adopted with apparent success, the sustainability of many of these increases is open to question. The prospect is that the requirements of increasing human populations will add to the pressure to convert forest and grazing land to crop land, and that the need to produce ever larger amounts of food will lead to the more widespread adoption of unsustainable land use practices.

VI. CHANGES IN BIOTA

The rise to global dominance of the human species has led to the appropriation of an astonishingly large fraction of global productivity. Clearly this could not have occurred without a compensating reduction of the share of that productivity used by wild animals and plants. The composition of the earth's biota has been evolving for as long as we can imagine, but the impact of the human presence, and particularly of human activities of the scale and complexity that they have reached during the past five hundred years, has brought about an unprecedented reduction in the populations of most species of wildlife and, inevitably as well, in the diversity of global flora and fauna.

It is not just species that become extinct; entire natural systems are being reduced in size and complexity or completely eliminated. This process took place centuries ago in the ancient civilizations of Asia and the Middle East and fairly recently in the industrialized countries, where watercourses have been dammed and diverted, wetlands drained and forests cut down. Today in the developing countries, where rapid rates of population increase coincide with the widespread introduction of new machinery for resource extraction and land transformation, natural systems are being degraded much more quickly.

It is unfortunately true that even now the rates and extent of ecosystem and species loss are, with a few conspicuous exceptions, poorly understood and even less well documented. For example, it has been estimated that about 17 million hectares of closed and open tropical forests are destroyed each year and that almost the same extent is grossly disrupted.[10] Yet in 1987, according to the Brazilian Space Research Institute, forest fires destroyed 20 million hectares in that country alone. As regards species loss, one estimate is that 312 of the described species of animals have become extinct in the world since about 1600, but since the invertebrate extinctions included in that total (83 is the figure given) are only those in the United States including Hawaii, this is clearly a significantly low estimate.[11] Other estimates, based on extrapolation, suggest that some 60,000 of the world's 240,000 plant species and an even higher proportion of land vertebrates and insects could become extinct over the next 30 years. It is difficult to devise and evaluate strategies to preserve species on the basis of inadequate data, but there are grounds for treating the matter as urgent.

Species decline in numbers or become extinct mainly because of two factors, which may of course operate simultaneously. The first is the consumptive use of animals and plants to meet human needs at unsustainable rates; the second cause of decline is loss of habitat resulting from the cropping of the forests and the conversion of forests, grasslands, wetlands and other natural systems to plantation forests, croplands, managed pastures, reservoirs, settlements,etc. In addition, large areas of habitat have been degraded and their carrying capacity reduced as a consequence, for example, of pollution or accelerated soil erosion. All these factors have become more significant as human populations and rates of consumption of natural resources have increased. Tropical moist forests, tropical dry forests, savannahs, wetlands, mangroves and coral reefs are all under severe stress.

Loss of biodiversity is becoming a widely shared concern, but it is not always recognized that the term refers to the loss of diversity at three distinct, though related, levels, each of which has significant implications for people. Intra-specific diversity is the variation within species; it is important because it provides a basis for species to adapt to changing conditions and serves as raw material for improving domestic varieties of plants and animals. It is threatened largely through lack of care; not enough attention is given to the preservation of the wild relatives of domestic species or of breeds that have gone out of favor. Species variability — the number of species that exist — is what most people think about when they hear that biodiversity must be maintained. Species loss is a matter of concern for several reasons. It is morally right to preserve species, or to put it another way, we do not have the right to cause or allow another species to become extinct. Many species are actually or potentially of value to people because they or their parts or products are known to be, or may be found to be, economically useful. An additional value is based on the fact that each species plays some role, perhaps a crucial one, in the ecosystem of which it is a part. Ecosystems are the third level of biodiversity. If they are lost, so also may be the diversity of species and the intra-specific diversity that they comprise, but, in addition, and more importantly, a set of complex ecological functions will have ceased. These are the irreplaceable functions involved in energy flows and nutrient circulation that maintain the dynamic balance of natural systems.

The extent and significance of the loss of biodiversity has become a matter of increased public interest and concern, particularly in developed countries, during the last few years. The World Conservation Union (IUCN) took the lead in assembling the data needed to make the case for international legal action to conserve biodiversity and in developing the concepts that should be reflected in a convention. UNEP stimulated and is supporting the international negotiations which may bring a convention into effect, perhaps within the next year.

VII. SETTLEMENTS

The greatest opportunities and the greatest challenges to manage environmental change face the inhabitants of settlements, particularly of major cities. Cities present major opportunities for moving toward development that is sustainable because they are the main centers for education, new employment, and economic opportunity. It is in cities where opinion leaders and decision makers reside. At the same time, cities present a formidable challenge to environmental management. Urban settlements process and consume vast quantities of natural resources. They occupy large areas of land and preclude its use for other purposes. They are major sources of pollution, which affects the environment far beyond their boundaries.

The world is becoming increasingly urbanized; half of humanity will live in cities by the end of the century. The size of cities is also growing and the rates of growth are striking. During the 1970s, Mexico City and Sao Paulo each increased by half a million people each year. It has been estimated that by the year 2000 there will be 61 cities with more than 4 million inhabitants each in the developing countries, and 25 of that size in the industrialized countries.

The present condition of cities, particularly in developing countries is far from satisfactory. Poor housing, which is in any case in short supply, dangerously polluted air, inadequate water supplies and sanitation services, limited access to health care, and dirt and noise are dominant features over large areas of many cities. They lead to despair, anger, and social instability.

Urban problems are a result of rapid population growth and the attraction to the city of the increasing number of persons for whom opportunities in rural areas are becoming more and more limited. Urban problems are compounded by the fact that many urban centers lack the power, or even the possibility, to raise revenues and regulate activities to improve the urban environment. Recent years have nevertheless seen an increasing assumption of responsibility for the environment by city governments, particularly in industrialized countries.

VIII. ETHICS, ECONOMICS AND EQUITY

In the foregoing sections, brief reference has been made to the multitude of human actions that affect the environment and that are thereby likely to have a profound influence on the human future. Many of these actions are something more than a simple response to our needs for food, shelter, community infrastructure, etc. They are also greatly influenced by our value systems. In considering the steps that need to be taken to ensure a sustainable future in the face of global change, it is just as necessary to take account of questions of value as it is to understand the dynamics of ecological relationships.

There is little doubt that material values have dominated the societies that have been ascendant in the world during the last several centuries. In most parts of the world, the decisions of the most powerful institutions, those that control business, industry, and government, have taken the accumulation of profit on investment as the most important, and very often the only, criterion by which an activity should be judged. An inevitable corollary of this attitude is the conviction that growth must always be sought, must never be questioned. (Even in those societies where the concept of profit was not acknowledged, the operation of its surrogate, the power to command the distribution of goods and services for personal advantage, had similar social effects.) This is the belief system that insists that everything must be expressed in monetary terms; if it cannot be, it is marginal, valueless, scarcely worth consideration. This value system, with its emphasis on increasing consumption of material goods, reinforced incessantly by advertising and popular culture, has spread ever more widely and become ever more powerful, despite the fact that the basic tenets of the world's major religions have been oriented toward non-material values.

There is a growing awareness now that a belief system which emphasizes material values above all others encourages the increasing consumption of resources and denies the importance of values that cannot be brought into the market place, inhibits the full development of the human potential, and is inimical to the evolution of sustainable societies.

For many persons concerned about the environment and development, ethical questions are now seen to underlie all others. This is not to say that material things are unimportant, that taking a profit is immoral, that economic yardsticks are not useful as one of the guidelines for decision making, that the rational use of resources is unethical, or that development is less important than we once believed. What is claimed is that the duty to care for other people and other forms of life, now and in the future, should take precedence in making decisions about environment and development. Reflecting this point of view, *Caring for the Earth: a Strategy for Sustainable Living* emphasizes that development should not be at the expense of other groups or other generations, that the aim should be to share fairly the benefits and costs of resource use and environmental conservation among different communities and interest groups. According to the new strategy, it is a matter of both ethics and practicality to manage development so that it does not threaten the survival of other species or eliminate their habitats.[8]

It was the particular contribution of the World Commission on Environment and Development to clarify in political terms the relationship between the environment and the economy.[12] This vital relationship is indeed becoming of increasing interest to economists, business people and politicians, but failure to integrate environment and economy in development planning remains widespread. As a result, economic policy has often worked against sustainability. With the help of innovative economic analysis, the consequences of this failure are now being recognized, as is the fact that economic policies, if they are carefully thought through, can be used to help achieve sustainability. Economic instruments, linking self-interest with the common good, can be a strong and effective force for sustainable resource use and good environmental management. They will be even more useful if better methods are devised to value the environment and its functions. Environmental parameters are inadequately valued in contemporary economic analysis and this is an area in which more effort is much needed. But even if the valuation problem were solved, economic instruments would not be able to do the job alone. The market mechanism will rationalize our activities and make them more efficient, but it must be coupled with laws that assert and safeguard human rights, protect the interests of the unborn and the disadvantaged and conserve species and ecosystems.

Questions of global equity are attracting increasing attention. That we should move to eliminate unfair advantages in conditions of trade and extend opportunities for sustainable development throughout human society is now widely seen as a matter of ethics, of simple justice. But it goes farther than that. Logic suggests, and experience so far confirms, that it will be virtually impossible to adapt to global change in a world of unequal advantage and opportunity. Adjustments will be required world-wide, stabilizing and reducing resource consumption in the industrialized countries, bringing population increase under control where it remains above replacement level. Reducing dangerous emissions to the atmosphere, retaining natural stores of carbon and preserving biodiversity will all require investment. These investments cannot be made by countries that labor under severe economic disadvantage. That is why there is now widespread support for the belief that it is in the global interest to develop economic stability and a strong capacity for environmental management in all countries as quickly as possible.

IX. INSTITUTIONS

Institutions relating to the environment and the use of natural resources have a history of centuries, but their prevalence and effectiveness took a quantum leap in the last third of this century, particularly during the 1970s. This is, of course, a direct reflection of the fact that environmental and resource issues were moving to the forefront of public concern as problems of pollution and resource depletion worsened.

Nearly all countries now have laws and organizations for the purpose of managing natural resources and the environment and these are increasingly supported by qualified staff. This represents a tremendous advance over the situation of 20 years ago. As already noted, international laws are now in force and international programs underway in a number of regions and in respect of some global concerns. Even though some of the programs are weak and patchy, the concept of international cooperation in the field of the environment is becoming well established. This is particularly encouraging because active international cooperation must be greatly extended and intensified to cope with global change.

The effectiveness of institutions is crucial since they will be the agents through which attempts will be made to cope with global change and to bring its causes under control. National and international institutions — laws, organizations and procedures — relating to the environment must be reviewed to evaluate their effectiveness in supporting adaptation to global change. Institutions for monitoring and research can lay the groundwork for better understanding of the causes and likely impacts of global change and for developing the most practical ways of adapting to it. Institutions for education and communication will be important for disseminating information about these matters.

At both the national and international levels, institutional responses were, and still are, largely sectoral and, therefore, often less than adequate. To put it another way, in designing organizations and procedures to deal with environmental issues, there has been a consistent failure to recognize the systemic nature of environmental problems, the complexity of the interrelationships among elements of the environment. The inadequacies of most institutions for managing resources are rooted in similar shortcomings, compounded by failure to understand the multiple values of natural resources and the ecosystems within which they exist. In very few jurisdictions is there an attempt to coordinate, let alone integrate, environmental and economic policies and planning. So long as this is the case, environmental and resource problems will continue to arise; they will likely become more difficult and they will certainly be more costly to solve than they would if they had been foreseen by a fully integrated planning process.

The situation is no better at the international level and is worsened by a lamentable failure to provide adequate financial support. Despite the idealistic initiative which led to the establishment of the United Nations Environment Programme 20 years ago, and innumerable idealistic statements on the part of almost all the principal actors on the scene since then, the United Nations system has not adopted an integrated approach to environment and development. Attempts at coordination, such as the System-Wide Medium-Term Environment Programme, are more like catalogues of good intentions than firm commitments to integrated action.[13] Agencies with overlapping mandates launch competing programs in the same country. Proposals for massive development projects with totally unacceptable social and environmental impacts are only now being questioned, and the questioning is due more to the activities of non-governmental organizations than to the operation of an effective coordinating mechanism within the United Nations system. The roots of these problems lie in the unchecked power of the sectoral constituencies to which the specialized agencies respond and in the failure of governments to counterbalance that power. Even more fundamental is the fact that concern for the environment is still generally seen as peripheral to concern for the economy. Both national and international institutions still largely reflect that perception.

X. CONCLUSIONS

The present state of the global environment reflects the stresses imposed by increasing numbers of people, growing demands for goods and services and more invasive techniques of land management. During the past decade, pollution of the lower atmosphere has diminished in some respects and in some areas, but on balance it has worsened. Damage to the ozone layer has increased. The emissions of greenhouse gases continue to increase and the likelihood of global warming, with all the consequences that it will entail, grows greater. The pollution of both marine and fresh waters continues; improvements in many of the industrialized countries are generally insufficient to achieve desired standards. Water quality in the countries formerly known as the "planned economies" and in developing countries is generally unsatisfactory. Problems of water supply, principally but not only in Africa, are worsening and likely to continue to do so as human populations increase. Loss of productivity of the land and desertification are more serious now than they were ten years ago. Deforestation and the associated reduction of biological diversity continues, not only in the tropics, but also in temperate rain forests;

and greatly increased utilization of the Siberian taiga is thought to be imminent.

The picture is by no means uniform. Pollution control technology is improving and the effect of regulations, combined in some instances with economic incentives, is significantly increasing its applications. In a number of industrialized countries there have been significant improvements in the control of air and water pollution. On the other hand, we are only now becoming aware of the gross and long standing pollution of air, water and soil to which the Soviet Union and the countries of Eastern Europe have been subject for many decades. Preoccupied with the need for rapid economic development to relieve intolerable social and health conditions, most countries of the developing world have allowed pollution to become a serious threat to people and other life. The pattern of development cooperation that has prevailed until now has done practically nothing to correct that imbalance. There is, however, some indication that greater attention will be paid to environmental issues and sustainability in the future.

Existing regimes of resource management seem unlikely to be sustainable, except perhaps in western Europe and parts of other industrialized regions. In the management of forests, fisheries and, in some areas, soils, immediate benefits are being sought at the expense of longer-term productive stability. This will have the inevitable effect of limiting future options for development.

There are, at the same time, two aspects of the current situation that are encouraging.

The first is that human ability to manage the environment and its resources is improving, in the technical sense. The store of knowledge about the characteristics of important species of animals and plants; about the functioning of ecosystems; about the nature of atmospheric and oceanic systems and biogeochemical cycles is growing. There are many examples of good management of land and other resources. The techniques exist for sustainable agriculture and sustainable forestry; they need to be coupled with the social and economic measures that will make them work. There are many cases of well managed "clean" industries: enough to make it clear that green targets can be achieved, not enough yet to achieve them.

The second cause for hope is the tremendous growth in awareness of environmental problems, particularly in industrialized countries. This is slowly being complemented by a realization that there are values beyond those material ones to which we have so long given prominence. As, and if, this realization spreads and becomes an element in our political orientation, we may hope that changes in human attitudes and practices will be sufficient to enable adaptation to global change in the environment.

REFERENCES

1. (a) *World Resources 1986*. World Resources Inst. and International Inst. for Environment and Development. Basic Books, New York. 1986.
   (b) World Resources 1987. International Inst. for Environment and Development and World Resources Inst. Basic Books. New York 1987.
   (c) *World Resources 1988-1989*. World Resources Institute, International Inst. for Environment and Development in collaboration with the United Nations Environment Programme. Basic Books, New York 1988.
   (d) *World Resources 1990-91*. World Resources Inst. in collaboration with the United Nations Development Programme. Oxford Univ. Press, New York. Oxford, 1990.
   (e) UNEP 1991 United Nations Environment Programme, *Environmental Data Report*, 3rd Edition, Basil Blackwell, Oxford.
   (f) UNEP. *The World Environment 1971-1992* (provisional title, in preparation).

2. United Nations Environment Programme. *The Ozone Layer*, Nairobi. 1987.

3. Molina, M J and F S Rowland. *Stratospheric sink for chlorofluoromethane: Chlorine-atom catalyzed destruction of the ozone.* Nature (249) 810-812. 1974.

4. Farman,J C, B G Gardner and J D Shanklin, *Large Losses of Total Ozone in Antarctica Reveal Seasonal ClOx/NOx Interaction.* Nature,vol. 315 pp 207-210, 1985.

5. Ozone Trends Panel (R.T. Watson, et al.) *Present State of Knowledge of the Upper Atmosphere, 1988.* An Assessment Report. NASA, Washington, D.C. 1989.

6. United Nations Development Programme, *Human Development Report 1991*. Oxford Univ. Press, New York Oxford 1991.

7. *Group of Experts on the Scientific Aspects of Marine Pollution Protecting and Managing the Oceans*. Report of 20th Session, May 1990.

8. Vitousek,P.M.,P.R. Ehrlich, A.H. Ehrlich,and P.A Manson. *Human Appropriation of the Products of Photosynthesis*. BioScience 36(6): 368-373 1986.

9. IUCN/UNEP/WWF. *Caring for the Earth: A Strategy for Sustainable Living*, Gland, Switzerland 1991.

10. FAO/UNEP *Tropical Forest Resources*. Forestry Paper 30. FAO Rome. 1982.

11. World Conservation Monitoring Centre. *Global Biodiversity 1992: Status of the Earth's Living Resources*. Compiled by World Conservation Monitoring Centre, Cambridge (in preparation).

12. World Commission on Environment and Development. *Our Common Future* Oxford University Press, Oxford, New York 1987.

13. United Nations Environment Programme. *System-Wide Medium-Term Environment Programme for the period 1990-1995*. United Nations Environment Programme, Nairobi, 1987 UNEP/GCSS.I/2.

A Case Study
Japan: Resource Conservation and Distribution

Mayumi Moriyama

BANQUET ADDRESS

It is my great honor and privilege to speak at such a significant forum, "Global Change and the Human Prospect." I would like to congratulate Sigma Xi, The Scientific Research Society for hosting such a global conference.

Honestly, I am not a professional expert on environment problems as such. I was the Minister of State in charge of environment in the very beginning of the first KAIFU Cabinet, but it was only for two weeks before I was suddenly moved to be the Chief Cabinet Secretary. However, two weeks' experience in the Environment Agency accelerated my interest in the issue, and since I left the cabinet position I have been actively working on the Commission of Environment in the House of Councillors.

Today, I would like to share my appreciation for one of the most important issues of the current world, resource conservation and distribution. In doing so, I would also like to consider the role of women in bettering the world's environment.

Firstly, I will examine the background of the current global environmental situation. The world situation has greatly changed during the past 20 years, since the 1972 Stockholm Conference. Nowadays, various activities of human beings, both economic and social, are conducted on a global scale, and environmental problems accordingly have become a threat to all of humanity. Changes in components of the rain or atmosphere, or the amount of vegetation the earth enjoys, reflect the crisis the earth is now facing. The earth's ecology in its present form, as various living

Mayumi Moriyama is Senior Director of the Special Committee on Environment for the Japanese House of Councillors and Chairperson of the Hokuriku Region Development Committee of the Research Commission on National Land Development.

things coexisted through the past many billions of years, is now endangered.

The World Commission on Environment and Development, which was established as one of the United Nations' Committees in response to Japan's proposal, released in 1987 a report entitled *Our Common Future*. The report calls forth the idea of sustainable development, which is defined as "development that meets the needs of the present without compromising the ability of future generations to meet their own needs." Since the release of this report, the idea of sustainable development has become recognized throughout the world, and we are now striving to materialize this idea.

Human beings, especially after the Industrial Revolution, have been gradually, yet continuously, imposing a burden on the earth's environment by extracting resources from the earth and by exhausting gaseous, liquid and solid waste. Therefore, the environmental problems of today can be thought of as the consequences of inconsiderate human conduct over many years. Now the problems have become so large that it is no longer possible to completely eliminate them by means of technology and investment only. Rather, changes in economic conditions and our lifestyle must accompany them.

I believe that now is the time for each of us to modify his or her lifestyle so that it becomes agreeable to environmental conditions such that the earth's ecology and social activities of human beings can be preserved in harmony without threat.

Secondly, I would like to go over the history of environmental issues in Japan. Japan is surrounded by the ocean and 70% of its land is covered with forests. Moreover, it is blessed with the turn of four beautiful seasons and a good harvest. Therefore, until recently, we Japanese have taken our rich natural environment for granted. On the other hand, our country has sought economic growth and material comfort, and we have unknowingly adapted mass-consumption and mass-waste as a part of our daily life. Particularly since the 1960s, high profitability and high productivity have been praised most, and this tendency naturally led to various public hazards, including the ones that threatened the health of people. Realizing the seriousness of the situation, the government and the people together tried to eliminate those hazards, and consequently most of the public hazards have since become less severe. However, problems such as air pollution, caused by emission of nitrogen oxide in urban areas, and water pollution, caused by household waste water, still need further improvement.

Simply placing restrictions on the sources of problems is not enough. We must start looking at the structure of our economic world through new eyes in order to formulate suitable policies.

During the past few years, the Japanese people have become aware of various environmental problems more than ever. It is because they have realized the fact that all problems, from immediate ones like air and water pollution, to the long-term problems of global warming and ozone layer destruction, or problems of the destruction of rain forests in far away developing countries, reflect the phenomena observed on this earth, our common treasure, and that all the problems share root causes. In other words, people are now actually seeing rips on the common homeland of all human beings, the earth.

The Prime Minister's Office of the Japanese government carried out "A Public Opinion Poll on the Disposal of Garbage" in 1988. According to the result of this poll, 70% of people agreed that "It is better not to have disposable goods arrive on the market so that the amount of garbage can be restricted." Only 20% of people disagreed with this statement. As this poll tells, there are now many people with an interest in environmental issues. To encourage such an attitude, I believe that the government must, in quest of the establishment of a "recycling-oriented society," call on each citizen to recycle and reuse resources and start acting locally.

I see that the idea, "Think Globally, Act Locally," is gaining support. Of course, reforms that may even affect the culture lying behind our accustomed daily life, or activities of enterprises, cannot be completed in a day, but why don't we start with little things around us? I think that one can start with small things. For example, one can stop tossing away empty aluminum cans, and one can start treasuring flowers, trees, birds, and insects. One can then eventually change one's lifestyle so as to actively become environment-friendly. People are actually beginning to feel this way and act locally.

Thirdly, I, as the former Director General of the Environment Agency, would like to introduce to you one of Japan's efforts with regard to the concept of sustainable development, namely the attempt to transform our society into a recycling-oriented society. Japan was the first country to institute a law concerning the idea of a recycling-oriented society, namely the "Recycling Law." It was instituted in April of 1991. Let me briefly explain the key concepts lying behind this law. They are the ideas of limiting the amount of natural resources put in economic activities, and reusing and recycling the resources, and at the same time limiting the amount of waste to be returned to nature. The ingredients of the waste must be agreeable to the environment.

Let me now refer to the historic traditions of Japan in relation to these concepts. Japan is an island isolated from continents, and its mountainous land, surrounding seas, and rich nature have long provided the basis for agriculture to be a main economic activity in Japan. Agriculture is a recycling-oriented activity that produces the necessities of human life by utilizing resources from nature, such as air, water, earth, animals and plants, and its products are then eventually returned to nature. The fact that this recycling-oriented activity has been carried on for thousands of years in Japan may be the most apparent sign that the idea of sustainable development is already there behind the Japanese culture.

The concept of treasuring and taking great care of every little thing has been a moral necessity for Japanese people. Parents have always reminded children of hardships farmers went through in growing rice, and have taught them to be thankful to the God of Nature and farmers, and never to waste even a grain of rice. Middle-aged people today, who were taught this way, sometimes complain that they are unable to diet, because their parents' words are still alive deep in their minds.

The word "mottainai," admonishing others for being wasteful, is heard very often in daily conversations. When I first came to the U.S., I kept thinking "mottainai, mottainai, " as I watched Americans who left the lights in empty rooms on during the night, and who used a thick paper towel to wipe little stains and threw the used towel away, as if it were a matter of course.

However, while such concepts may be still alive, Japan of today is not the same as Japan of old days. In the course of industrialization and economic growth, Japanese have come to be familiar with the act of wasting with the increase of disposable supplies, one-way containers, products that contain hazardous materials, undisposable waste and so on; the amount of garbage, too, increased and its ingredients have changed. Now the disposal of such garbage has become a social problem.

Now let us see how resources are presently provided, consumed, and then disposed of in Japan. Japan is a country where about 2.3% of the world's population live on land covering only 0.3% of the globe. In 1990, the "Committee to Discuss the System of a Recycling-oriented Society for the Purpose of Environment Protection," established by the Environment Agency, released a report titled "Toward the Realization of the Recycling-oriented Society." In this report, Japan's material balance is estimated as follows. Each year in Japan, about 1.83 billion tons of raw resources are used as productive input. About 1.15 billion tons of products, including both exports and those for domestic use, are produced and about 80 million tons of food is consumed. About 330 million tons of energy is consumed to support these activities. And about 270 million tons of both industrial and general waste is disposed. Within this amount, about 160 million tons is reused. This amounts to about 8% of approximately 2 billion tons of energy and resources consumed.

As you know, resource utilization brings waste as exhaust into the atmosphere, sewage into rivers, lakes, or seas in addition to solid and liquid waste disposed of in a variety of areas. According to the report of 1987, in Japan, about 244 million tons of carbon dioxide is exhausted into the atmosphere as a result of combustion of chemical fuel, and this amount comprises about 4.7% of the world's total carbon dioxide emissions. It can be thought that each person in Japan is, therefore, responsible for 2.5 tons of carbon dioxide emission, and this figure is much higher in the United States, which is 6.1 tons per person.

In Japan, the Cabinet instituted the "Action Program to Arrest Global Warming" in October last year, and attempts have been made to prevent further increase in the amount of carbon dioxide emission, both per person and as a nation. Internationally, too, similar issues were discussed at the World Climate Conference and some agreements have been made.

However, I am sorry to say that the United States, who is the greatest emitter of carbon dioxide in the world, has not been very active in setting a definite goal regarding the reduction of its emissions. I hope that the United States will come up with a constructive goal and start working for its achievement as soon as possible.

Now, I would like to elaborate on some efforts to establish a recycling-oriented society. Today some of the recyclable resources that become household waste are collected, dissolved, and reused. Such materials include not only paper, aluminum cans, glass bottles, and clothes, but also durable goods such as cars and household electric appliances. With regard to the waste materials from households, women are playing the most important role in reducing them. While Japanese women have been making their presence known in various fields such as economics, politics, and other social activities, the fact that they play the most responsible and authoritative role in their homes also cannot be ignored. Nowadays, when the problem of environmental pollution due to household waste is apparent, it can be considered that women hold the key to the solution of these problems. Women themselves have also become aware of this. Needless to say, in their roles as housewives, they have started various activities in cooperation with each other to better their communities' environment.

Housewives of today, who have grown up in an affluent society, certainly differ from those of indigent days in their way of thinking and their manner of action. However, their efforts are real in a sense that they are setting to work, not because poverty forces them to take such action, but because they recognize the importance of environmental issues, and the need to protect the health and safety of their families, and to leave the earth with a rich and beautiful nature for their children.

Those women's activities include cooperative recycling and reuse of paper, aluminum cans and oil. They produce homemade foods from natural materials grown without the use of agricultural chemicals, promote campaigns to discourage citizens from purchasing wastefully packed goods, and enhance education of citizens to get them to be more careful with sewage to protect rivers and lakes. They keep their eyes on nature, including cleaning up mountains and beaches and promoting various campaigns to protect nature, such as forests and lakes. Depending on the local situation, these activities are conducted at different levels by concerned women throughout the country.

Such activities by women have influenced the policies of local and national government, and have pushed them to incorporate environmental concerns in instituting policies. For example, in Shiga Prefecture, which encompasses Lake Biwa, the sale of detergents that contain organic phosphorus, a major water pollutant, was prohibited about ten years ago. This was a result of efforts of women's organizations in the area. This movement spread throughout the country and now none of the Japanese detergent makers manufactures detergents that contain organic phosphorus.

To give one more example of women's achievement, realizing that the production of recycled paper by paper manufacturers was unprofitable unless a certain amount of used paper was available, women's organizations called out to the public to collect used paper, sorted the paper according to its quality, and made the business economically feasible.

Each of these activities may be a small one, but women's activities show how efforts to "act locally" can lead to success. I believe that Japan owes a great deal to those zealous and active women.

As for Japan's industrial waste, mud and scrap wood comprise most of it. Organic mud from the city sewerage, as well as from the paper and pulp industry and the food manufacturing industry, can be used as compost or fuel. Inorganic mud, as accompanied with silt, can be recovered and recycled. Scrap wood and wood chips can be used either as construction lumber or chipwood. Waste concrete is used as a substitute for crushed stones to pave roads, and waste asphalt is used again as asphalt or as a substitute for crushed stones or gravel. The recycling rate of scrap wood is comparatively low, but is expected to increase in coming years.

With respect to the creation of a recycling-oriented society, first of all, producers are the suppliers of products, the users of the recycled materials, and moreover the ones who have the most accurate information on commodities. Therefore, I believe that producers should be encouraged to produce goods that can easily be recycled and to use recycled raw materials, at the same time improving the manner and quality of repair services to extend the life of their products. Distributors should also improve their service by, for example, discontinuing excessive packing in order to make recycling easier and to reduce the amount of waste.

I believe that we must pay greater attention to the role of consumers. Consumers are the ones who select the goods to purchase, therefore, I am confident that they are able to change the structure of production and distribution by actively selecting recyclable goods. Also, as the disposers of garbage, they can cooperate by collecting recyclable materials and not wasting usable goods.

Moreover, it is more important that these three groups, producers, distributors, and consumers, should all cooperate in order to form a network where recycling and reuse become normal activities.

To promote roles of these groups, as I mentioned earlier, "the Bill for Promotion of the Use of Recyclable Resources," which is popularly called the "Recycling Law," was instituted this April. It details the institutional structure of the recycling-oriented society in conjunction with the socio-economic activities of human beings.

The contents of the Recycling Law are as follows. First of all, the government is to establish basic policies that would promote recycling and reuse of resources. Then, based on those policies, enterprises such as producers and distributors, have certain responsibilities, including making an effort to use recycled resources, and making an effort to recover recyclable materials from products. They also must explicitly indicate the quality of the material so as to promote the recovery of reusable goods, such as empty aluminum cans, and to promote the use of industrial by-products, such as blast furnace slag.

As for the institutions, they are responsible for limiting the amount of waste and for collecting recyclable materials from waste materials to promote reuse of resources; the Diet this October has passed "the Bill to Amend the Law concerning Waste Disposal and Public Cleansing." Both laws are expected to contribute greatly to promotion of recycling and reuse of resources in Japan.

In 1989, the rate of recycling and reuse in Japan was 50.3% for paper, 42.5% for aluminum cans, 43.5% for steel cans, and 47.6%

for glass cullets. (For reference, in America, it was 33% for paper, 54.6% for aluminum cans, and about 30% for glass cullets.) These percentages are expected to increase as the system of recycling becomes more institutionalized.

Lastly, I would like to touch upon Japan's role in international society. If one recognizes the Stockholm Conference, which I mentioned at the beginning of this paper, as the origin of the world's attempts to better the environment, next year marks the 20th anniversary of such attempts. In Japan, it was 20 years ago that the Environment Agency was established, backed up by strong public support, and we celebrated the 20th anniversary of the Agency this year.

Over the past 20 years, the Agency has continuously been making efforts to better the environment. At the time of its establishment, it was thought to prevent economic growth and was not always welcomed by private industry. However, through various experiences and achievements over the past 20 years, it has gained the support of people and industry, indeed the whole society. Now both in the world and in Japan, people are more aware of what is happening to the environment. We should not allow this recent development to become a temporary boom. We must not cease to make our best efforts.

In cooperation with other countries, Japan is, I believe, now able to contribute to the betterment of the world's environment with its experiences and achievements through the 20 year history of the environmental administration and its technological and human resources. I believe that not only can it contribute, but that it must.

Section II

What Kind of World Do We Want?

Carrying Capacity of the Globe

Peter H. Raven

First I wish to congratulate the organizers of this program for its organization. It is of great importance at this stage of world development for Sigma Xi to consider the relationship between global resources and human activities. If we are to be able to make the transition from the kind of world we have to the kind of world that we want in the future, we need to understand both worlds better.

In other contributions to this symposium, you reviewed the growth of the world population from 2.5 billion in 1950 to just under 5.4 billion today. One of the aspects of that growth has been that the proportion of people living in the industrialized countries of the world has dropped from an estimated 33%, or one out of every three people in the world in 1950, to about 23% today, and is projected to be approximately 16% in the year 2020. In other words, the proportion of us living in industrialized countries will have dropped during a period of 70 years — the space of an average human lifetime — from one out of three to one out of six; this change represents a very significant difference in the distribution of patterns of consumption and resource utilization around the world.

In our world, the number of young people in developing countries — those under 15 years of age, and therefore still to reach child-bearing age — is very high proportionately, amounting to some 45% in Africa, 36% in Latin America, and 33% in Asia, as compared to about 20% in Europe and North America. Family planning, which reflects a desire to limit family size so that people will have the ability to take care of themselves better is almost universally accepted and pursued as a matter of governmental policy in developing countries. As a result, the rate of growth is

Peter Raven is Home Secretary for the National Academy of Sciences and Director of the Missouri Botanical Garden.

dropping throughout almost all of the less developed parts of the world. Nonetheless, because of the high proportions of young people in these countries, we will not be able to attain global population stability for perhaps a century, overshooting our goals, in effect, by two or three generations.

World population growth peaked at 1.9% in 1970 and is now about 1.7%, but thanks to the larger and larger numbers of people in the base population, we still are growing more and more rapidly in absolute terms. The World Bank has recently calculated that the global population could stabilize at a level of approximately 12.5 billion people by the end of the next century; earlier United Nations projections ranged from 7 to 14 billion people. There are, however, some critical aspects to which we must attend if popula-

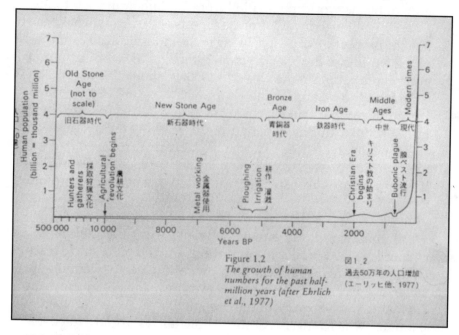

Figure 1.2
The growth of human
numbers for the past half-
million years (after Ehrlich
et al., 1977)

図1.2
過去50万年の人口増加
(エーリッヒ他, 1977)

Slide from Peter Raven, Missouri Botanical Garden.

tion stability is to be attained even then, and at those levels. First and foremost, only continued world-wide attention to family planning will allow this outcome. Our population will not auto-matically reach a level of 9 billion or 14 billion people and then cease growing; rather, if we continue to pay consistent attention to this problem, and devote the resources to bring about success, we have the ability to make it happen. If not, we simply will not achieve stability. The second obvious point is that the difference between 9 and 14 billion is equal to the <u>entire</u> world population today, a population that, as we shall see, is already high enough to be consuming the world's resources at an unsustainable rate! Again, this means that the degree to which we attend to, and are successful in, family planning will be of very great importance for the sustainability and stability of the world in the future.

Another pertinent feature of world population distribution is that at the beginning of the Industrial Revolution, approximately 1800, only 3% of the world population was living in cities; fully 97% was rural, living on farms or in small towns. Putting it another way, there will be more people living in Mexico City by the end of the 1990s than were living in all the cities of the world combined 200 years earlier. This is a staggering difference in the way the people live, which underlies a fundamental difference in the way we look at the world; among other aspects, it tends to make us collectively less able to understand and appreciate biological productivity, on which our common future depends. Almost 50% of the world population lives in cities now, with a very high proportion of the people who are being added to the world's population also living in cities. This tends to lead to the increasing exploitation of those who live in rural areas and produce the food, wood, and other commodities on which city-dwellers depend.

The 1990s and the two decades that follow will be of fundamental importance to the pattern of growth of human populations, and thus to their impact on global ecology. During the 1990s alone, nearly a billion people will be added to the world population, with approximately a billion more being added during each of the first two decades of the 21st century. About 95% of the increase will occur in developing countries. From every point of view, these three decades are likely to be the most stressful that the world has ever experienced, even though we may ultimately be headed toward a period of greatly increased stability. We need to take action immediately, knowing that our best chance to affect the future is now, not at some distant future time. With nearly 3 billion additional people added to the 4.2 billion who now live in developing countries, we have in place the recipe for a global disaster of unprecedented dimensions.

In the world today, the distribution of resources is very unequal. Those who live in industrialized countries, a rapidly shrinking 23% of the global population, control about 85% of the world's finances, as measured by summing gross domestic products. The per capita income in industrialized countries is just under $17,000; the per capita income of the other 77% of the people in the world, the 4.2 billion people who live in developing countries, is about $3,760, approximately a fifth of that characteristic of the industrialized world. In general, developing countries are using up their own resources, ones that might otherwise have been renewable, much more rapidly than are the citizens of industrialized countries, who often consume other people's resources. This

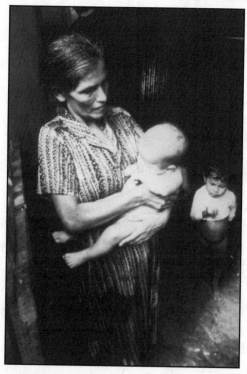

Slide from Peter Raven, Missouri Botanical Garden.

means that the disparity in wealth and access to resources between industrialized and developing nations is probably even greater than that implied by the financial relationship just mentioned.

The ratios of availability of other commodities are highly unfavorable also. For example, the 77% of the world's people who live in developing countries utilize only about 20% of the world's industrial energy. While the United States, with 4.5% of the world's population, produces about a quarter of the world's carbon dioxide emissions, China, with 1.2 billion people and the world's largest proven coal deposits, produces only about a fifth as much. In addition, 1.5 billion of the 4.2 billion people living in developing countries depend on firewood as their principal source of fuel, consuming a very high proportion of the trees and shrubs in their vicinities with an ever-increasing intensity. For other kinds of materials that contribute to living standards, such as iron, nickel, aluminum, and so forth, the people who live in developing countries, over three quarters of the world's population, typically consume 5-20% of the total used worldwide.

According to the World Bank, about 1.2 billion people live in absolute poverty, with incomes of less than $370 per year. This means that they are frequently unable to obtain the absolute necessities of life: food, shelter, and clothing. They are unable to depend on being able to obtain them on a day-to-day basis. About half of these people are seriously malnourished, receiving less than 80% of the United Nations-recommended caloric intake; this means that their bodies are not being maintained, and that their brains cannot develop properly. In addition, UNICEF estimates that about 13 million babies a year, or more than 35,000 each day, starve to death or die of diseases related to starvation. Against such a background, it is literally incredible that many authorities assert that the world is functioning well, and that we are fortunate to have avoided widespread starvation. How could a world-wide disaster be defined, if we are not experiencing one now?

As we have seen, more and more people are being added to the world population each year, even though the overall rate of growth is slowing down. Thus 750 million people were added during the 1970s, 840 million during the 1980s, which I think we are going to look back on as a particularly indecisive and destructive decade, and 960 million are projected to be added in the 1990s. The great majority of these people will be added in developing countries, which are already seriously disadvantaged economically and in a variety of other ways. For example, only about 6% of the world's scientists and engineers live in developing countries, which are home to the great majority of the world's people. Considering that most of the scientists and engineers live in a relatively few countries, of which China, Brazil, Mexico, and India come to mind, it becomes clear that for well over 100 countries, more than half of the total, trained, technical personnel are virtually lacking. How are these countries to decide, based on their own knowledge, whether to join international agreements concerning the environment, or how best to manage their own natural resources? They are home to at least 80% of the world's biodiversity — the plants, animals, fungi, and microorganisms on which we all depend. How will they use, study, manage, and conserve these precious and poorly-known resources?

The inequality between developing and industrialized countries unfortunately is growing at the present time, but already constitutes the kind of situation that Willy Brandt aptly termed "a blood transfusion from the sick to the healthy." Brandt used this analogy to describe the modern world economy, and his characterization remains highly pertinent at the present time. Although the actual net cash transfers may have turned in 1990 to a situation where the flow was towards developing countries, the net flow is still, as it has been for several centuries, from the poor to the rich.

There are a variety of ways of measuring the impact of the rapidly growing human population on the global environment, but I think the most cogent way is in terms of our impact on net photosynthetic output on land. For theoretical reasons, terrestrial photosynthetic output is the chief source of energy available to us. Taking into account losses due to desertification and similar phenomena, the proportion of net terrestrial photosynthetic output that human beings, one species among between 10 million and 100 million others, is consuming, diverting, or wasting about 40%

of the total. This is at a population level of about 5.4 billion people. With some 3 billion likely to be added over the next three decades, what are the prospects for decreasing the levels of poverty, malnutrition, and actual starvation globally against such a background?

In effect, such a rate of consumption reflects clearly that human beings are utilizing the world as a single productive system, our common planetary home. In the light of this relationship alone, the extreme reluctance that citizens of the United States, who are the lowest donors of international development assistance on a per capita basis of any industrialized nation, is irrational. Rich industrialized countries have a great deal to gain from a condition of international stability, but exhibit very little enthusiasm for promoting it. Instead, they seem all too often to be consumed by internal problems, centering around a desire to "improve" their economies, which are already the richest that the world has ever known. We who live in the United States have simply not yet been able to accept the lesson that the world is one, and that the future of the United States depends on our ability to understand and to act on these relationships, and ultimately on a major political, economic, and spiritual breakthrough to a degree that we have not yet even begun to grasp.

What are some of the consequences of the pressure we are exerting on the global environment? For one, the greenhouse effect, which by virtue of our atmosphere maintains the planet Earth at a temperature about $35° C$ warmer than it would be without such an atmosphere, is being enhanced rapidly. A net total of 2 billion metric tons of carbon dioxide was added annually to the global atmosphere in 1957; three times that amount, a net of about 6 billion metric tons, was added in 1987. Both industrial and developing countries contribute to the rise in carbon dioxide in the atmosphere, as well to the increasing amounts of nitrogen oxides and methane and CFCs, which are more effective in trapping radiant energy from the sun than the others, but which fortunately have been limited by the international conventions that have come into force over the past decade. The trends in atmospheric composition that have come have led most modelers to conclude that there will be a rise of 1.5° to 4.5°C in global temperatures by the middle of the next century. Recent reports to a certain extent have tended to trivialize the effects of that kind of a rise at least for countries like the United States, presenting them as if we can cope with them by building dikes, by adapting, by changing the farming system and the like. That may be so for the richest nations on earth, but those calculations, which I would really characterize as quite cynical, do not take into account the global effects of warming. Furthermore I think that one could characterize them as saying that, "well, we got by the Dustbowl alright, and that wasn't so serious, so let's go try it again." Also it needs to be pointed out that a 1.5-4.5° C change is approximately equal to the change from the height of the last expansion of glacial ice at the end of the Pleistocene to the temperature today, and we are talking about this change occurring over the space of less than a century. Obviously, climatic changes of that amount would significantly alter patterns of rainfall and temperature, and be a very major and unpredictable impact. Furthermore, the rise in temperature would not stop there unless actions were taken then — it would simply go on getting warmer.

With respect to the condition of the Earth itself, it is calculated that about 10% of the world's land surface has been desertified already and that an additional 25% is at risk. One of the most frightening statistics, I believe, is that an estimated 20% of the topsoil from the world's arable lands was lost, while the global population was increasing from 2.5 billion in 1950 to about 5.4 billion today. Top soil is now being lost at the rate of about 24 billion tons per year, which, as Lester Brown and his associates have pointed out, is equal to a loss of all of the top soil on the total wheat lands of Australia every year. Six to seven million hectares of agricultural land are being lost to erosion every year, and an additional 1.5 million hectares to water logging, salinization, and alkalinization; at the same time grazing land and all other kinds of productive land around the world are being degraded.

It is well known that grain production per capita has largely kept pace with human population growth over the past 30 or 40 years. In Europe and the United States, we tend to overproduce, and to be concerned with the expense of subsidies for agricultural production. We largely ignore the fact that much of our agricultural productivity is taking place at high costs in energy and sometimes as a result of expending non- renewable supplies of groundwater. Our overproduction, in turn, tends to cause us to fail to acknowledge the lack of adequate productivity over much of the world, and the serious needs for additional food associated with rapidly growing populations in the developing countries. In addition, and for similar reasons, we tend to be ambivalent about applying the fruits of biotechnology to crop improvement. The application of genetic technology and many other improvements will be necessary to grow crops productively on marginal lands, something that is absolutely necessary if the world's people are to be fed adequately. As the world population continues to grow at the rate of nearly 100 million people a year, it is obvious that the capacities of the world's food production system have been stretched to the very limits; this is clearly demonstrated by the loss of topsoil and the deterioration of agricultural lands worldwide. In the relatively near future, our 62-day grain reserves are likely to be

Slide from Peter Raven, Missouri Botanical Garden.

pushed beyond their limits. In short, we are facing a very serious crisis, one that we continue to ignore at our peril.

Among all of the global problems that we face, however, the permanent loss of existing species and genetic diversity of plants, animals, fungi, and microorganisms is the fastest moving and the most serious in terms of its long-range impact. Despite this, it is not really yet regarded by world leaders as an important global problem, as are, for example, the depletion of the stratospheric ozone layer, global warming, and other problems that can more easily be quantified. It will be necessary to elevate our degree of awareness of the importance of biological extinction at an international, political level if we are to serve future generations well.

Biodiversity is being lost for a variety of reasons. It is being lost because of the cutting of tropical forests of all kinds, not only the tropical moist forests that have persisted over the largest area because they tend to grow in places that are the least suitable for agricultural development, but also tropical dry and seasonal forests that normally grow on more fertile soil, and have long since been ravaged. Since the Stockholm conference of 20 years ago, an area of tropical moist forest the size of the United States east of the Mississippi River has been permanently removed from the reserves. Two hundred million hectares of tropical moist forest remain — an area about the size of the United States — and it is being lost today at the rate of about 20 million hectares a year, which amounts to the removal of an area about the size of the state of Washington every single year.

The forests are being lost for two principal reasons. First, they are being converted to cash; like natural resources all over the world, they are being extracted and sold, and the resulting funds invested. Old-growth forests in Oregon and Washington, Alaska, and Siberia are being lost for the same reasons, with some form of tax subsidy from the central government in each case. Until the concepts of natural productivity and the central role of sustainability are built more securely into economic calculations, some of the more susceptible natural resources will continue to be consumed for this reason and thus often lost permanently.

The second reason that the forests in question are being lost has to do with rapid population growth, widespread poverty, and the consequent unwise or unplanned use of resources. In a number of countries, the forests serve as a "safety valve" for the poor, who by consuming small tracts of forest on a one-time basis and moving on, find a source of food, shelter, and clothing for themselves and their families.

Unfortunately, we still have very limited knowledge about the world's biological diversity. We have given scientific names to only about 1.4 million kinds of organisms. Although we know flowering plants, vertebrate animals, butterflies, and a few other groups reasonably well, we have only a small amount of information about most of the other living inhabitants of this planet. What

Slide from Peter Raven, Missouri Botanical Garden.

we are losing, therefore, is being lost mainly in ignorance; it is being lost because of the operation throughout the world of an outmoded economic system, which assumes that the best way to deal with natural resources, renewable or non-renewable, is to convert them into cash and bank the cash. National economic planners traditionally have no way of calculating the very real irreversible loss of productivity, and, as a result, we simply continue with our routine business, dealing with our natural resources as if they would be renewed in some way.

The diversity of corn from a single field, or a single crib, in central Mexico is a reminder of the fact that virtually all of the crops grown in the agriculturally productive or industrial parts of the world are ultimately derived from elsewhere, and that the genetic basis for improving those crops, therefore, must be obtained from another country. Concerning other uses of plants, it is significant that approximately three-quarters of the people in the world depend directly upon them as their major source of medicine. Less that a quarter of the world's people have regular access to prescription drugs; even of these, almost all are now or were originally derived from a natural source. In another sense, the loss of biodiversity in natural communities is even more critical: it is those naturally-occurring and artificial communities that function in capturing energy from the sun and making it available to all organisms, including ourselves; regulating the cycling of nutrients; protecting topsoil and water supplies; and regulating local climates. We know very little about the principles by which organisms function in such communities, much less how they can be reformed if the organisms themselves are lost. Many other points could be added to indicate why the loss of biodiversity is so important to human beings, and to the functioning of the world as a whole, but these will be sufficient to establish the case.

When we who live in industrialized countries like the United States think about a developing country such as the Philippines or a region such as Central America, we tend to focus on the form of government, laws, patterns of use of natural resources, and the ways in which the business of that country or region is conducted. We tend to forget that in the daily affairs of such countries, the grinding effect of poverty and malnutrition, which affect large numbers of people; the seeming inevitability of debt and inflation; and often a feeling of hopelessness about the future may be pervasive. We certainly do not often focus on the fact that, for better or worse, we are managing the world's resources collectively.

For this reason alone, the fact that the developing countries of the world, with more than three-quarters of the world's people, have such a limited human and institutional base for science and engineering, ought to be a matter of serious concern to us all. Research communities must be built up in developing countries neither as a matter of charity, nor as a matter of satisfying our intellectual curiosity, but in explicit recognition of the fact that all countries of the world are working together to manage our single planetary resource as well as possible. To accomplish that task properly, all people must be given a sense of being able to participate in that process; if not, we shall simply all fail together.

Biodiversity can be preserved most easily through the creation of an appropriately-chosen network of parks and reserves throughout the world, provided that the wealthy nations of the world are willing to pay their share of the bill. The developing countries, which are home to at least 80% of the world's biodiversity, will not be able to afford such reserves in the face of the needs of their own people unless the international community faces up to the problem. The increasing urbanization that is occurring throughout the world is increasing the pressure on natural resources, which are ultimately controlled to a large extent by city-dwellers, who may have little understanding of the ecological foundations of productivity. When people come to control less of their own destiny, their lots become increasingly hopeless, the ability of their governments to address their needs becomes increasingly limited, and the chances for attaining the global stability that we all need so desperately is progressively decreased.

We need to act now to preserve as much as we can of biodiversity, as we enter a 30-year period when 20 to 25% of the total number of species on Earth may disappear permanently. We need to find ways to store comprehensive, viable samples of at least those groups that are of most interest to ourselves, such as the flowering plants. Above all, we need to help to build the kinds of national and international institutions that will create the kind of spirit of solidarity around the world on which we can base a common effort that would really improve our chances for a secure future. We are literally and collectively engaged in a massive denial of the wise stewardship of the Earth and its creatures that is commended to us by the Bible, by all major religions, and by all major philosophical systems. We are throwing away our common biological patrimony, during our own lifetimes: a crime that the people of the future will not understand, and for which they will not be able to forgive us.

What specific actions might we take? The Report of the World Commission on Environment and Development—the Brundtland Report — represents an outstanding effort to organize our thinking on global problems. On the other hand, it is really time that we move beyond the position taken in this report, which is, in one sense, that development occurring throughout the world can improve our common lot and save all of us from pain and inconvenience. Actually, I believe that we must give up more than is implied by this scenario, and especially that those of us who live in industrialized countries must be willing to sacrifice much for the common good, and for the security of our common future. To preserve biodiversity, safeguard the ozone layer, prevent global warming, protect our soils and our water supplies, we must achieve population stability, social justice, and a much better distribution of resources throughout the world. Those of us who live in industrialized countries must be willing to look seriously at the problems caused by our own overconsumption of the world's resources, bearing in mind that our activities alone — and we number less than one fourth of the world's people — are more than sufficient to create global instability. For example, the United States, with 4.5% of the world's population, generates about 25% of the world's carbon dioxide. Similar relationships can be demonstrated in almost any area of resource consumption, indicating clearly that the industrialized countries of the world must act forcefully to reduce their levels of consumption if we are all going to be able to attain stability.

As we strive so aggressively to increase our incredibly high standards of living in industrialized countries, from a level that would be considered utopia by most people on Earth, we drain resources from the entire globe and thus contribute willy-nilly to the creation of an unstable system, one in which neither we, nor our children, nor our grandchildren will be able to live in anything like the degree of affluence or, more importantly, opportunity than the one we experience now.

The world as a whole will never achieve population stability without empowering and involving women and other groups of people who are characteristically under-represented in the corridors of power and thus have little control over their own destinies. We must collectively find ways to take advantage of the world's magnificent array of human diversity if we are going to be able to save ourselves. Putting it another way, the human race succeeds to the extent that every person has the opportunity to attain his or her potential. Gender-related inequalities must be relentlessly and systematically dismantled. If women continue to be relegated in many societies to a relative state of weakness and powerlessness, we will not be able to make the strongest possible approach to the serious problems the world faces. If people of color are unfairly treated or not able to express themselves in determining the course of human affairs, the racism that results will prevent us from achieving our goals of a just world, and therefore a stable world. Age discrimination, by which the relatively weak and powerless — babies and children — are regularly not accorded a fair share of the world's productivity, will greatly impede our attainment of global stability as long as we are willing to tolerate it. In short, global stability will come only from a dedicated approach to addressing the problems of poverty and social justice around the world, beginning with the international debt and going on from there.

One of the better and more direct ways of achieving these goals would certainly seem to be the allocation of appropriate legislative and judicial powers for the United Nations. During the early years of its existence, the UN has properly regarded issues of war and peace as the fundamental reasons for existence. In the future, matters of social justice, equality, relationship between "haves" and "have-nots," between "North" and "South," between the empowered and the powerless, must assume equivalent importance. Perhaps the "Earth Summit," to be held in Rio de Janeiro in June, 1992, will be a time when the hope and optimism that were so evident in the days of foundation of the UN can be re-created, and directed to these deeply significant issues.

In order to improve world stability, we must find better ways than we are employing at present to consider the plight of rural people and farmers around the world. Particularly, but not exclusively, the citizens of industrialized nations often seem to assume implicitly that overall prosperity can be created as a result of science and technology, and that primary productivity is something secondary that should in effect be avoided as a source of wealth and prosperity. If we are to improve the world situation, however, we must find ways to support the farmers and others who are producing the crops on which we ultimately depend, and to incorporate them into the affairs of the countries where they live.

Of great importance for world stability is building adequate scientific and technical infrastructure and levels of trained personnel and expertise in developing countries. One way of accomplishing this is through the formation of national biological resource centers (biodiversity institutes or inventories), comparable to the Instituto Nacional de Biodiversidad (INBio) that has been established in Costa Rica, and similar efforts in the Republic of China and Mexico. Efforts of this sort are being considered by a number of other countries, and would be helpful everywhere. They are of importance in demonstrating the value of biodiversity at a national level, they also help the countries develop schemes to study effectively and conserve their own biodiversity for their own purposes. Without such developments, it will continue to be difficult for nations to decide freely that they wish to cooperate internationally in the conservation of biodiversity, because the value of biodiversity will not be apparent at a national level.

Concerning the empowerment of people who live in developing countries, Francisco Segasti has put it especially well. In an article in the *New Scientist*, he wrote as follows:

> Our aim must be to enable individuals and social groups to choose what is best for them and to assist them in acquiring the capacity to decide and bring about their own destinies with full knowledge of the possibilities, limitations, and consequences of their actions for present and future generations. The generation, dissemination, and use of knowledge will play an even more critical role in whatever we may call development, progress, or empowerment in the years to come. The presence or absence of this capacity constitutes the crucial distinction between developed and developing nations, between those parts of the world in which individuals have the potential to decide and act with autonomy and those in which people are not yet empowered to realize their potential.

To put what I have been saying concisely, we must change our view of the world radically, and adopt new ways of thinking, or perish together. We simply cannot go on as we are. We must learn to understand, respect, and work with one another regardless of the differences that exist between us. We must base our new way of thinking on a genuine love for humanity. If, for example, you are motivated by a love for the beauty of nature, by John Muir's "First Summer in the Sierra," or by Aldo Leopold's magnificent thoughts about nature, then translate that love of natural scenes and the beauty of nature and the wonder of pristine areas into a love for humanity and for all the good things of this planet Earth, our common home. People are basically good. Each and every one of us is basically good. Each and every one of us has enormous potential. The most heartening aspect of the situation that we confront is that people, given the motivation, do have the capacity of making remarkable changes. In that sense I would conclude with a wish that our thoughts here would result soon in the creation of new ways of thinking of solutions for improving our common situation and thereby of preserving this magnificent planet, our only home, for the benefit of future generations.

A View From the Developing World

M.G.K. Menon

I. INTRODUCTION

In addressing the topic of this Sigma Xi Forum on "Global Change and the Human Prospect" from the viewpoint of the developing world, I would like to start with a quotation from the speech made by the then Prime Minister of India, Mrs. Indira Gandhi, at the UN Conference on the Human Environment in Stockholm in 1972. She said:

> We do not wish to impoverish the environment any further, and yet we cannot, for a moment, forget the grim poverty of large numbers of people. Are not poverty and need the greatest polluters? For instance, unless we are in a position to provide employment and purchasing power for the daily necessities of the tribal people, and those who live in or around our jungles, we cannot prevent them from combing the forest for food and livelihood; from poaching and from despoiling the vegetation. When they themselves feel deprived, how can we urge the preservation of animals? How can we speak to those who live in villages and in slums about keeping the oceans, the rivers and the air clean when their own lives are contaminated at the source? The environment cannot be improved in conditions of poverty. Nor can poverty be eradicated without the use of science and technology.

The essential point made by her is that problems relating to the environment are inextricably linked with poverty alleviation and bringing about development and in this, science and technology have an essential role to play.

Professor Menon is President of the International Council of Scientific Unions and Member of Parliament, India.

I would like to spend some time, at the beginning of this paper, on the vicious circle of immediate problems that face the Third World. Populations are rapidly growing. The principal cause for this is poverty; with consequent lack of human development, particularly education. Increasing populations and corresponding human needs put increasing demands on both development and the environment. From the environmental angle, the developing countries are faced with immediate issues that relate to their local vicinity, such as air and water pollution, deforestation and desertification, removal of top soil and loss of soil fertility, severe natural hazards such as earthquakes, cyclones, typhoons and the like. In this situation, the longer term and much less tangible issues of global change, particularly climate change and its implications for life on the earth, do not loom large amongst the priorities of the Third World.

And yet, sustainable development is important for the Third World. As defined by the World Commission on Environment and Development, which produced the Brundtland Report entitled *Our Common Future*, sustainable development means consistent economic growth that meets the needs of the present without compromising the ability of future generations to meet their own needs. Third World countries have a responsibility to ensure that the present, and the increasing numbers of their future generations, have the chance to continue to develop and hope for a better quality of life. But if significant changes do occur in the global environment, with global warming, (and consequences such as sea level rise and changes in weather with increases in severe conditions), ozone depletion, greater vulnerability of coastal zones and other fragile ecosystems etc., then developing countries are likely to be hurt most. For invariably, it is the poor and disadvantaged who are most vulnerable to drastic environmental changes, for they do not have the wherewithal or reserve capacity to adjust to these and the consequent economic effects; they may be faced with effects they cannot manage, costs they cannot absorb, or benefits they cannot realize. Developing countries would therefore have to realize, and be made to realize where necessary, that it is in their interest to participate in a truly cooperative, worldwide, international program to ensure that global changes that could result in severe environmental degradation, and thereby compromise long-term sustainable development, do not take place, or can be managed to the extent they occur. Their role in this must be understood by them as an investment in their own future. To play this role they would need to be helped by the North for their immediate development cannot be compromised.

This offers new opportunities for a productive and cooperative North-South dialogue which can lay the foundations for a better world. This will call for major structural and attitudinal changes both in the North and South. I shall deal with these opportunities a little later. Before doing so, I would like to deal with some historical and conceptual aspects relating to the Third World.

II. THE THIRD WORLD

The Third World, or the South as it is often referred to, consists of the large number of countries which gained independence after the Second World War. These are the countries of Asia, Africa, Latin America and Oceania. They represent a wide spectrum of characteristics in terms of sizes, populations, history, level and manner of development prior to their independence, and the way in which they have developed since then. Among these, there are resource-rich countries, such as oil exporting countries; a few newly industrializing countries which have recently made rapid economic progress, and some others following in their footsteps; and then there are the large numbers of countries whose levels of per capita income, literacy rates, health status and the like are way below what is encountered in the affluent North. It is, therefore, difficult to talk in uniform terms about this highly varied spectrum of nations that constitutes the Third World.

However, there are certain common features which characterize the majority of them. The most important feature is that the GDP per capita, of 30 of the low-income developing countries, is in the range of less than a thousand dollars of equivalent purchasing power; for another 33 countries, it is less than two thousand dollars. In contrast, in the case of 26 of the most well-off countries, including all the industrialized countries of the North, this figure is in the range of around ten to twenty thousand dollars. Basically, therefore, a large number of Third World countries are very poor countries in absolute terms, and also relative to the North. Other characteristics of these countries are the generally low literacy rates and high population growth rates.

What should the long-term goals of this group of countries be? The answer in general terms would be: to get out of the poverty and deprivation that characterize them today; meet basic human needs; cut down population growth rates; and ensure a steady, positive and sustainable development in a society characterized by a high level of equity and low level of energy usage.

Should they adopt the pathway of development along which the rich countries of the world have come in the past? In a broad sense, the answer would be "yes"; only in the sense that it implies the use of the existing, and increasing, science and technology, to bring about production of goods and services with increasingly higher efficiency and lower energy usage and in a milieu in which innovation and entrepreneurship is allowed to flower. The recent advances of science and technology, particularly developments relating to electronics and information, biotechnologies, space technologies with applications to communications, remote sensing and broadcasting, and new materials technologies offer opportunities to developing countries that the present industrialized countries did not have at the time they started on their present economic growth. The developing countries should make full use of these to leapfrog into the future. I believe strongly that many of these so-called "high technologies" have an important role to play in the development processes in the South. But the important qualification that needs to be stressed is that the Third World countries must avoid the pathways leading to high levels of consumption, which is unnecessary and wasteful, of resources that generally characterizes affluent societies. To achieve this is not easy but feasible.

Should they aspire to the same ways of living that characterize the affluent of the world today? My personal view is that this is not needed for achieving a desirable quality of life for all. As Mahatma Gandhi had once remarked "There is enough for everyone's need but not for everyone's greed." However, the lifestyles of the affluent are highly attractive and therefore, invariably unheated.

There are further questions. Is it feasible, in terms of accomplishment, for developing countries to adopt lifestyles that characterize the North today? Indeed, the upper strata and elite in the South are already doing so. But, in my view, these lifestyles are unsustainable for the world as a whole. The affluent have an ethical responsibility not to set these bad precedents — even though many in such societies regard it as their birth right to live in such affluence, as they regard it is a result of their own efforts.

If the developing countries adopt such a pathway, what impact would it have on the global environment? These are considered a little later in this paper, where we consider the issues of the driving forces of global change and environmental stress, including patterns of consumption.

III. BRIEF BACKGROUND OF DEVELOPMENT IN THE THIRD WORLD

Let me now consider certain other aspects of the background which has characterized the Third World and its recent history.

Four decades ago, after the Second World War, there was a feeling of euphoria that colonialism, imperialism and exploitation were on their way out; the world had gone through a very disastrous period of destruction, and humankind was not prepared for more wars and conflicts. There was already a major base of science and technology in the world; and there was ample evidence of how much it could deliver, given a proper environment in which it got directed and managed purposefully. Countries of the Third World felt that if the industrialized countries in the world could get to their present levels of development and standards of living with this base of science and technology, it should be possible for them also to move forward rapidly on the pathway of development by similar means. Indeed, we have seen how a further exponential and spectacular growth of science and technology has taken place over these four decades. What would have been regarded as many different "Ages of Humankind" have been telescoped into the short period of the past 40 years. The Atomic Age, the Space Age, the Age of Electronics and Information, the Age of New Biology, the Age of New Materials and much else have all occurred in parallel. The power that human society has today, through these advances of science and technology, is indeed enormous; and should be more than capable of dealing with the problems of development in the Third World and of solving them. The intrinsic powers and capability to bring about development, and take the human race along the pathway that would provide a minimum quality of life for all in the world, are with us; I am optimistic on that account. Though there are major aspects relating to adaptation and manner of appropriate application that have to be worked out, it has to be ensured that science, instead of being a peripheral activity or directed toward the affluence of a few, is organized so as to permeate and become an integral part of all of society. The causes and roots of the problems we face lie in the crucial sphere of human and social relations.

Since the end of the Second World War, we have seen a bipolar world, with continued confrontations between the two major super-powers. This led to an increasing militarization of the world, with enormous sums of money allocated for the development of weapon systems of all types. While the Third World countries were not directly parties to this Cold War, they were affected significantly, through the creation of spheres of influence, association with various defense pacts being part of treaty organizations, and through provision of military bases. With the build-up of large military industrial complexes and commercializing of military hardware, they themselves became major purchasers of arms. The arms imports of all developing countries (for 1987) was over 34 billion US dollars. These were used largely for conflicts among themselves and in internal strife, apart from the one major case involving a super-power, namely the Vietnam War. From a financial view point, with the enormous arms expenditure by countries of the North, there was much less available for world development. The total overseas official development assistance (ODA), in 1987, to all developing countries was around 34 billion US dollars, equal to their total arms imports, and smaller than the interest payments on long-term debt of 45 billion US dollars. There are wide variations in ODA given to different developing countries in magnitude and as a percentage of their GNP, and also in their degree of indebtedness. These variations, when carefully scrutinized, are themselves causes of concern; for they demonstrate the operation of factors, essentially political, far removed from the imperatives of development or ecology. In addition, countries of the South have also been engaged in the madness of large military expenditure, instead of using their scarce resources for development. The principal military conflicts that have taken place since the Second World War have all been in the Third World countries.

Now, with the ending of the Cold War and of super-power confrontation, and with the highly satisfactory progress toward reduction in weapons of massive destruction and their delivery systems, can it be hoped that there will be a period of reduced tensions and reduced militarization of the world? — of turning swords into plough-shares. This constitutes a major hope, and indeed can make this decade a turning point in human history. We have an unique opportunity. The question is whether we will seize it.

With regard to the question of the powers of science and technology to bring about development, there has been considerable change in our understanding over the past few decades. The first feeling was that all elements of science and technology needed for the development process were available in the world. This was the philosophy that prevailed to some extent around the time that the first UN Conference on Science and Technology for Development was organized in Geneva in 1963. All that one had to do was to shop in the world super market of science.

Since then one has learned the hard way that the process of development is more complex than earlier assumed. We recognize that development has to be comprehensive, and cannot relate only to economic dimensions. There are many important elements which relate to the social and human dimensions, e.g., improved quality of life, providing the right kind and extent of employment, promotion of creativity, safeguarding the rights of man, etc. and related aspects of education, health, and so on. Development should also have endogenous roots, and not be merely an imitation of a model being practiced elsewhere; this implies the capability to select a development style suited to a particular community, and reduction of dependence and vulnerability — and this is what is understood by self-reliance; this would respect and preserve the different cultural heritages. With the capital-scarce conditions that are characteristic of developing nations, development has to be a planned process to ensure that available resources are deployed for priority areas; this calls for appropriate attention and intervention by national authority, while ensuring fully the freedom and opportunities for the creative activities of groups and individuals. More than the already developed countries, it is those that are developing that need a careful mix of market structures and government initiatives and interventions. Development has to be democratic and respond to the choices of the population as a whole, and also needs to be directed toward a just and equitable social order. The role of government has to be in relation to the latter and creating the necessary infrastructure, including the social component of it.

These are some of the social and political aspects that have become clearer over the years, apart from the obvious economic measures relating to development, such as savings rate growth, investments, exports, and so on. It is also necessary to state explicitly that science and technology constitute an essential component to achieve development. This is often not understood by the government and peoples of most countries of the South. There can be no development without making full use of the intrinsic capabilities in science and technology; how these are to be developed, and the environment in which it can take place, is a different question. This implies support for the growth of endogenous capabilities in science and technology. But science and technology by themselves cannot bring about development; they have to be suitably integrated into the societal fabric; this aspect needs to be appreciated by the scientific community. The manner in which this has to be done is not yet fully understood and is still being explored.

IV. SOME CONCEPTUAL ASPECTS RELEVANT TO A VISION FOR THE FUTURE

The French Revolution was characterized by a stirring call of "Liberte, Egalite, Fraternite." This was in the context of a nation, France; but it is highly relevant both to the national, as well as the international, scene today. It was a call to alter a system in which all of these parameters of liberty, equity and fraternity did not exist. In a large number of nations in the world, and also on the international scene, these qualities are notable for their absence. The hope of the peoples of the Third World would be that, in the foreseeable future, one can move in a direction which will hopefully lead toward fulfillment of these basic aspects of a just human society. This calls for a New International Order — not a world government, but a new compact between nations of the North and the South to bring about just and equitable global sustainable development in the interests of all.

For the countries of the Third World, what they have achieved has essentially been political independence, which has resulted in the disappearance of the visible signs of colonial occupation. Political independence was, no doubt, an essential and necessary condition for the start of an endogenous development process in these countries. However, political independence by itself, which meant freedom from domination or exploitation by an alien power, has not brought about the betterment of the lot of the vast masses of the downtrodden people of many of these countries. For this there is need for freedom within.

The prerequisite for any improvement in the quality of the life is liberty, with freedom of the individual, freedom of thought and expression, and freedom of information, with limitations only imposed by society for its own good governance. With the existing power structures, both economic and social, very large numbers of people in the Third World do not have freedom or liberty in the true sense. This is particularly true of the large numbers in the lower strata of society, who are economically and socially backward, including the landless and bonded labor in rural areas; this is even more so in the case of women. How does one expect that they will be able to play any meaningful role in development, let alone sustainable development?

There is clearly need for major transformations within these countries, to ensure that the vast numbers of their society, at present deprived and lacking in freedom, are brought out from this state. However, international actions, the functioning of market economies, and manner of use of science and technology have all been supportive of the status quo, enabling the existing power structures to continue. We thus see in most developing countries the picture of two societies: the rich upper strata, the elite, who relate to the affluent countries of the North; and the poor disadvantaged strata for whom development takes place so slowly that the fulfillment of their expectations is only like a mirage.

An important aspect of any society should be that each individual in it is given the fullest opportunity for self development and creative pursuits. For this, there are certain basic requirements of: elementary education; meeting basic health needs; provision of shelter and clothing; and opportunities for gainful employment. This will not result in equality of all citizens in terms of their incomes, material standards of living, achievements and the like, which will all relate to the capabilities of the individual. However, what society has to guarantee is that basic human needs of each individual are met (which are covered by Social Security Systems in affluent countries) and opportunities provided for development. This cannot come about in societies with the power structures that exist in a large number of the developing countries. It is not a question of the well-off doing things for the less well-off, as charity or patronage. The latter have a unalienable right to participate in the development process. The present disadvantaged segments of society must be empowered to shape policies that affect their lives and to enjoy the fruits of political independence and the process of development. In most developing countries, which are characterized by a highly iniquitous society, a reduction of the disparities in a visible manner can be realized only by an affirmative and redistributive social and economic program for the economically and socially backward sections. The disadvantaged in society must be given their rightful share in the system of governance so that they become masters of their own destiny.

Pope John Paul II has remarked:

> Peace is born not only from the elimination of hotbeds of war. Even if all these latter were eliminated, others would inevitably appear, if injustice and oppression continue to govern the world. The intention to direct science to the promotion of justice and peace demands a great love for humanity. Every human virtue is a form of love. This is the case, in particular, of justice, which is love of neighbor, of individuals, and of peoples. Only the person who loves wants justice for the other person. The person who does not love seeks only to obtain justice for himself.

How true if one looks at the relations between the rich and the poor within nations, and also between nations.

The third element in the stirring call of the French Revolution was fraternity. This is sadly missing in the world of today, which is clearly highly fragmented. Apart from the coming together of East and West Germany in a remarkable act of union in October 1990, and the gradual cementing of the European Community, one sees elsewhere increasing divisive tendencies. We witness this currently in the Soviet Union, and in more bloody terms in Yugoslavia. In many places in the world, the call for secession and fragmentation is strident.

A large part of the Third World has highly fractured societies, divided on the basis of religion, creed, caste, tribe, language and ethnicity. Instead of a kaleidoscope of cultural diversity welded together by an overriding feeling for the oneness of humankind, narrow and chauvinistic calls for separatism and fundamentalism have come to the fore, increasingly. Instead of fraternity, as in the call of the French Revolution, one sees pictures of animosity based on parochial differences. These animosities are now given greater power for destructive purposes, for conflicts between groups, through the many modern technologies of automatic weapons, explosives, modern communication equipment and the like. The Third World is riven by these dissensions. The assassinations of top leaders in the Third World, and the frequency of coups, are illustrative of the malaise.

These then are some of the aspects that characterize the Third World, which have resulted in stagnation, with a structure of society continuing to be based on status quo, which has kept alive the grim inequalities between different sections of the society and led to a great deal of internal strife. Conflicts between nations, which have been a way of diverting attention from internal problems and settling scores based on narrow interests, have resulted in unnecessary expenditures on arms.

All of this has taken away the power of the programs directed toward development. In spite of this, as brought out by the *Human Development Report* (1990) of UNDP, it is clear that the developing countries have made significant progress toward human development in the last three decades. North-South gaps in basic human survival have narrowed considerably, even while income gaps have widened; it is clear that it has been possible to achieve good levels of human development at fairly modest levels of income.

However, many of the statistics are based on averages and there are enormous disparities within the developing countries, with large sections of the population — particularly those in rural areas, in urban slums and women — being highly disadvantaged. Often there has been stress on economic indicators such as GNP or per capita income, but these by themselves do not necessarily imply overall human progress.

The most important task for the Third World countries is how to ensure development that directly reflects in benefits to the individual human beings — in terms of better health, lower infant mortality, higher expectation of life, prevention of avoidable diseases and disabilities, access to safe drinking water, ensuring minimum needs of food, nutrition, water and clothing; for all these, basic education, which opens up the human horizons, is essential, particularly in building the right value systems, ensuring literacy, as well as vocational training for gainful employment. These will all call for corresponding related efforts in the sectors of energy, communications, transport and other infrastructure.

While a very large part of the effort and resources for this will have to come from the developing countries themselves, there will be need for external aid, and particularly for the poorest in the Third World. The UNDP Report indicates that the net transfer of resources to the developing countries has been reversed — from a positive flow of $42.6 billion in 1987 to a negative flow of $32.5 billion in 1988; primary commodity prices, on which the economies of the Third World countries significantly depend, have reached their lowest level since the great depression of the 1930s. The foreign debts of the developing countries, more than $103 trillion, now require nearly $200 billion a year in debt servicing alone. In this environment, development takes place much too slowly.

V. RESOURCE REQUIREMENT OF THE THIRD WORLD FOR SUSTAINABLE DEVELOPMENT

The developing countries need to grow at a rate, significantly higher than their current population growth rate if there is to be a tangible impact of the development processes on their societies.

There is the need to bring about human development in the areas of health, nutrition, education and poverty alleviation. Only this can bring about a sustained impact in the area of population stabilization. If social unrest is to be assessed, there is need for greater social equality through improvements in income distribution, and also a reduction of unemployment to manageable levels. The growth rate in recent years of 3.5% for developing countries as a whole is clearly inadequate. A great deal of the effort needed to increase the growth rate, and to ensure its right direction to fulfill the objectives stated previously, will have to come from the developing countries themselves. This will include increasing domestic savings, reducing defense expenditure, political mobilization resulting in better social efforts leading to greater entrepreneurship, decentralization, increased efficiency and productivity and the like. These social efforts are best achieved through nongovernmental and voluntary organizations. However, the shift from static, agrarian societies to developing industrial societies, which has to take place, will call for a significant increase in the impact capacity of the developing countries. This, and immediate needs for resources to meet targets relating to human development and population stabilization, will call for an increase in official development assistance (ODA).

There have been, in recent past, several estimates of the additional requirements of developing countries for ODA. These are: (i) WorldWatch Institute estimates (Lester R. Brown, et al. *State of the World 1988: a WorldWatch Institute Report on Progress Toward a Sustainable Society*, W. W. Norton and Co., New York and London); (ii) *Caring for the Earth* (Published in partnership by IUCN, UNEP & WWF, October 1991); (iii) *A Global Environmental Compact for Sustainable Development: Resources Requirement and Mechanisms* (Lal Jayawardena, World Institute for Development Economics Research of the UNU: August 1991) ; and (iv) Preparatory Committee for the United Nations Conference on Environment and Development: Report of the Secretary-General at its Third Session Geneva, August, 1991, on Cross Sectoral Issues - *Progress Report on Financial Resources*. Though these various assessments differ somewhat in terms of types of expenditure, amounts needed under each as a function of time, and the trials, what is interesting is the surprising degree of agreement on an overall basis.

The additional demand for, and supply of, foreign savings in the Third World has been placed (in the analysis by Lal Jayawardena) at $40 billion in the early 1990s, rising to $60 billion by 2000 AD, for socially necessary growth; additionally they would need $20 billion, rising to $80 billion over the same period, for environmental protection. The amounts needed by the Soviet Union and Eastern Europe on a similar basis would be $60 billion in the early 1990s, but these would decrease to $25 billion by 2000 AD. The total needs would therefore be $120 billion (in the early 1990s) going up to $165 billion (by 2000 AD). This may be compared to the total ODA for 1990 of about $55 billion. The need is, therefore, for at least a doubling of official aid flows. It is relevant to point out that the accepted UN target for ODA is 0.7% of GNP. Even if this is achieved, it will not be sufficient, as it will only provide $55 billion in the early 1990s rising to $70 billion in 2000 AD. The proposal submitted by Willy Brandt to the UN Secretary General, in the *Report of the Stockholm Initiative on Global Security and Governance* (1991), is to increase this target to 1%.

This analysis by Lal Jayawardena brings out that even the 1% target will yield only amounts rising from $110 billion in 1995 to $130 billion in 2000 AD; this would still be short of the requirements. He has suggested a further possible resource in the form of switching of surpluses of Japan and other countries through appropriate policy decisions by OECD countries.

All of this is only to indicate the magnitude of the financial requirements and the efforts that will be called for. It is clear that faced with these realities, mere tinkering or marginal changes will be of little value. Such large inputs of resources would imply a restructuring of the international system. It calls for a new vision of achieving sustainable development globally on a cooperative basis, with the recognition that this is needed by the North and the South. If implemented, it will bring about socially necessary growth and appropriate human development, as well as long-term environmental protection. For both of these, slowing down population growth is essential, and a large part, estimated at $13 billion (in 1990) to $33 billion (in 2000 AD), of the total development assistance will relate to efforts to achieve this through support for specific relevant sectors of human development and provision of family planning services. Part of this financial assistance would be used for "the cost of switching to environment sensitive patterns of growth and consumption in the South" as stated in the *Report of the South Commission*.

It must be made abundantly clear that the objective of any such exercise is not for the North to pay out such large sums of money for governments of the South to proceed unquestioned in a manner which they consider appropriate; nor should it be regarded as charity. No doubt each nation has its sovereignty and own national priorities. But the magnitude of financial flows just referred to have to be in the context of an overall understanding that they are for a specific purpose. Thus, each country's development plan would have to include clear allocations and targets for human development, slowing down of population growth, bringing about equity and a more just democratic society and ensuring sustainable, environment-friendly development. The present status quo structures, and also policies and attitudes so far adopted, would need to be changed significantly. Clearly, there must be effective domestic policy reforms to attract the potential savings of surplus countries. This would have to be a part of a global understanding. On this, the *Report of the South Commission* states: "Should the North be prepared to finance a substantial part of the cost of switching to environment-sensitive patterns of growth and consumption in the South, a negotiated agreement could provide for reciprocal obligations on the part of the governments of the South. A concerted attack on global poverty has to be an integral part of efforts to protect the environment."

The ability to meet these large financial requirements of the Third World must be viewed against the current international situation. The principal positive element is the end of the Cold War and the prospects of significant demilitarization. One needs, of course, mechanisms to reduce the number of low intensity military conflicts around the world. The negative elements, on an immediate basis, are the Presidential elections in the U.S. in 1992 and Parliamentary elections in the United Kingdom. There is a significant recession and large scale unemployment in the United States. Western Europe is coming together in an unique manner, and the attention of that community is likely to be largely inward looking as this process develops; outward, their first approaches will be toward the immediate neighbors of Eastern Europe, and not toward the Third World.

It must be stressed that what is needed is immediate availability of large sums of money. What is called for is an assurance and commitment that such amounts will be available, on a long-term basis, with a degree of automation. It is important that such sums are used with the highest efficiency. This is often not achieved on a multilateral basis. Appropriate bilateral arrangements between donor and recipient would need to be worked out for this purpose. The word "appropriate" has been used in context of fears relating to political overtones, hegemony and undesirable conditionalities; these should not go hand in hand with such bilateral assistance.

So far I have dealt with a broad historical picture of the Third World, certain conceptual aspects relating to development and its imperatives, and the scale of the effort called for, in financial terms, to bring about a just, equitable society characterized by sustainable development. One might well ask what all of this has got to do with the subject of this Forum, namely "Global Change and the Human Prospect." After all, global change, as understood by scientists and environmentalists, refers to a series of phenomena taking place in the earth's environment, or likely to take place in the foreseeable future. A large part of this is due to physical causes such as: increase in various greenhouse gas concentrations in the atmosphere, including CFCs responsible for ozone depletion; discharging various other pollutants into the earth's atmosphere, oceans and fresh water systems; deforestation; loss of biodiversity and the like. These are now on a scale, in magnitude and rate of change, so as to produce impacts such as global warming leading to climate change, sea level rise, ozone depletion, etc., which can be hazardous for human functioning on earth. So the basic approach should be to control these physical causes, largely well defined. This would imply certain targets to be achieved, time scales for achievement, technologies to be developed for the purposes, arrangement of finances, and international agreements relating to compliance. On the part of science and technology, the efforts would be to understand the nature of global change and its ramifications, as well as to develop new technologies in the areas of energy production and usage, industry, agriculture, etc. to reduce or eliminate the physical causes identified as being responsible for global change. This is the sort of technological fix that most, whose lives have been spent in the natural sciences and engineering, would think of from the viewpoint of the long-term solution. But past experience in human affairs tells us that while such technological fixes are indeed essential, and need to be worked on, <u>they cannot by themselves lead to stable long-term solutions.</u> They can be effective only within the framework of strategies to solve the greater human and social issues which are the root causes of these problems. It is for this reason that I have dealt at some length with these aspects in the context of the Third World. To repeat: the problems of the environment cannot be separated from the problems of development.

VI. GLOBAL CHANGE — THE DRIVING FORCES

The twin elements that constitute the driving forces of environmental stress and of global change are rapid increase in the world's population, and corresponding human needs; and the increasing material demands of human society, with rising expectations and related economic activity, at present on a significant scale in the affluent societies.

A. Rapid Growth of Population
The growth of population that has taken place during this century has been unprecedented in human history. It took fifteen centuries for the population to double from the figure of 300 million at the start of the present era. In contrast, from 1.7 billion in 1900, it will have more than tripled to reach over 6 billion by 2000. This growth in population is taking place essentially in the developing countries. Countries with <u>low human development</u>, as defined by UNDP, have population growth rates ranging from 2% to 4.5%. Julian Huxley, the first Director General of UNESCO has written: "somehow or other, population must be balanced against resources or civilization will perish...population can drastically effect the type of civilization possible and the rate of its advance." These were prophetic words; and we see, four decades after this was written, we are faced with the relationship between population, resources and type of civilization in stark form.

The countries of the Third World are aware of the problems posed by high population growth rates in them. In the *Report of the South Commission*, chaired by Mwalimu Julius Nyerere of Tanzania and consisting of respected figures from a range of countries in the South, it is stated:

> Rapid population growth presents a formidable challenge for most developing countries.... A strong commitment to slowing down population growth through integrated population and human resource planning can bring large personal and social benefits in most developing countries.... The present trends in population, if not moderated, have frightening implications for the ability of the South to meet the twin challenges of development and environmental security in the 21st century.... In the long run, the problem of over population of the countries of the South can be fully resolved only through their development. But action to contain the rise of population cannot be postponed...The task is indeed formidable, but the consequences of inaction can be disastrous. The South must summon sufficient political will to overcome the various obstacles to the pursuit of a sensible policy on population.

India, with the second largest population in the world, has had a National Family Planning Program started in 1951. It cannot be said that the South is unaware of the nature and magnitude of the problems implicit in rapid population growth. The question is how to deal with it effectively and rapidly.

From a great deal of demographic analysis that has been carried out, it is reasonably clear that high population growth rates are related closely to poverty, and possibly also to an erosion of the local environmental resource base. The key to controlling population lies in achieving a motivation in society for having small families; and this is facilitated by bringing about satisfactory human development: e.g., a high standard of literacy, and more so for women; reducing infant mortality; and providing for an environment conducive to the economic independence of women.

There is need for an integrated population policy aimed at achieving these, along with measures such as ready availability of improved credit and savings markets, and also methods for family planning.

In spite of this population increase, and the other problems faced by them, with the efforts currently under way in the countries of the South, gross income per capita has grown in all regions of the world (except Sub-Saharan Africa). There has been an improvement (UNDP Report 1990) in the various indicators of human development (literacy, health status — life expectancy, lower infant mortality). Food production has exceeded the world population growth rate since 1960 (FAO 1989, *The State of Food and Agriculture*); however, this excess of food production over population growth rate has slowly declined over the past three successive decades from 0.8% (1960-70) to 0.5% (1970-80) and 0.4% (1980-87) - this should be a matter of concern.

All this has occurred while population growth rates have overall been substantially higher than in the past. So there has been success: but decline in fertility has not matched the declines in mortality rates; the total fertility rates, after declining, have stabilized at levels well above the replacement rate (of a little over 2.1); the figures for India of 4.2 and for low income countries in general of 5.6 are disturbing. So much more needs to be done to bring about population stabilization.

In the meantime, as population grows, pressures on natural resources intensify daily. Agriculture is pushed to marginal lands. There is continued deforestation and loss of biodiversity and of habitats. Unsustainable agriculture leads to land degradation. More than 20% of the top soil of the arable lands of the world has been lost in the past 40 years. The significant and continuing loss of top soil is of the greatest concern, as it jeopardizes the possibilities for the sustained increases in food production needed in the South.

The sooner population stabilization is achieved, the better for the world — hence the need for substantial ODA from the North, as outlined earlier, and specifically directed toward this.

B. Consumption Patterns in the North

The developed countries have 24% of the world's population, but their share in global consumption of various commodities ranges from 50% to 90%. This raises a demand on all natural resources — renewable and non-renewable. Most of the commodities finally consumed are not primary products but finished items, which have resulted from several stages of processing, packaging and transportation. A look at the supermarkets of the North brings out the nature of the final product. Whereas in the South, the food grown is more or less directly consumed, except for some cooking, in the North it is significantly converted to animal products. These are then further processed and packaged. The cultural energy needs in the food sector of the North are very large. Because of these consumption patterns, and also those relating to transportation, heating, cooling, etc., the developed world is responsible for 75% of the world's energy consumption. The per capita energy consumption in the North is 10-20 times that of the South. The per capita carbon emission from the North is 7 times that of the South. These then are the high consumption patterns, and in particular of energy, that characterize the North.

With advances that science and technology have brought about, the world has indeed become a small place. Easy, rapid means of transportation have resulted in mass movements of peoples — from rural to urban areas, and from the South to the North. Even more, we have had spectacular revolutions in the areas of communications and broadcasting. These have come about through the developments that have taken place in micro-electronics, space technologies and opto-electronics. More than 600 million people all over the world watched together on television the first landing of man on the moon in 1969. More than twice that number watched together the World Cup Football games in Rome in 1990. Lifestyles all over the world are becoming increasingly common knowledge. As a result, the poor in all countries aspire to the life enjoyed by the rich in their countries, and the South, in general, hopes to attain the affluence and ways of life of the North, that appear to be so tempting. There is a rising tide of expectations, of clamoring demands, which governments are unable to fulfill. Dammed aspirations lead to frustration and social discontent. And this is seen in increasing degree all over the world. While consumerism and market demands have been the motor of development, we need to pause in the circumstances that we encounter today; and ask what form of market demands would be appropriate, and need to be encouraged, through national and international policies.

It will be extremely difficult to bring down the standards of living or lifestyles of entire societies except as the result of some catastrophic situation. What is needed, in the first instance, is to ensure that these standards are maintained without putting further burdens on the environment and natural resources. This is the challenge before science and technology, and those who deal with national and international policy, framing of taxes, incentives/disincentives and the like. Economic factors in the market place will have an impact on the selection of options by society.

VII. BACKGROUND OF GLOBAL CHANGE

Let us now consider the main elements of global change that are of immediate concern to us. Until relatively recently, up to the beginning of this century, the world's population grew at a slow pace. Human activities, designed to meet the needs of this population, were also small compared to the dimensions and recuperative capacities of the earth's environment: the atmosphere, the oceans, the fresh water systems, the cryosphere, the forests, arable land and the like. However, there has been the unprecedented growth of population discussed already. In addition, there has been a similar increase in the scale of human activities; this started with the Industrial Revolution of a few hundred years ago. But the very large scale transformation of the industrial scene has come about during this century, and more particularly over the past few decades; industrial production has grown more than 100 times in the past 100 years. The fear now is that these driving forces may have impacts on the environment with which we will be unable to cope. The environment in its totality is very complex, with a high degree of non-linearity and large number of inter-linkages. It may be difficult to specify when one is pushing it beyond the limits of reasonable recovery, to a new regime which could be more hostile to human welfare.

Initially, environmental degradation was relatively slow, mainly then seen in deforestation, particularly with agricultural operations moving into marginal areas, and air and water pollution. More recently, the deterioration in the environment has been much more dramatic. Extensive deforestation, oil spills in the ocean, acid rain, major air and water pollution, introduction of toxic materials into the environment, industrial accident hazards (with familiar names like Minimata Seveso, Bhopal, and Chernobyl), have all brought the magnitude of environmental degradation to public notice to the extent that it has become one of the major issues before human society.

There have been many local agitations and movements in various parts of the world led by non-governmental groups protesting against environmental vandalism and devastation; the actions of the green movements in the industrialized countries and protests in the Amazon and Himalayas are examples of these. Indeed, it is the increasing concern with the deterioration in the environment which led to the convening of the UN Conference on the Human Environment in Stockholm in 1972.

The position has again dramatically changed over the past two decades. Earlier, many of the issues appeared to be local or regional — examples of the latter being acid rain or the nuclear fallout from the Chernobyl accident. Now the concerns are about the much larger questions of global change — a large part of it intangible, but which in the long term could have severe tangible manifestations, and sustainable development. It is this essential nexus between environmental issues and the concept of sustainable development that constitutes the background for the convening of the UN Conference on Environment and Development (UNCED) in Rio de Janeiro, Brazil in 1992.

While natural changes have been taking place in the earth's environment, these have occurred over geological time scales. What is of concern today is that changes of such magnitude are being brought about over historical time scales as a result of human activity.

VIII. GLOBAL CHANGE: THE MAIN AREAS

A. Climate Change
On the subject of climate change, there has been the report of the Inter-governmental Panel on Climate Change (IPCC), and very detailed discussions in the Second World Climate Conference organized by WMO, UNEP, UNESCO, FAO and ICSU in Geneva in October - November, 1990.

The main conclusion is that over and above the natural greenhouse effect, which keeps the earth habitable as it is today, there is an enhanced greenhouse effect, which could result in raising the global temperature. This warming could have many consequences, such as climate change, with implications for many ecosystems of the earth, particularly those that are fragile; have deleterious effects on agricultural production patterns; affect fresh water systems; and cause the sea level to rise which could be devastating for coastal regions and islands.

The principal reason for all this is the additional quantity of greenhouse gases being put into the atmosphere as a result of human activities. The principal greenhouse gases are CO_2 and CH_4. Then there are others, e.g. water vapor, ozone, CFCs, etc.; water vapor plays a crucial role in atmospheric chemistry in relation to CO_2, and also in ozone destruction through CFCs. CO_2 is a product of all combustion processes and is, therefore, an essential product of all energy generation today (other than nuclear, hydro and several renewable sources). The North is responsible for 70% of the current CO_2 emissions into the atmosphere, and 77% of cumulative total emissions; the latter figure is important since CO_2 has an estimated life of 50-200 years in the atmosphere. India emits only 0.2 tons of CO_2 per capita, compared to 5.4 tons per capita in the United States.

B. Ozone Depletion
The other significant area of concern under global change is ozone depletion, which is basically due to CFCs and related chemicals which find their way into the stratosphere. Here one is concerned with a straight forward technological fix: how to develop and introduce CFC substitutes into the global economy which would do no damage to the ozone layer, and which have no

other major side effects. This is a matter of technology and finances, to develop such products, arrange for their production and usage through conversion of current CFC-based systems (particularly refrigeration and air conditioning). This poses a complex question of major magnitude in the North. Even more daunting is how the South, which does not have the capabilities to carry out this technological exercise, nor finances to implement it, can become a party to this and protocols that relate to this. This can be dealt with in two ways:

(1) The related technologies can be brought into the public domain, after providing appropriate returns to those concerned with their development. These payments can come from public funds contributed by the North and South, in proportion to their ability to pay. This will imply a significant contribution by the North to enable the South to shift to the new regime which will avoid the present ozone depletion. In my view, amounts on the order of a few billion dollars would have to be provided by the North for this.

(2) CFCs can be used in sealed systems with recovery and reuse. This needs to be investigated and worked out.

C. Sea Level Rise and Problems of Coastal Zones

The IPCC concluded that global warming would result in a temperature rise of 1° C to 5° C over the next century, if no actions are taken to reduce emissions. This could result in a rise in sea levels from 35 cm to 100 cm. This would have severe effects on low lying coastal areas and island territories; 70% of the world's population lives in such areas. Invasion by the sea of this magnitude would pose serious problems for their lives. Coastal erosion, sea water intrusion into fresh water aquifers, destruction of coral reefs and mangrove areas, increases in damage by storms and sea surges, and physical submergence of land areas are all consequences which would have to be reckoned with. The question of a real sea level rise and its magnitude are subjects of serious scientific debate; and there is no need to have a neurosis about sea level rise. But all actions that can be taken sensibly to avoid its consequences need to be considered even now.

D. Loss of Tropical Forests and of Biodiversity

There has been significant destruction of tropical forests. These are the planet's greatest storehouses of biological diversity. We have destroyed and continue to destroy this enormous richness so essential for our future well-being. Compulsions of poverty have led to this destruction in Third World countries. A large part of the requirements of the rural poor for fuel wood is met by "lops and tops." But, because of the high costs of other fuels, there is a demand for firewood in urban areas which leads to deforestation. However, a large part of the destruction of forests has come about because of industrial demands: for paper, pulp, packaging materials, furniture and various fiber based industries. Countries of the North have a significant responsibility for cutting down the forests of the South to meet their industrial needs.

In my view, the loss of biodiversity is one of the crucial and immediate questions facing us today — and should figure high in the list of priority areas of global change. Dr. Peter Raven has dealt with this topic in great detail in Chapter 6 of this book.

E. Pollution of Oceans and Coastal Zones

Oceans and coastal areas are being increasingly afflicted by human-induced pollution. Industrial wastes and agro-chemicals travel long distances in rivers and accumulate in coastal zones. Oil spills at sea have been taking place far too frequently. It must be remembered that the ocean surface represents a delicate interface between the atmosphere and oceans. It represents an important element in exchange phenomena and teems with biological activity. Damage to it can have unpredictable and serious consequences.

F. Acid Rain and Industrial Pollution

This continues to be an area of concern. While there has been significant progress in the North in establishing emission standards for an increasing number of pollutants and controlling industrial pollution, much more needs to be done as new synthetic compounds continuously make their appearance. In the countries of the South, there is need for much more to be done: in setting emission standards, winding down industries and technologies known to be severely damaging to the environment, and imposing and adapting pollution control technologies. Basic knowledge in many of these areas is available. It is a question of access to it, of transfer of technology and finding resources for moving to a new environment-sensitive regime. North-South cooperation has enormous possibilities in this area.

None of these problems — of greenhouse gas emissions with implications for global warming, sea level rise, ozone depletion, pollution of oceans and coastal zones, destruction of tropical forests and of biodiversity, acid rain and industrial pollution — will go away or disappear in the foreseeable future. What we have to do is set processes in motion to slow or to reverse the present trends. This will involve education and awareness-building, generation of new technologies, transfer of environment-sensitive technologies in a way in which their usage will become widespread (at low cost or taking them into the public domain), economic measures to encourage the choice of environment-friendly options, and significant availability of financial resources to the South which will have to be made available by the North. We cannot immediately solve all of these problems, but we can learn to manage them better.

IX. INTERNATIONAL SCIENTIFIC WORK RELATING TO GLOBAL CHANGE

The initial attempt to study the earth's environment on a global scale was the first International Polar Year, 1982-83. Since then, the International Council of Scientific Unions (ICSU) has initiated many programs to study the global environment. The most important have been: the International Geophysical Year (1957-58); the Global Atmospheric Research Program (GARP) (1967-80), jointly with World Meteorological Organization (WMO); which has been followed by the World Climate Research Program (since 1980). The most recent of the programs on the global environment is the International Geosphere-Biosphere Program(IGBP).

The key objective of IGBP is "to describe and understand the interactive physical, chemical, and biological processes that regulate the total earth system, the unique environment that it provides for life, the changes that are occurring in this system, and the manner in which they are influenced by human actions." IGBP recognizes that there are many studies and programs that are already being addressed in existing initiatives, at the national level, as well as through large international organizations such as WMO, UNEP, etc. IGBP will make full use of the knowledge resulting from these. For IGBP, "the priority will be on key interactions, and significant changes on time scales of decades to centuries, that most affect the biosphere, that are most susceptive to human perturbation, and that will most likely lead to practical, predictive capability."

A program of this nature, by definition, has to be global in character. Three-fifths of the land area of the earth is covered by developing countries, who must, therefore, be participants in this program. A program of this nature has become possible only now, with the availability of global observation systems based on satellites with advanced sensors, and large scale computational capabilities for analysis and modelling. We also know much more now on how to extract paleo-information on environmental parameters from the distant past, which are indicators of global change. This is a program which will continue over several decades. It is the most ambitious and most wide-ranging global scientific program ever taken up. The success of such a program calls for free availability of data and information, namely, a system of openness which is at the very heart of scientific endeavor. It will demand long-term commitments of scientific and financial resources, with no practical applications for many years.

ICSU is thus committed deeply today to two major programs that are complementary: the World Climate Research Program (WCRP) and the International Geosphere-Biosphere Program (IGBP). In addition, ICSU undertakes major activities in the area of environment under its Scientific Committee on Problems of the Environment (SCOPE), and environment issues are also looked at by many of the Unions and Scientific Committees of ICSU. In view of the diversity of this work, ICSU has set up an Advisory Committee on Environment (ACE) chaired by its Secretary General to coordinate all of its activities in this area.

We have to realize that global change is not just climate change. It is not covered in its totality by WCRP and IGBP, however important these programs are. The great problems of loss of biodiversity, of destruction of precious soil cover, of population increase, and consequences of the many natural disasters are immediate problems that we face. The international scientific community has to work on all of these, for which support has to be provided by society.

There is a great deal of knowledge, and a great deal of capability, to deal immediately with some of the problems confronting us. We must proceed to do so in a manner which, at the lowest cost, with the greatest returns, society as a whole would benefit to the greatest extent. On the other hand, we also realize that the physiology of the earth system is highly complex. There is a great deal that we do not know. There are many uncertainties in the consequences that are often stated or put out, which society tends to regard as absolutely correct and reliable since these have come from science. We have to caution against this. There is a great deal more research that we need to do to improve our knowledge, understanding and ability to predict, for which support must be provided by society.

The International Council of Scientific Unions is constantly keeping these issues under review to ensure that the scientific community of the world can fulfill the expectations that society has in respect to the assistance that science can provide on aspects of policy-making and implementation that can bring about sustainable development.

X. THE NORTH-SOUTH DIVIDE ON GLOBAL CHANGE ISSUES — PROSPECTS BEFORE UNCED

There is concern that countries of the North and of the South might differ significantly in their perceptions concerning the issues that are likely to come up before UNCED. Many in the North have spoken up strongly about the large and rapidly growing populations of the South, pointing to this as the principal cause of global environmental stress. There is also concern that since the increase in greenhouse gases due to human activities can pose long-term serious hazards, all nations must take steps to ensure that they do not contribute to an increase in these gases. Developing countries would not like to accept targets and conditionalities that would jeopardize their development. The countries of the South could take the view that their contribution to greenhouse gases in the atmosphere is at present small, in terms of total cumulative and current emissions, as well as per capita emissions; it is the North which has been responsible for the enhanced global greenhouse effect through its very large energy consumption and industrial activities; the industrialized nations should, therefore, take the responsibility for the situation that the world finds itself in today. The countries of the South can also take the view that, when a major natural resource, such as the atmosphere, is converted from a free to a managed resource, then the principle of equity should be strictly followed. Each individual in the world has an equal right to this resource. They could argue that it is the affluent lifestyles of the North which are leading to over consumption of natural resources and to global environmental stress; they would view it as a matter of concern that very few in the North, particularly those in responsible positions, have spoken strongly and vociferously against these continuing trends, which can only be regarded as profligate living.

It would indeed be a pity if discussions at UNCED led to confrontations of this nature, rather than an attempt to arrive at an understanding between North and South so that we can move toward sustainable development on the basis of international solidarity.

It is a fact that three quarters of the world's population resides in the developing countries; and their shares of consumption, of almost all commodities, are considerably smaller than this fraction. The largest of the developing countries, namely India and China, are well below the average in per capita consumption levels of all types of commodities, as well as in overall shares. Rapid growth in population and consequent lack of development keeps a large fraction of the population of the developing world at subsistent levels of living, and their per capita consumption of global change phenomena is accordingly small with respect to the immediate future. In contrast, the major stress on the environment due to greenhouse gases, particularly CO_2, and CFCs which damage the ozone layer (both cumulative totals as well as current total emissions), is due to the developed countries of the North. It is, of course, true that, in the long run, since population growth is basically irreversible, and a high rate will lead to a higher stable population level in the future, it will be a major cause of environmental stress in the course of time. Thus reduction of the population growth rate is essential to bring about development, and also to lessen the severity of environmental problems in the future.

Many environmental problems arise because environmental costs and consequences are not taken note of in the present system of accounting. They tend to be external to cost/benefit calculations. Policies at the national and international levels, with a system of incentives/disincentives and appropriate use of the market mechanism, would be important to ensure that the economic systems of today take environmental implications fully into account.

There are many specific actions that can be taken on an immediate basis which are briefly indicated below:

i) Energy Efficiency: There is a great deal already known for improving efficiency, not only in energy generation but also in energy use; the focus is often on the former, neglecting the latter, which is incorrect. There should be a major international effort to reduce energy consumption through appropriate energy management and energy efficient technologies. It is a pity that efforts in this direction, which had gathered impetus after the oil shocks of the 1970s, have slowed down significantly over the past decade. There is great scope for the new information technologies and biotechnologies to yield new process routes with lower energy intensity to meet societal needs.

ii) Renewable Energies: Renewable energies have an important role to play, particularly in developing countries where they can contribute to decentralized energy availability. At present, in most of these countries, very large energy generation systems, and corresponding transmission and distribution systems, are not in place. Renewable energies can, therefore, meet a real need, and also save on energy consumption, particularly based on oil and wood; savings in the case of the former will mean conservation of a non-renewable source, in addition to reduced imports for most countries. Unfortunately, the thrust relating to renewable energies has also shown no improvement over the past decade; and they have not yet entered the energy supply statistics.

iii) <u>Pricing</u>: There is clearly a need for appropriate pricing, which would reduce unnecessary energy consumption, particularly in the transportation sector. This would involve hard decisions by the developed countries; what would be needed is not only efficiency improvements but changes in lifestyles.

iv) <u>Use of Natural Gas</u>: There is need for much greater stress on the use of natural gas, which is far cleaner compared to coal, oil or fuel wood. Many developing countries have natural gas resources which are yet untapped. A major international effort to assist them in this area would be of great value.

v) <u>Afforestation</u>: Afforestation will be important, in the short and medium term, from the viewpoint of increasing the global sink for carbon dioxide. It will also be an important way to bring about soil stabilization. A variety of proposals exist to encourage afforestation on a substantial scale, particularly in developing countries. This needs to be pursued further.

It will be seen that there is a great deal that we can do on an immediate basis to reduce the stress on the earth's environment. As one learns to move forward in a spirit of cooperation rather than confrontation, more such opportunities will surely become available. These are opportunities at UNCED that should not be missed.

Before concluding, it is important to stress two points. Firstly, world population will grow to a figure well above 8 billion before stabilizing. The stabilized level may range between 8.5 billion to 15 billion, as given in various demographic projections, depending on how rapidly the development issues and poverty alleviation can be tackled. We will have to learn to live with a population of this size and to meet its needs.

Secondly, the total energy consumption in the world will reach a level more than twice the present level. It is estimated to reach a saturation level between 22 and 26 TW (terawatts). The major source of this energy will continue to be fossil fuels; no other acceptable and available source for large scale energy generation is on the horizon. One would have to live with higher CO_2 emission levels. A great deal of work will be needed to understand with some certainty what environmental consequences will result. There will also be need to initiate work on processes for trapping greenhouse gases or arranging sinks for them.

It is clear that science and technology have an important role to play in ensuring development that is equitable and also sustainable in the light of the scenario before us, which has a degree of inevitability.

REFERENCES

1. Human Development Report, UNDP (1990).

2. A Global Environmental Compact for Sustainable Development: Resource Requirements and Mechanisms. Lal Jayawardena (WIDER UNU), 1991.

3. The Challenge to the South: The Report of the South Commission. Oxford University Press, 1990.

4. Consumption Patterns: The Driving Force of Environmental Stress. Jyoti Parikh, Kirit Parikh, Subir Gokarn, J.P.Painuly, Bibhas Saha, Vibhooti Shukla, (Indira Gandhi Institute of Development Research Bombay) - October, 1991 (Preprint).

The Role of Science & Technology

George E. Brown, Jr.

I would like to talk about the future that our past decisions have already created for us, and how we need to make some very different decisions to change our trajectory. That we are not heading in a sustainable direction has become accepted dogma. So I will address where science and society should be in the future if we are to achieve a sustainable world, not about when carbon dioxide in the atmosphere will double. My thesis is that while knowledge generation is important, societal transformations are paramount. Science is, after all, a part of society.

I believe we need to transform both science and policy formulation, and to accomplish these two things we will need to change society as well. We could begin today to implement some technologies to mitigate global change. I refer to phasing in substitutes for freon and using more fuel-efficient autos, as two examples. These changes are not occurring smoothly because society doesn't see the urgency of doing so. Of course, such changes probably will be incremental, iterative, and interactive; in a word, evolutionary. The important thing to recognize is that we won't be able to proceed in a linear fashion, i.e. to do science first, then make policy, then change society, as some often claim.

The debate over global change occupies the profoundly complex interface between scientific research and political decision-making. I would suggest that Congress and the American people have never before been faced with an issue of such technical, political, and sociological complexity. At the same time, it seems to be increasingly hard to make policy decisions. This is illustrated, of course, by our failure to even take-up the legislation providing for a new energy strategy for this country.

Taking a large perspective, the release of 33 billion metric tons of other greenhouse gases into the atmosphere each year can be viewed as an ongoing experiment in the physics of atmospheric

Congressman George Brown is Chairman of the Science, Space, and Technology Committee of the U.S. House of Representatives.

process. However, the public dialogue over global change reveals the broader nature of the experiment. Although we may first think of this as an environmental experiment, it is also an economic, political, aesthetic, philosophical, and ethical experiment. We have then an experiment in cultural values. The very existence of this controversy, and our response to it, says a great deal about our culture, and especially about the respective roles of science and politics in American society.

The political debate over climate change has focused on issues of data quality and scientific uncertainty. Some argue that the implications of global climate change are potentially so disastrous that we must take action now to mitigate emission of greenhouse gases. Others feel that the economic consequences of such mitigation cannot be justified unless we are able to reduce the scientific uncertainty and better understand the consequences of any warming that may occur. This debate reveals less about science, and more about our underlying attitudes toward a range of basic human values, than we might want to acknowledge.

Greenhouse gas emissions are merely a by-product, or symptom, of human activity on earth. We must go beyond symptoms to more basic processes and causes. The two most important such processes and causes are high population growth rates in the South and high rates of material consumption in the North, and both will be difficult to change. That's what we must begin to focus on.

The globalization of economies, of communication, of migration, and of conflict, assures that we can no longer isolate ourselves from the problems of the developing world. Growth of populations triggers growth in resource consumption, in waste production, in conflict and violence, and in the disparity in economic status and quality of life between nations, and among classes within nations. Whereas once the consequences of population growth may have affected only local cultures, they are no longer contained by geographic or political boundaries. The problems of the Third World become our problems, not because of humanitarian concerns on our part, but because of the inexorable trend toward global interdependence.

It is crucial, then, that we see ourselves as part of a dynamic global system operating in the present — today. But it is perhaps equally important to understand historical patterns of human development, and to learn from the successes and mistakes made in the past. If conflict, resource use, environmental degradation, and increasing concentration of wealth are predictable consequences of population growth, shouldn't we see evidence of this relationship in human history?

Indeed we do. Anthropologists such as Marvin Harris recognize that history displays a typical pattern of cyclical progression: the decline of one culture as a result of environmental degradation and resource depletion, followed by the rise of another culture which has the ability to support a larger population by means of a more advanced technology.

This process has been going on probably for 10,000 years. It is recorded from the days of the rise and collapse of civilizations, communities, in the valley of the Tigris and the Euphrates. For example, in the Bible the prophet Isaiah may have been referring to this cycle when he said in Chapter 51, "Pay attention to me, oh my people, and give ear to me, oh my nation; for a law will go forth from me and I will try to set my justice for a light of the peoples. Lift up your eyes to the sky. Then look to the earth beneath for the sky will vanish like smoke and the earth will wear out like a garment and its inhabitants will die in like manner." He could be talking about ozone in southern California. Of course most of the prophets were making apocalyptic statements generally about the sin of fixating on material consumption rather than spiritual values. And that message, too, is appropriate today.

The critical point made by Marvin Harris is that human history in every region of the earth is dominated by repeated evolutionary cycles of this kind: population growth, resource depletion, and declining standards of living, followed, in many cases, by technological innovation that launches a new cycle of growth and resource depletion. This cyclical view of history asserts a Malthusian correlation between population growth and the inadequate supply and distribution of the resources necessary for a high quality of life. The social consequences of this correlation are poverty, hunger, and war. From this perspective, technology does not avert these consequences; it advances as a result of them.

Contrast this theory with the basic philosophy of progress that most of us share. We tend to think of science and technology as benign and autonomous forces that are the major contributors to what we call progress. Most of us see progress as linear, and more-or-less continuous. We share a modern, western confidence in the ability of science to fuel technological innovation, and in the ability of this innovation to solve social problems and improve the quality of our lives.

We may thus believe that science and technology can free us from the cycles of growth and decline that characterize the past. But we must consider an alternative hypothesis: that our faith in science and technology, and our faith that progress is driven by science and technology, blind us to the cyclical nature of our own cultural evolution, and to its consequences.

At the very least it is easy to show that the idea of continuous progress, of the potential for infinite growth, for perpetual improvement in the quality of our lives, is rather parochial. The population of the industrialized nations is projected to grow by about 150 million people in the next thirty years. Over this same period, the population of developing nations will grow by twenty-three hundred million. Thus, 95% of all the human beings born over the next thirty years will benefit little from the progress that gives Americans such faith in the future.

We may already be seeing the implied regression. For example, per capita food consumption has been decreasing in Africa and Latin America for the past decade, and the trends and projections for the future are ominous.

The percentage of human beings on the planet who may never benefit from technological innovation and consequent economic growth increases every day. So we ask ourselves: toward what are we progressing? If we embrace the belief in science and technology as the great contributors to progress, are we also then embracing resource depletion, environmental degradation, economic disparity, and human suffering, all in the name of this progress?

These arguments suggest that science and technology have been largely reactive, and that, from a global perspective, the modern idea of progress is either selfish or illusory. The history of science and technology is one of increased metabolism — more production, more consumption, more waste.

A neutral observer from Mars would say that we are using science and technology not to deliver ourselves from primal chaos into grace, but quite the reverse. The historical version of progress does not offer a plausible scenario for the world's development because the planet cannot provide the resources necessary to sustain five billion human beings in the style of the typical American citizen to which they all aspire.

I have argued, so far, that human cultural evolution has a strong cyclical component, and that science and technology have been integral to the perpetuation of these cultural cycles. Of course, there also seems to be a component of more or less steady progress for some parts of the human race. The recognition of the existence of the cycle of population growth, resource depletion, and technological innovation may help us to reduce its inevitability.

In fact, by recognizing the cycle, I believe that we are morally obliged to question its inevitability, and to seek new trajectories of cultural development. This will require a revolution, not in science and technology, but in values. We must begin to think of science and technology in entirely different terms — not as mechanisms to increase our exploitation of material resources, but as the sources of innovation that can drive us to less consumption, less pollution, less depletion of resources, and lower rates of population growth.

The scientific community seems reluctant to embrace the basic terms of this debate. Comfortable with their current research agendas and with hard data, but uncomfortable with change and with the ethical and cultural implications of their inquiry, they debate what they perceive to be the scientific substance, and leave the value judgments to the politicians. Scientists tell us that their data is objective, unburdened by ethical or moral implications. That leaves us in the political sphere free to use the data in any way we see fit. And we do. And we love it.

Scientific uncertainty has become an operational synonym for inaction on global environmental issues. Certainly a temperature increase of several degrees over the next century could have disastrous global consequences, especially for the less resilient societies of the developing world.

But the immediate challenge for science and technology must NOT be viewed as the need to reduce scientific uncertainty about climatic warming. This is a hollow ambition which, certainty about global warming, as with other areas of science, will never be achieved. It is a goal too easy to support and too unlikely to bear fruit. It plays into the hand of those who believe there is no problem. The real challenge is to find ways to increase the quality of life for humankind throughout the world while escaping the cycle of population growth and resource destruction.

We need a whole new approach, a new context for science and technology. For example, traditional economists look at the cost of mitigating greenhouse emissions, they look at the future benefits, they apply a discount rate and calculate that the present value of the future benefit is much less than the cost. But this makes no sense if the situation is treated as an issue of intergenerational equity.

Richard Norgaard, a Berkeley economist, has shown that if you assume that future generations have the same right to a habitable environment that we do, then sustainable development becomes economically feasible. In other words, we need new basic assumptions. We need values — such as intergenerational equity — that lead us to the right technical solutions, that lead us to explore the right scientific questions.

The opportunities for implementing a new age in scientific inquiry and outreach have never been greater. We have the technological capability to link together research centers in distant corners of the world, to instantly share data and ideas and hypotheses, to hold satellite-transmitted teleconferences between scientists and policymakers, and to connect elementary and secondary school students with research scientists. At this point, we lack only the cerebral software necessary to fully utilize this capability.

What are the appropriate ultimate goals for science and technology in our society? Does science serve the scientists, or humanity? Must science and technology continue to feed the historical cycle of more consumption, more waste, more economic disparity? Or can research break that cycle, and create a new trajectory for cultural evolution based on the minimization of material and energy waste, and the increased consumption and enjoyment of non-material resources?

The pursuit of scientific knowledge must be explicitly devoted to the service of humankind and the betterment of the human condition. In no way should this be seen as a limitation on the breadth of scientific inquiry. On the contrary, I am advocating that researchers break the shackles on scientific pursuit that are imposed by our own flawed definition of progress. This definition has led us to a straight-jacket of disciplinary specialization and an allegedly "rational detachment" from the ethical and moral problems facing the human species.

Now let me summarize my argument and give my prescription. The history of the human race has been one of inexorable, non-sustainable, accelerating cyclical growth in:

· human population;
· resource consumption;
· waste generation;
· conflict and destruction; and
· disparity in economic circumstances and quality of life.

My principal countervailing source of hope is the growth in organized human knowledge, science, devoted to humane goals. Therefore, the leaders of science, in the manner of Tom Malone and many others, must make a value choice: They must decide to direct their efforts, their scientific efforts and their social efforts, to getting off the historical path of non-sustainable material growth and onto a path of sustainable increase in:

· the quality of human life;
· all branches of knowledge;
· the consumption and enjoyment of non-material resources;
· the minimization of waste;
· cooperation, constructive competition, and non-violence; and
· justice and equity in the distribution of economic goods and opportunity.

This gives an outline of our goals. Referring back to the goals of the forum, it is clear to me that we are going to need more societal transformation than science — more progress in the social and policy sciences than in the physical sciences.

WHAT SPECIFIC STEPS DO WE NEED TO TAKE?

First, self education as to the real dimensions of the problems. We cannot be smug that our conception of the problem is right.

Second, we must reach out beyond our narrow disciplines and create links to the many other relevant communities.

Third, we need to strengthen international scientific communication and cooperation. This is not because we need foreign data to validate models. No, it is because we need new ideas. Western science has been so successful by its own non-sustainable standards that it may not be able, without diverse help from non-Western science, to find the new sustainable trajectory we need.

And again, I found an appropriate quotation in the Bible from Ecclesiastes in Chapter 4, "A poor yet wise lad is better than an old and foolish king who no longer knows how to receive instruction." The old and foolish kings of western policy, politics, and science might heed this message.

Fourth, we need to revitalize elementary through undergraduate science, mathematics, and engineering education in order to expand scientific literacy. And we need to meld this with the humanities and social sciences to give citizens the perspective they need to make wise decisions. Only in this way can we develop the broad understanding of the problem necessary to generate political support for action.

Fifth, the physical-science community needs to become, first, more involved with its social-science colleagues and, second, more involved with business, schools, community groups, and politics. It is not enough to drop a stack of computer output on a policymaker's desk. Scientists need to learn why action is so hard — why "the system" is so viscous — and how to make it work better. They need, in a word, to be more worldly.

We must pursue a new definition of progress, and we must reconsider the goals of science and technology in light of this new definition. This will require both individual and institutional change, which will come neither easily nor quickly. It will require new metrics for success, based not on the ability to publish a lot of papers and generate a lot of grants or patents, but on the ability to forge innovative, interdisciplinary approaches to global problems facing humanity.

By insight and intellectual prowess, scientists throughout the ages have taught us a new perspective from which to understand ourselves. Their discoveries have enlightened our perception of everything from our planetary position among the stars to the intricate biology of living cells. From science has come a new concept to describe radical change. The concept of the paradigm shift. The time for such a paradigm shift is now upon us.

Now we call upon the scientific community to lead us into new patterns of sustainability, and survivability that honor the dignity and the needs of all humans. Our task is to learn how to husband and to share the bounty of this planet. These new metrics for sustainability will require scientists to move beyond the security of their laboratories and classrooms into the hurly-burly social infrastructure. In the marketplace of human expectations, we will look for scientists to lead us into change by their own example and engagement. I hope that you are equal to the task.

Section III

What Must We Do To Get There ?

182

Implementation:
Science & Technology

John H. Gibbons

I take great pleasure in being back among some long-term friends and colleagues, having learned over 12 years what Harry Truman once said, "In Washington if you want a loyal friend you better go out and buy a dog." I'm also a little chagrined, as a person working within the federal government, in speaking about how to make decisions and take actions. There is a lot of talk and a lot of rumors, but sometimes one gets discouraged by the lack of momentum. William O. Baker, who used to run Bell Telephone labs, once said that "Washington is very confusing to a physicist because its a place where sound travels faster than light."

Congress is wrestling with many vexing issues, many deeply involving science and technology. In fact, science and technology are increasingly imbedded in the issues that Congress must address. Congress suffers from burgeoning demands and is overwhelmed by special interests. It's reminiscent of what George Bernard Shaw once said: "A government which robs Peter to pay Paul, can always depend on the support of Paul." The only question is: what do you do for Peter?

There is a major issue, and that is how to face today's crises, while establishing long-term goals and implementing long-term programs to meet those goals. I don't know how many of you read the comics, but I'm a faithful reader of McNeeley's *Shoe*. You may recall the day when the professor was talking about goals and he says: "My short term goal means that I make it to 5 pm, and my long-term goal means putting together a string of short term goals." Unfortunately that's the way we seem to operate in our goal setting business. There is a dilemma, to me at least, that with greater wealth one can worry less about tomorrow and more about next year, and, therefore, greater wealth would imply greater ability to think in terms of long-term perspectives. It sounds sensible, but it doesn't seem to work that way. In the U.S. our

Jack Gibbons is Director of the U.S. Congressional Office of Technology Assessment.

thinking about the future seems to be foreshortened as we increase our wealth. I was somewhat dismayed by an official from the Peoples Republic of China who told me the other day that their leadership has great problems in thinking about long-term issues, because they are more and more drawn to focus their efforts and energies on shorter term issues.

Does, therefore, increasing wealth imply an increasing rate of change, and therefore a foreshortening of thinking about the future? I think to a degree that is the case. For example, in microelectronics, average product lifetimes are several years, so one is not very wise in spending a lot of time thinking about microelectronics even as short a time 30 or 40 years hence, since so much will change in the meanwhile. But, simultaneously, I think we all understand that we must come to grips with some inherently long-term issues, where traditional muddling through, which has been our national political philosophy for 200 years, would be a perilous if not a foolhardy thing to do. It's increasingly imperative to gain a better perspective of where we are headed, and it's as true for political leaders as it is for researchers. C. P. Snow said that "Sense of the future is behind all good politics. Unless we have it we can give nothing either wise or decent to the world." Yet, at the same time, I think we are all nervous about trying to make predictions about the future. It's better to talk about scenarios, opportunities, and options, than it is to talk about predictions. As Antoine St. Exupery said: "As for the future, your task is not to foresee but to enable." I believe that is what we're here this weekend to talk about: How do we enable futures to be perceived, devised and achieved.

But my assignment is to address what must we do to get there. First, I think defining desired futures is a very important thing. If you don't know where you want to get to, you have a hard time knowing how well you're doing. Lewis Carroll, fine mathematician that he was, better known for *Alice in Wonderland*, described it this way as Alice questioned Cheshire Puss. She said: "Cheshire Puss would you tell me please which way I ought to go from here"? The cat responded: "It depends a good deal Alice, on where you want to get to." I think we tend to forget that lesson when we talk about national goals. We tend to say that it's not wise to set targets or measures of progress. As we know, the devil lies in the details. Getting beyond the generalities and agreeing on long-term goals requires a rationalization of extraordinary diversity of interest in our society, and there are disturbing signs that we are increasingly in trouble in terms of acting together as a people or a nation.

Consider the current arguments about global climate change, about energy policies and futures, about industrial competitiveness. A people unwilling to subordinate personal gratification in order to achieve common goals has become a mob, and I think there is evidence that in our current search for personal gratification and individualization, we can be described as a people who have become a mob. But in addition to defining desired futures, it seems to me we need to spend time and effort on rationalizing science and technology goals from overarching social goals. That is linking the science and technology enterprise to definable, identifiable national goals. Examples of the latter are economic strength and resilience, sustainability, habitat, health, security, freedom, privacy, environmental quality, education and enlightenment and extension of knowledge. It seems to me those can be seen as goals that are overarching and identifiable, that enjoy broad public consensus. Our task in science and technology, which is my assignment here, is to try to link our enterprise to those overarching goals.

I would like to give a couple of examples. Let's first talk about energy, because energy so ubiquitously reflects economic, environmental and security issues faced not only here at home, but also around the world. Energy issues range from personal to global. Energy has immediate concerns, as well as fundamental features that are inherently multi-decade, if not half-century in time dimensions. Now we can talk about some candidate long-term goals. For instance, we can talk about the transition beyond our dependence on fossil fuels. Robert Louis Stevenson said, "Sooner or later we sit down to a banquet of consequences," and I will return to the banquet of consequences when I talk about moving from where we are now to a time in which we will be far less dependent on fossil fuels.

Another candidate long-term energy goal might be achieving an acceptable dependence on imported fuels, as well as the diversity of sources that energy imports come from.

A third energy strategy could be to commit to least cost strategies in energy development, which include considerations not only of the traditional market measures of cost, but also incorporation of the external cost, such as environment and health, and international security.

Now to illustrate my point, Figure 1 is a simplified diagram of oil. The upper envelope defines the total amount of consumption of oil, not only in times past, but the projections to the future, assuming current trends continue. We see rising demand and a fall off of domestic production, and, therefore, a rise of imports, and it's a rather sobering thing to see such a curve as this. But I also remind you of a Chinese proverb that says: "If we don't change our direction, we are likely to end up where we are headed." So one has to take seriously then, the point of this slide, namely that we are heading into a time of extraordinarily increasing dependence on imported oil, most of which has to come from the Middle East because, like Willy Sutton said about taking money from banks, the Middle East is where the oil is. So one can develop, given this situation, a series of scenarios to illustrate what can be done.

Figure 1

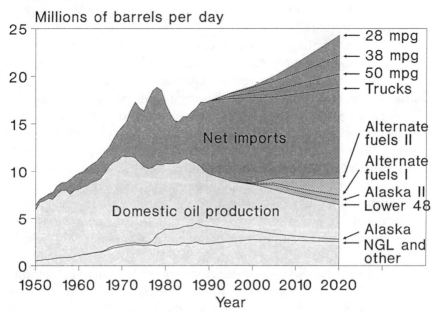

Source: Office of Technology Assessment; adapted from Energy Information Administration, Annual Energy Outlook.

A variety of strategies are illustrated. One sees that on the supply side one can add something like the north slope ANWAR [Arctic National Wildlife Reserve] and, if we're lucky, we may get about this amount of increase of oil production. In other words, it would help slow down our decreasing domestic production. One can also become rather heroic and say let's devise a way of producing, by the year 2020, 2 million barrels a day of synthetic fuels from other sources. It might be from biomass, it might be liquid fuels from natural gas, or even coal liquefaction. So there are a few things one can do on the supply side, which with heroic efforts might level out the domestic production.

What about the demand side? If we go from the current 28 miles per gallon automobiles to another 10 miles per gallon by the time we get to 2010, and get to about 38 miles per gallon, that's a pretty hefty decrease in the amount of oil we have to use. If we really get serious and use a lot of our technological muscle, and by the year 2020 are producing cars at 50 miles per gallon, this drops the demand envelope quite considerably. If we do the same thing to trucks, we drop it further, and if we take half the oil out of every other use, we drop down to about a constant demand on liquid fuels, much of which would be made up by synthetics, and one sees that one could, at least with a series of scenarios, devise a strategy in which our total demand is no more than 50% dependent on imports. Then one could devise other strategies to assure the development of oil resources around the world. Thus, with a lot of aggressive activity we might hold ourselves to about 50% oil imports out in the years of the next century.

Of course, modeling is always a tricky activity. John Kenneth Galbraith once said that "The modern economic system does in fact survive not because of the excellence of the work of those who forecast its future, but because of their supremely reliable commitment to error." Yet he says, "There is a redeeming possibility: We can attempt to understand the present, for the future will inevitably retain compelling aspects of what now exists." So modeling does seem worthwhile.

Let's take a look at another aspect of energy: time-series changes. The vertical bars in Figure 2 represent the ratio of energy consumed per GNP produced. We see that we went along with an energy-to-GNP ratio that was seemingly almost in lockstep until we got to the early 1970s, when we began to discover the technologies of efficiency. New applications enabled us to maintain an increase in GNP while basically leveling out energy consumption. The fall-off of the ratio, until we got into the Reagan years, was about 2% per year decrease in energy required to produce a unit of GNP. Detailed analysis indicates that, in the future, one might well be able to continue such a fall-off in energy intensiveness of our economy for several more decades. Similarly, as illustrated in Figure 3, electricity was growing faster than GNP up until the early 1970s, when again the change of price of electricity, plus the rapid introduction of technologies of efficiency, enabled us to level out. Instead of electricity growing at about twice the rate of GNP, it has been growing at about the same rate as GNP since that time.

Figure 2

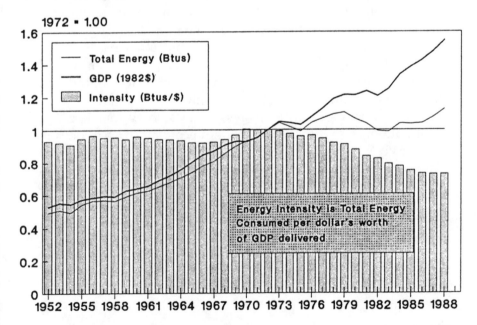

Energy Intensity of the U.S. Economy

1972 ▪ 1.00

Total Energy (Btus)
GDP (1982$)
Intensity (Btus/$)

Energy Intensity is Total Energy Consumed per dollar's worth of GDP delivered

Source: Annual Energy Outlook, U.S. Department of Energy, Washington, D.C. 1990

<u>Figure 3</u> Electricity Intensity of the US Economy

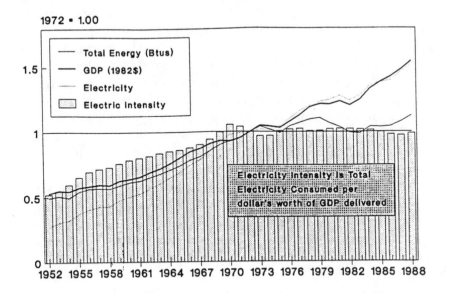

Source: *Annual Energy Outlook, U.S. Department of Energy, Washington, D.C.* 1990

That tells us something else again about the plausibility of moving toward the future with electricity demand growth rates which include not only a growing economy, but a growing market share of electricity in the energy system. That still would enable us to have the historic ratio of two-to-one electricity growth over GNP growth reduced to as little as one-to-one. So it's the specificity that one derives from systems analysis of energy that one can at least lay out plausible national goals, measurable targets, and attendant R & D. Some possible energy futures that come out of this kind of an analysis are: (1) that we can hold our oil imports to no more than 50%, but only with hard work, particularly on the demand side; (2) that we can increase our energy efficiency for at least another 40%, that is 2% per year over perhaps 20 years; (3) that we can reduce our dependence on fossil fuels; and (4) with intermediate strategies of natural gas, we can reduce the carbon intensiveness of our energy system by about 10% per decade. That last goal may not be fast enough, but it is a very plausible start in the direction of making the transition to the post-fossil fuel age.

We know that we are having a considerable struggle in articulating and implementing energy strategies. Not so much on where we ought to go, but how to get there. I think the Administration and the Congress both agree that increasing dependence on imports is just not a good thing for us in the long term. Oil imports account for half of our total balance of payments. It has lots of features that are not desirable for us in the long term. But the issues resolve to exactly what do we do in order to achieve these goals. We also know that there are intimate links between these energy arguments and the issue of how we move toward reducing the impacts of global climate change due to green house gases. It also relates to stratospheric ozone and the relationship of chlorofluorocarbons to the way we use them, particularly in our energy system. And finally it relates intimately to our national strategy for technology transfer to the developing countries, who in turn are moving on a much more rapid growth path of energy consumption with attendant problems for ozone and greenhouse, and our own national willingness to make available to these countries the technology requisite for them to follow paths that are less energy intensive.

A second example is our economy. We know that technology has enabled unprecedented wealth to much of the world, particularly since the 1940s and led by the United States. It's now spread out and globalized. The U.S. lead in manufacturing now is badly eroding, with no sign of significant turn around, so there is increasing discussion of a strategic technology policy for the U.S. This relates to the question of the direction of our research and development, especially that are supported by the federal government. As we look at the research and development agenda of the federal government, we find, especially since 1980, that it has become increasingly dominated by defense related research, in a post-war environment that seems more than a little anachronistic. Max Born said after World War II that "Intellect distinguishes between the possible and the impossible, reason distinguishes between the sensible and the senseless. Even the possible can be senseless." And so, as we think about our national investment in research, we need to think not only about what is possible, but what also is sensible. We need to worry about downstream effects of research. We're still very good at the bench, but as we move toward commercialization, product development, design, quality control, we find ourselves very clearly down the line from Japan and other producers. We have to be concerned about defense conversion. We are now in a time in which the events of the world are moving faster than our own ability to keep up with them. Fortunately, we have past experiences in defense conversion following other times of conflict, which give us some ideas about how we might move in the future. One of the problems, however, is that today is different from the end of World War II, or the end of the Korean War, or the Vietnam War, in that we no longer have such a commanding lead in our science and technology. It's going to be a lot tougher for us to move our industries toward civilian sector activities than it was in some of those earlier times.

I think we need to come to better understand the link between our economic viability, and our education and training. We can no longer compete with labor around the world, even labor that is more expensive than ours, unless our labor becomes more skilled, and that includes our management as well.

There is a link between our economic goals and our environmental goals. We still are a nation that has been characterized by Kenneth Boulding as "The Cowboy Economy." We think of achieving our needs in the future by either moving west or making more, or doing a bit of both. That runs into problems after a while.

That reminds me of the identity that was originally developed in a slightly different form by Paul Ehrlich and John Holdren, in which one relates pollution or other externalities to a series of terms. Of course all cancel out and you end up with an identity, but the terms are separated so that one can think in terms of strategies. In this case lets talk about pollution (Figure 4). It might be global change, it might be other forms of environmental impacts.

Figure 4

$$\text{Pollution} \equiv \underbrace{\frac{\text{Pollution}}{\text{Energy}}}_{\text{(Technology)}} \times \underbrace{\frac{\text{Energy}}{\text{GNP}}}_{\substack{\text{(Technology,} \\ \text{Market Basket)}}} \times \underbrace{\frac{\text{GNP}}{\text{Population}}}_{\text{(Economy)}} \times \underbrace{\text{Population}}_{\text{(People)}}$$

The effect, pollution, consists of four terms that multiply each other:

(1) The amount of pollution per unit of energy, and of course there are a lot of technological options attendant to that term.

(2) The amount of energy used per GNP; that relates to substitutability of other things for energy in our system and the market basket of our goods and products. We know that both of these terms can yield to technology and we've been operating on both of those terms to try to minimize them over the last twenty years, and have done very well at it.

(3) Then there is a term which relates to essentially the economy. This is a term you would sort of like to see grow but, in order to do so and hold pollution in check, you have to work on the other terms.

(4) Finally there is the inexorable population term, which one must never forget because it's the most fundamental driver of the whole system of four terms.

I think you will agree that progress, however measured, is important, terribly important, to our futures and that these terms are technologically determinable, but have their limits as well. We need to be particularly attentive to the issue of population because it is so fundamentally important for the long-term future.

Figure 5

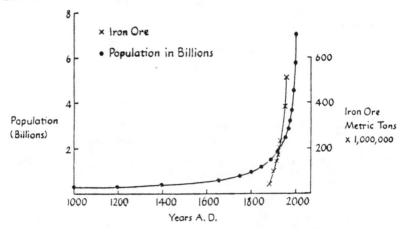

"What cannot go on forever must come to an end." Herb Stein

When you think about curves, I like this curve in Figure 5, which I wrote down about 30 years ago. It relates two exponentials, one is population growth and the other is growth of resource demand. In this case it is iron ore, but you can take your choice of what you want to plot. To someone who is mathematically inclined there is something ominous about these curves. Why? Because they are unbounded.

Let's turn to the third example: population. It's always interesting that when people plot future populations as seen in Figure 6, the slope of the curve changes. The second derivative begins to roll over. There is fortunately some recent evidence that this may indeed be the case in many countries around the world, but a slowdown always seems to be in the future rather than in the past, and future population numbers turn out invariably higher than earlier predictions. But we do see a time in which we expect that population in the coming century will indeed begin to level off and move toward some kind of equilibrium. I would remind you of a quote from a French Inspector General of the Bureau of Geological and Mineral Research in France. He said: "The ship of our civilization, which was already full of leaks and punctured by exponential curves, began to sink." I think we do have to come to understand that the exponential, historically seen as our greatest friend in

Figure 6   World Population Growth, 1750-2100

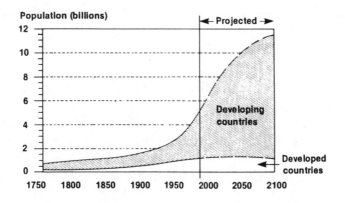

Source: *Thomas W. Merrick with PRB staff, "World Population in Transition," Vol. 41, No. 2, p. 4, January, 1988.   Updated Reprint by Carl Haub, Population Reference Bureau, 1991.*

terms of deliverance of goods and needs, can also become our enemy.

Let's think about population for a moment. George Bernard Shaw once said that "One mark of an educated person is that he or she can be emotionally moved by statistics." Figure 7 is a chart about U.S. population that should make us give pause. Females are charted on the right, males on the left. The age distribution has a peak in the age group 25 to 40. We are going through a demographic transition, following the post- World War II baby boom, and we've had a fall-off of birth rates since that time. Despite the major decrease in birth rates since 1960, we still are undergoing

Figure 7

USA Age Distribution					
Age	% of Pop'n	Male	Female	% of Pop'n	Age
70+	3.1%			5.0%	70+
60-69	3.9%			4.6%	60-69
50-59	4.4%			4.8%	50-59
40-49	5.3%			5.6%	40-49
30-39	8.1%			8.3%	30-39
20-29	8.8%			8.8%	20-29
10-19	7.5%			7.1%	10-19
0-9	7.5%			7.2%	0-9

24,000   12,000   0   12,000   24,000
(in thousands)

- Total Population... 248,231,000
- Total Male Pop'n... 120,640,000
- Total Female Pop'n: 127,591,000
- Life Expectancy (Male): 72 years
- Life Expectancy (Female): 79 years

significant population expansion in the U.S., especially when one adds immigration to the equation.

What we are also learning is that, if this kind of a distribution changes too suddenly, as the people in China have recently come to understand, then, if one looks ahead a number of years, one finds that the number of those who provide sustenance for the older people becomes fewer and fewer, and the result is a lot of deep seated social problems. We find other implications here of an ageing population, which undoubtedly makes us more productive because we have more experienced labor force. We don't have to absorb quite so many new people into the labor force and that's a great salvation these days; yet, at the same time, any movement that's too rapid in terms of change in birth rates and death rates can cause a lot of deep seated problems.

Figure 8 provides a look at Mexico. There is reasonably good news from Mexico, namely that the birth rate in recent years (no thanks to the U.S.) has been dropping. Otherwise, the bottom slice of this demographic profile would come on out into the margin. So the good news is that at the margin things are looking much better for Mexico. At the same time one sees the extraordinary demand,

Figure 8

		Mexico Age Distribution			
Age	% of Pop'n	Male	Female	% of Pop'n	Age
70+	1.0%			1.3%	70+
60-69	1.4%			1.7%	60-69
50-59	2.4%			2.6%	50-59
40-49	3.6%			3.8%	40-49
30-39	5.7%			5.7%	30-39
20-29	8.8%			8.7%	20-29
10-19	12.6%			12.3%	10-19
0-9	14.5%			13.9%	0-9

```
        14,000        7,000          0          7,000        14,000
                               (in thousands)
```

• Total Population... 86,366,000   • Life Expectancy (Male): 67 years
• Total Male Pop'n... 43,183,000   • Life Expectancy (Female): 73 years
• Total Female Pop'n: 43,183,000

now and in future years, for job creation and assimilation of these people into the world economy.

Figure 9 looks at the continent of Africa. This is a plot, from 1990 out to the middle of the next century, of total population in Africa under three different assumptions starting from today.

One assumption is that the movement toward equilibrium that is replacement level (births equal deaths), is made over a period between now and the year 2030. The second curve shows the population that would obtain if the date of reaching replace-

Figure 9   Population Momentum in Africa

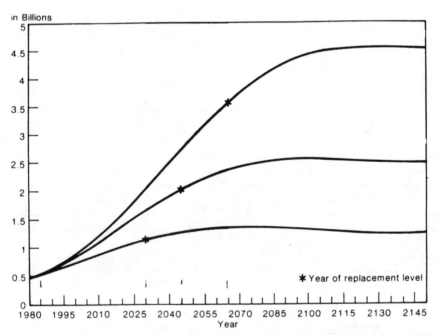

When a country reaches replacement-level fertility, it might be expected that the population growth rate would immediately reach zero. However, if the decrease to replacement is comparatively rapid, the large proportion of younger persons in the population will cause growth to continue for some time. In the above UN projections for Africa, note that in all three variants the population continues to grow after replacement is reached.

Source: Carl Haub, "Understanding Population Projections," Population Bulletin, Vol. 42, No. 4, p. 28, December, 1987.

ment level is moved out to 2045. The third is if that movement down toward replacement rate takes a time up to about year 2060.

A difference of about 40 versus 75 years in moving from where they are now to replacement level implies for Africa an ultimate equilibrium population that changes from 1.4 billion people to 4.4 billion people. The difference is as many people as inhabited the entire planet in 1960. So you see the implication of what can be called population momentum. If we take a lot more time in moving toward equilibrium, the ultimate population implications are devastating. George Bernard Shaw said that "The worst sin toward our fellow creatures is not to hate them but to be indifferent to them." If we are indifferent to these population implications, that is the essence of inhumanity.

What to do? We could spend the rest of the morning talking about what to do. Obviously, we need increased understanding of the dynamics of population: Rapid changes either way have negative implications. Understanding of the link between population growth and the achievement of other social goals is critical; so too is more effective contraception.

Now, some observations and principles, what you might call the necessities for getting from here to there. I'll just tick off a few of them:

One is, it seems to me, that "we" need to learn arithmetic, "we" being the whole world, especially those of us who have a chance to teach or influence other people. Shaw was right when he said "Man would rather commit suicide than learn arithmetic." It was reliably reported that President Dwight D. Eisenhower was amazed when he was informed that fully one half of the American people are below average intelligence. We need to learn about exponentials and time constants and the likes, and apply those concepts zealously to the articulation of goals and the setting and pacing of priorities.

It seems to me we also have to foreswear Disney's Law of "wishing will make it so." That seemed to be White House policy in the 1980s and it didn't work very well. The way we get past it is to talk about these issues, not only in our classrooms but in political forums, and to make our citizen governors, that is those whom we elect, and others in leadership roles understand these issues and take a stand on them in the right direction before they commit to the wrong direction.

Thirdly, I think we need to give rhetoric the boot that it deserves. We need to fight sensationalist, diversionary, escapist trivialization of issues, which is so easy to do with 7 second sound bytes on television — being our newly defined national attention span. We should remember what Herbert Spencer said, "The ultimate result of shielding men from the effects of folly is to fill the world with fools."

It seems to me we also need to begin to think of some better measures of progress than our gross national product. The recent Oakland fire was a real boon to the GNP of California. Our horrendous deficit spending and the Gulf war spurred our economy. I'm positive we can devise better measures of progress.

It also seems that we need to think about human resources more as capital and investment, rather than people as expendable. We need to develop new respect for the value and resilience that comes from diversity, as well as a more interesting world; and the value of flexibility. Someone said there are three kinds of people: people who make things happen, people who watch things happen, and people who don't know what is happening. As we move today in terms of spending billions each year on B-2 bombers and space interceptor missiles, while our schools and our infrastructure are in desperate trouble, the message I get is that we need to catch up with changing times or else we will suffer the ill consequences for certain.

Next to last, I think we need to devise more effective systems of government, that are responsive to the simultaneous centrifugal and centripetal forces that operate in the world today. Centrifugal forces such as global climate, global integrated economies, global security questions, throw us outward toward needing to organize ourselves on an effective global basis. The renewed emphasis on the United Nations that President Bush has done is a good example of reaching out to embrace those mechanisms that enable us to tackle things globally. The centripetal forces though are just as strong. Witness the disintegration Post-Pax Russia of Eastern Europe, the Balkans, and the former Soviet states. Cultural diversity, old time feelings, can take strong action when other forces are not neutralizing them.

There is an efficiency which pushes us toward making decisions more on the localized level rather than the global level. Efficiency is much greater when the money stays at home and works at home, where you can keep an eye on it and the people that govern it. But how does one simultaneously accommodate for these two forces that throw us on the one hand outward as citizens of the planet, and on the other hand throw us inward as we lose trust in bigness and want to do the things at home. I think John Locke still is our guardian angel in terms of political philosophy: "To govern least and govern closest to home is the best way to govern."

On the practical business of public decision making with regard to science and technology, it seems to me we ought to be heeding and learning from the lessons that are now being taught in the way things are working.

If you look for instance at the Clean Air Act, the driver for the Act was public opinion. It was only modestly driven by health data. It was heavily driven by people's personal encounters with the effects of pollution, and their desire to see things happen. That in turn caused political decisions, which in turn caused technology development. The Act was a technology-forcing political decision. That is the lesson we learned from The Clean Air Act over the last 20 years. If you look at the stratospheric ozone decision, that was data-driven, it also turns out that there is a relatively effective technology to substitute for CFCs. But the jury is still out on whether or not the world will respond and abandon the compounds that decrease stratospheric ozone concentrations before they catch up with us even more than they have already. An important lesson about stratospheric ozone is that it was a data-driven issue. It enabled political decision makers to make a decision, especially when they came to realize that the cost would be manageable.

If we look at global climate, there is much uncertainty, not so much about the fundamental science, but about the ultimate effects when the greenhouse effect is admixed with all sorts of other phenomena of the planet. It has a very long time constant, and it's a poorly defined risk at this point, and there is a lack of focused and perceived stakeholder support. Compare global warming, for instance, with defense. We may have very low probability scenarios for defense, but we have a very well established set of clients who are willing to use scenarios as a lever to support public policy, and in turn support the department of defense budget. If you look in terms of probabilistic analysis, the implications of global climate change are vastly greater than most of the areas we presently spend a lot of defense money on. But it's a different situation because of the time constants, the perceived risks and the degree of organization of the stakeholders.

Finally, I think that, with respect to population growth and related exponentials, a lot of these issues are obfuscated by religious ideology, and also discounted by a number of people who maintain that we can indefinitely grow our way out of trouble — the old cowboy economy. But I would remind you of what Herb Stein, a very outstanding economist said, "Whatever cannot go on forever must come to an end." When you think about it that's hard to argue with.

In order to move ahead, we have to change some of the fundamental ways we think about ourselves and how we operate. In Figure 10, the left is a portrayal of the exponential world and, in this situation, demand, let's say for energy, is described as essentially something that grows with the economy, which always goes up. Now, if you introduce efficiency, the first or second term of that modified Ehrlich-Holdren identity, you find that you can drop demand over time, while still supplying the same people, the same kind of goods and services. But the argument goes, improved efficiency only buys you a little time, and before you know it you're right back up to where you were in terms of meeting exponentially rising demand. Therefore, efficiency is discounted, because its seen only as a minor adjustment in the amount of time we have to make this exponentially increasing demand.

An alternate model, much more familiar to those of you in the life sciences, is the so-called S curve, in which one thinks about not only supplying goods and services but having the whole system move toward some kind of equilibrium. In that case, efficiency introduced to the system, in those terms I showed you, ultimately results not so much in buying a little time, but in basically buying a lessened demand of resources to provide a given number of people a given amount of benefits.

I think we need to become enamored with S curves, and also to think about energy resources, population, in terms not of "growth" in the traditional sense, but in terms of progress. What do we mean by progress? Kierkegaard, the Christian existentialist, said that "Progress should be measured by the increase in man's individuality." That seems to me to be a much more intriguing way to measure progress than the so called GNP. But René Dubos said it best of all. He said, "Just as important are the social amenities that make it possible to satisfy the longing for quiet empty spaces, for privacy, independence, and other conditions essential for preserving and enlarging the peculiarly human qualities of life." These are in short supply already.

In summing up: science and technology, new understanding, new options, give us hope, but no guarantee. We have our work cut out for us. We have a new realization about the imperative for sustainability, about the value of diversity, about resilience. It's a long journey that must be taken step-by-step, and it's time to get moving.

Figure 10   Alternative Growth Models

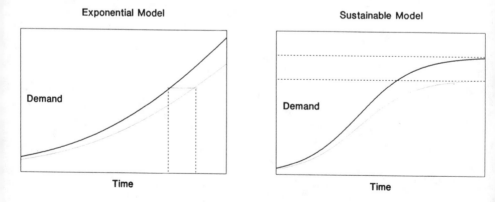

Exponential Model

Demand

Time

The change in efficiency of energy use translates to only delaying for a few years the inevitable growth of demand.

Sustainable Model

Demand

Time

The change in efficiency of energy use translates to a permanent lowering of demand and, therefore, pollution for a given level of economic activity.

202

Industry's Role

Elwood P. Blanchard, Jr.

It's a pleasure to be here in such distinguished company - and gratifying to be included in a session probing the question of "how" to enhance the quality of life on our planet.

As the representative of a major industrial corporation, I'm not always cast in such a positive role. Let me add that such a role is appropriate.

As an organic chemist by discipline, I have no doubt that many of the challenges confronting the world of today and tomorrow are amenable to scientific solutions, including those offered by chemistry. Further, I believe that corporations such as the one I represent should be and can be an important part of the solution; in fact, it is critical that we take a leadership role.

This is because we bring to the equation not only a solid base in science and technology and the resources for further research, but also some degree of global influence. For example, we can practice a high level of environmental stewardship wherever in the world we do business, and we can encourage others to do the same. There are several ways in which multinational corporations can enhance the human condition, and I will touch on some of these, but my primary focus will be on environmental stewardship.

I. ENVIRONMENTAL STEWARDSHIP

A major global company has two sets of environmental responsibilities. The first is to do a good job itself, for itself. The second is to provide leadership and share environmental expertise with others. I would like to address each of these responsibilities from the perspective of the company I represent, as illustrative of what is happening more generally. Then I will discuss public policy from an industry perspective. My position is that goal-setting and motivation, as opposed to rule-setting and detailed

E.P. Blanchard is a Director, Vice Chairman of the Board, and a Member of the Office of the Chairman of Du Pont.

regulation, comprise the most effective approach, at both corporate and government levels.

On the corporate level, Du Pont has set some challenging environmental goals for itself in the 1990s.

These are reflected in a continuing high level of capital expenditures, which will rise from $500 million in 1990 to about $600 million this year and a further $600 million in 1992.

The goals for this decade include reducing hazardous waste by 35 percent from 1990 levels,which themselves represented a 35 percent reduction from 1982 levels; eliminating heavy metal pigments in our plastic processes; reducing toxic air emissions 60 percent by 1993; and eliminating carcinogenic air emissions and ground discharges, among other objectives. We have an ultimate goal of eliminating all hazardous waste, period.

In regard to U.S.-based global companies as a whole, it's probably true to say that the standards are generally set in the United States. But in our case, the U.S. standard may only be the least we will do in other countries. This is because most of Du Pont's current expansion is outside the United States, and the new facilities being built incorporate state-of-the-art environmental technology. At the same time, improved processes and methods at existing facilities in the United States last year enabled us to achieve a remarkable 25 percent reduction in our listed emissions. I believe this effort is typical of many major industrial corporations.

We've developed considerable expertise in managing waste, and offer the service to our customers and others through a new business unit that combines environmental services with our former safety consulting business. We forecasted this unit would generate $100 million in sales in the first full year of operation and be doing $1 billion worth of business by the year 2000. So far so good: the first full year was 1990 and sales did reach $100 million, and our efforts, along with those of our customers, continue to make a significant contribution to environmental protection.

For our own operations, we continue to invest in equipment to capture, neutralize, and dispose of waste generated as by products of our manufacturing processes. But the long-term strategic emphasis is on minimization of waste, in two ways.

The first is to capture the value of by products from the main product streams — turn them into saleable products, with a net reduction in waste. This concept really began in a serious way for us in the 1980s. Today, the Du Pont Chemicals businesses are generating $70 million a year in revenues from 15 former waste streams. By the end of the 1990s we expect to have another 10 products from former waste streams, annual sales of $250 million and annual savings of $100 million in disposal costs.

The second thrust is to minimize waste and eliminate hazardous waste by new or improved technologies and raw materials strategies. This represents a substantial and ongoing research effort.

As you may know, we have a research and development center at our Experimental Station in Wilmington. Some of the work done here, and much of that at the Du Pont Haskell Laboratory for Toxicology and Industrial Medicine, has an environmental focus. We have many other technical centers in various locations worldwide. The knowledge that is generated at these facilities is available to our people via computer, along with information about best practices at the plant level. So there is a central direction and focus, and a very strong commitment from the top.

But although senior management can always point the direction and set the goals, we cannot, in every case, tell our people which levers to pull and which buttons to press in order to achieve these objectives. Du Pont is a company with 144,000 employees, 200 manufacturing and processing facilities in 40 countries on six continents and literally thousands of products. Our polymer businesses alone involve over 60 technologies.

II. ENVIRONMENTAL PERFORMANCE

So we have focused on creating the conditions that will encourage people to find the right strategies, technologies and catalysts to achieve our objectives, ultimately including closed systems and zero waste. We're making it clear that environmental performance is an important career attribute. Managers' incentive pay is tied to environmental performance, and we've devised a variety of ways to reward and encourage environmental initiatives from the grass roots up.

The program is working. We have a long and growing list of achievements by people in our plants. Probably the most impressive concerns a plant at Beaumont, Texas, which manufactures acrylonitrile, an intermediate used in the manufacture of nylon and polymers. Ammonium sulfate waste from that process was more than 110 million pounds annually. We ran the process to maximize yields on the most expensive ingredient, and models suggested that modifying the process would result in a cost penalty.

But when our people at the plant re-thought the process in order to reduce emissions, they found they could actually reduce costs as well. In fact, the process change implemented a savings of about $1 million a year, as well as cutting our emissions by two-thirds, and we're looking for more savings as we learn how to further refine the system. Again, the goal at this and all our plants is closed systems with zero waste.

Examples of this kind can be found throughout industry as individual companies respond to the environmental imperative and the profit motive in various parts of the world.

In poor countries, multinational companies can have a positive influence on living conditions in a number of other ways. The obvious influence is economic — through providing jobs, creating business opportunities in the area around the plant, and adding to the tax base. But there are other positive influences. For instance, concepts and practices relating to health and safety have also been introduced by multinational companies in areas where these ideas at one time were largely unheard of.

Du Pont is currently involved in a major health effort. The case concerns a parasite called the Guinea worm, which contaminates water in parts of Africa and south Asia. This parasite cripples 10 million people annually. In an effort to eradicate this severe public health problem, a U.S. group, The Carter Center, asked us to help develop a simple, workable solution.

The basic challenge was that the kind of high-technology filtration system that we manufacture at Du Pont, and which could be used to remedy such a problem in a developed country, would not be appropriate in places where municipal water systems do not exist or where the high-tech answer is too expensive.

The Carter Center's studies suggested that the most practical solution would be a filter of woven synthetic fiber. We worked with one of our customers in North Carolina to fabricate simple nylon filters that can be placed over water jars and re-used. The product is an elegant, low-tech solution that satisfies the need in an appropriate and successful way. We have not made any money in this case. We will donate more than a million of these filters a year to help solve this terrible problem.

III. CULTURAL CHALLENGE

In some countries we have occasionally encountered cultural differences of opinion. For example, the Du Pont safety culture is based on the safety of the individual. This view is not shared in all parts of the world. But when we used our U.S. model and made it a matter of team pride, safety on and off the job did become important. The plant sites where the "safety first" slogan was initially questioned are now among those that take the most pride in winning the Du Pont Board of Directors' Safety Award. This is another example of how global companies can have a beneficial influence on the quality of life where they operate.

A fundamental cultural challenge in establishing industrial operations in a less developed country is to try to avoid the "disconnect" between sophisticated industrial equipment, including environmental equipment, and underqualified local operators. Without adequate training of local labor and management, technology transfer in and of itself may create only short-term benefit, perhaps punctuated by industrial and environmental incidents that could have been avoided. Training programs, whether undertaken by the company alone, or in cooperation with government, are essential.

In regard to multilateral action, involving cooperative initiatives by a number of companies and other organizations, there are several examples of positive responses to environmental issues.

The Montreal Protocol is the most celebrated case so far. It shows how corporate leadership can contribute to an agreement among producers and consumers of many countries in response to a global environmental challenge. I refer, of course, to the agreement to phase out the use of chlorofluorocarbons, commonly called CFCs, that are associated with stratospheric depletion of ozone. Subsequently we and some others decided to accelerate our part of this effort, but the protocol established the first goals.

IV. CAPITAL

This is an environmental issue with many facets and as such deserves more than a passing mention in these remarks. It involves massive investment in airconditioning and refrigeration equipment throughout the world, as well as the capital represented in the production of CFC-based refrigerants. Compared to the investment in user equipment, the latter is relatively minor. For example, it will cost Du Pont about $1 billion to replace CFC production with alternatives. However, at a very rough estimate, we're probably talking about a quarter of a trillion dollars invested in installed equipment worldwide, for refrigeration and air conditioning. We have estimated that about $135 billion of that is in the United States.

The CFC-ozone initiative also involves social considerations, and business ethics. I am sure you are all familiar with the background, but to summarize briefly, in the early 1970s some scientists theorized that CFCs might be rising into the upper atmosphere and breaking down the ozone layer. At first there was no hard evidence, but Du Pont and others supported further scientific research to better understand the ultimate fate of CFCs, and we concurrently began looking for alternative products. Then a hole in the ozone layer was detected over Antarctica. At that point, we at Du Pont stepped up our R&D efforts and led industry support for an international agreement, the Montreal Protocol, to initially slow down the growth of CFCs' use worldwide and ultimately phase them out.

In March of 1988, we saw the results of a scientifically impressive study, sponsored by NASA, which introduced enough uncertainty for us to conclude that we must phase out of these products completely. But we couldn't just stop producing CFCs.

V. BALANCING RESPONSIBILITIES

We had responsibilities to our customers: an ethical obligation to continue to meet their needs. Considering that we supplied 25 percent of all CFCs used worldwide, we also had a responsibility to society to maintain refrigeration for food and medical supplies, as well as for air conditioning and other uses. We decided after a few days of discussion that we would commit to a CFC phase out and at the same time pull out all stops in an effort to find, develop and manufacture environmentally acceptable substitutes.

It's worth emphasizing that the major challenge here is not developing and making CFC alternatives available to customers, but in replacing the user equipment.

The fact is we're in the midst of a $1 billion program in which we already have 10 plants for alternatives in operation or under construction, including two large plants, one in Ontario and one in Texas, where we have begun commercial production of a new family of alternatives. These are the Du Pont "Suva" refrigerants, announced early this year.

I should add that our customers themselves, particularly including those in the automotive industry, have been extremely cooperative in helping find solutions to the various challenges associated with developing workable and ozone-friendly CFC alternatives. GM, Ford and Chrysler will have airconditioning systems that are compatible with our new refrigerants in place in their 1994 models. With much smaller production, Nissan will be completely converted in the U.S. market by the end of 1992, as will Saab in the U.S. and European markets. We have also addressed, with these customers, such issues as service in the aftermarket and aspects of retrofitting.

We believe history will recognize the discovery, development, and substitution of CFC alternatives as one of the most significant industrial achievements of the last two decades of the 20th century. It is certainly a watershed event in terms of international cooperation in the cause of environmental protection.

VI. LESSONS FOR FUTURE PROTOCOLS

Many valuable lessons can be learned from the Montreal Protocol as we seek agreement on other aspects of climatic change. We hope the full measure of these lessons will be learned.

In this I would especially include the components that led to the protocol, such as the responses based on hard scientific evidence, a global approach, a role for business, and a sequential process. I believe decisive leadership from the premier producer was essential in this case, and it also seems reasonable to suggest that only a large company with substantial scientific, technical and financial resources could have taken that leadership.

There are several other examples of voluntary cooperation by industry in response to environmental challenges.

Among these is the Council for Solid Waste Solutions, a U.S. business group which has formulated a "Blueprint for Plastics Recycling", in cooperation with a growing number of municipalities. This focuses on collection, handling, reclamation and end-use markets for all types of post-consumer plastics. One of the specific goals is to recycle 25 percent of all common consumer plastic bottles by 1995.

Du Pont is active in this movement, along with Dow, Amoco, Mobil, and others, but we are also working on another level. In partnership with the Waste Management Systems company, we have undertaken a nationwide plastics recycling program under which they collect and we process. We already have two plants in operation, one in Philadelphia and one in Chicago, with capacity of 40 million pounds a year each. One of the big challenges is the variety of plastic materials in the waste stream and the fact that for true recycling we need to convert them back to their basic ingredients — reverse engineering. There's a limit to the market for park benches made from recycled plastic! But we are making headway, and there is a growing market potential as the term "made from recycled materials" takes on its own special appeal.

The Chemical Manufacturers Association has launched a far broader program called Responsible Care. This is somewhat similar to the Malcolm Baldrige award concept. It establishes criteria for continuous, measurable improvement in safety, health and environmental protection. A full commitment to the program has been made a condition of membership, and the results will be made public on a regular basis. This program was started in Canada and has been adopted by the chemical industries in the United States, Europe, and Australia.

And, of course, the International Chamber of Commerce has initiated a Business Charter for Sustainable Development, or "Rotterdam Charter", named for the meeting in Rotterdam at which the charter was publicly announced last April.

Under the Rotterdam agreement, 250 international companies pledged support for principles designed to enhance environmental protection, including research and technology transfer. The group includes Du Pont, ICI, Dow and other major chemical and petrochemical manufacturers.

The basic premise is that industry needs to be managed in a way that fulfills the needs of a growing world population without compromising the ability of future generations to meet their needs. A tall order, no doubt. But there is no acceptable alternative, if we agree that economic development must continue in order to provide for the new billions of people, and to raise up from misery those who already populate the Third World.

Economic development is the tool of preference in responding to the underlying problem of exploding global population. As William Ruckelshaus has pointed out, history demonstrates there are only two sure cures for explosive population growth: one is wealth and the other is mass death. Prosperity seems to promote lower birth rates. I should add that the former head of the U.S. Environmental Protection Administration was advocating the creation of wealth.

The role of multinational corporations in wealth creation seems obvious, in planting the seeds of prosperity through international investment and technology transfer. It goes without saying that the seeds will be planted in fertile ground, where there is an opportunity for profitable growth, and will grow most readily in climates conducive to business.

The sustainable development concept being promoted by the International Chamber of Commerce recognizes the need for policies that will engender economic development and good stewardship of the earth. It follows the work of the World Commission on Environment and Development. This work was summarized in the report *Our Common Future*, which was presented to the U.N. General Assembly in 1987 and is more popularly known as the Brundtland Report.

VII. MIND-SETS MUST CHANGE

Two basic challenges emerge from this report, in my view. One is that environmental activists need to understand and accept that the only way people in developing countries will have a chance for a step change in their quality of life is through industrial development. The second is that industrialists need to understand and accept that such development will have to be in the form of different industrial systems. By this I mean systems that will enable us to produce both durable and recyclable goods without generating more waste and pollution than ecological systems can handle, and to use non-renewable energy resources much more efficiently.

The Business Council for Sustainable Development will take the Brundtland Report to the next logical step. It will present an industry view of sustainable development at the meeting of the United Nations Conference on Environment and Development in Brazil next year.

It will address issues pertaining to government, such as open trade and the efficacy of market economies, as well as industry issues. It will include commitments to waste minimization, environmental protection during production, and product stewardship. This implies developing products that will do an effective job while at the same time contributing to environmental progress. I would like to point out that this makes good sense, generally, in terms of maintaining public consent to remain in business, and also in terms of specific business opportunities, such as CFC alternatives and Du Pont's sulfonylurea herbicides. The sulfonylureas are very effective, require only ounces per acre, and are environmentally friendly, not only in use but after use, because they break down quickly after the job is done. These products have helped our agricultural business achieve significant profitable growth. In other words, although public environmental awareness is a major factor driving industrial response, free market principles are also energizing environmental progress.

Let me add that good product stewardship should be both forward-looking and retrospective. New product development must take into account environmental effects during production, during use of the product, and its afterlife. We serve our customers well when we head off their waste management problems in our own development laboratories. We also need to study products already in the market, to determine what kind of chemistry goes on during their life cycle and during their degradation, and whether re-engineering might be appropriate. We are pursuing both kinds of studies at Du Pont, and I believe others are similarly engaged.

VIII. CONCLUSIONS

These kinds of initiatives demonstrate a willingness on the part of business and industry to respond to environmental challenges in a productive way, for reasons of good citizenship and good business.

There's a lot going on. Much more needs to be done, and not only in the areas of science, technology and business. Public policy also needs attention and particularly as it relates to global issues. Indeed, sometimes it seems that the scientific and technological challenges may be less than those presented by international policy.

It is an understatement to say there is inadequate alignment in the environmental policies of the various governments of the world. Environmental regulations and the way they are enforced vary greatly from one country or region to another. They also vary within the United States, where states superimpose their own rules on top of federal standards.

The marketplace may be global, and many environmental issues certainly are. But in matters of public policy, we are largely governed by Tip O'Neill's dictum: "All politics is local."

The reality is that most environmental decisions are not made as a result of analysis of global trends. Only in dramatic cases, such as the ozone depletion issue, is there agreement as to a general course of action. And you will recall that even in this case full consensus was not achieved. Many countries did not sign the

Montreal Protocol. Local problems rather than global concerns set their priorities.

For most people, the world is the local community in which they live and work. Their sense of well-being includes economic and physical health, which is to say gainful employment and a good environment in terms of air, water, and esthetics. A feeling of safety is also an important part of the sense of well-being. Companies should and must respond to these local concerns in order to maintain public consent.

Legislators in general also tend to be locally focused. They react to the opinions of constituents in formulating national and sometimes international policies. However, as their constituents are inspired largely by what they hear over the garden fence and what they see on television, then it can be said that hearsay and television indirectly influence public policy in state and national legislative assemblies.

Legislators should be responsive to their constituents. But one can question the advisability of such an ad hoc approach to issues such as stratospheric change, and those surrounding the exponential growth in the world's population. We need a better driver than the six o'clock news to set an agenda for our responses to these kinds of global challenges.

The best hope may well be some kind of United Nations charter that would enunciate guidelines and principles, on the premise of sustainable development. These guidelines would seek a balance between economic growth and environmental protection, along the lines of the *Rotterdam Charter*. They could not be very specific, of course. A central planning authority could not possibly lay down specific and sensible worldwide rules regarding the acceptability of deep well injection, as one example. I would like to add parenthetically that we hope the *Earth Charter* and *Agenda 21*, to emerge from next year's UN conference, will address this issue. The efficacy and safety of deep well disposal would depend on site-specific conditions including, very importantly, geologic structure. The desirability of incineration versus materials recycling in individual cases would also depend on location and conditions.

The broader point here is that multinational corporations would welcome uniform guidelines and goals, but probably would agree it would be counterproductive to include detailed rules on "how to" achieve these goals.

The approach that Du Pont senior management has taken recognizes that hands-on management from the top of the details of "how to" achieve objectives is not practical, as I mentioned earlier. Our job is to set the goals and create the environment most amenable to achievement of these goals, using both carrot and stick incentives. If this is the most productive approach for a relatively small organization of 144,000 people, then surely it must apply to a far greater degree in the policy-making process of national and regional governments.

As S. Bruce Smart, Jr., of the World Resources Institute, has pointed out (NAS Colloquium on Industrial Ecology, May, 1991), sanctions and regulations are occasionally needed but they tend to alienate corporations and make them defensive rather than proactive. He advocates that society instead should "establish the goals it wishes to achieve and translate them into a system of positive stimuli." Again we are left with the question of who should establish the goals and create the motivation.

Most people I know in industry would be horrified at the prospect of a central bureaucracy dictating rules and regulations for the world. But at least the United Nations may be able to create some alignment among sovereign states in general principle. The basic idea would be to gain agreement for the concept that we need economic activity that increases prosperity without destroying the environment on which the economic activity depends.

The general agreement could include some ancillary commitments. For instance, no industrial plant should be built anywhere in the world without a definitive plan for waste minimization, waste treatment, and emissions reduction.

No country should subvert the principles by using them for "green protectionism." This is the practice in which a government may require very strict environmental compliance from multinationals while applying relaxed standards to its own national companies. This would in effect subsidize the country's own industry and erect a non-tariff barrier to trade. Instead, standards should be applied uniformly, and countries should seek investment by multinational companies and use it as an opportunity for the transfer of environmental technology.

Perhaps there should be a special consideration for less-developed countries, to enable them to leapfrog the phase of environmental disregard that characterized the Industrial Revolution in Europe and the United States. Economic assistance programs could be set up to encourage and facilitate environmentally sustainable development in the LDCs.

At least these are subjects that need to be pursued, in the interests of rich and poor nations alike. It has been pointed out that billions of people are simply not going to suffer in place. As Ruckelshaus notes: "It is well to remember that history from ancient times has been the story of poor people on the move and of what happens when they crash up against the wealthy places." So it's in everybody's self-interest to generate global prosperity, and to do so in ways that will not ravage the earth and its environs.

In those cases where a state flagrantly disregarded the principles of environmental protection as agreed upon by the community of nations, sanctions could be employed against that state. On the evidence that has come in since the dismantling of the Iron Curtain, it seems that most of the previous Eastern European regimes would have failed the test of environmental stewardship on the most minimal levels. This, in itself, is an argument in favor of a free market context for such stewardship.

Before I close, let me say that making the world a better place is obviously a very popular — and populist — goal. To many environmental activists, the issue is all about saving the planet.

To those of us promoting sustainable development, it's about the human prospect. As Ruckelshaus has noted, "The planet can take care of itself, as it has done for some four billion years. It has established a natural balance that has suited most of us very well. If we upset that balance, a new one will be established and we will probably like it a lot less."

I would like to conclude with a supporting opinion offered by a retired and outspoken chemist of my acquaintance Dr. Philip J. Wingate. He said: "The activities of humanity are to Mother Nature what a gnat is to the rear end of an elephant. If it irritates enough, Mother will scratch it off."

I think we would all agree, we need to find better ways to generate global prosperity without upsetting Mother Nature to that extent.

Closing the Gap

Thomas R. Odhiambo

I. INTRODUCTION

The dominant imagery of international dialogue today is one of a fractured human family. The emergence of a strong Economic Community in Europe, which will become a single market scarcely a year away, and which is being wooed by diverse members of the European Free Trade Area and some Mediterranean countries for membership, is a forerunner of what is becoming a relentless move towards the establishment of exclusive regional economic and trading blocks. The North American economic group of the United States of America, Mexico, and Canada is fast heading for the formal beginnings of such a trading block. There is serious talk of a Pacific Rim trading block of exclusively East Asian States. Scarcely 4 months ago, the Member States of the Organization of African Unity (OAU), at a Heads of State Summit held in July 1991 in the capital city of Abuja, in Nigeria, signed an agreement to launch an African Economic Community.

Over the last two decades, the corridors of political power and the labyrinths of financial politics have reverberated with communiques from the Group of 7 Leading Industrial Nations or declarations from the Group of 77. The world is divided into "developed countries" and "developing countries." And one senses almost a smack of satisfaction when some senior legislators divide the world into "the rich industrial nations of the North" and "the poor countries of the South." The East which, for four decades after World War II, provided a sort of geopolitical and geoeconomic passageway for engagement of the South with the North, has ceased to exist in dramatic circumstances, and is now groping to find its own passageway to the North.

This fractured human family, which has drifted away from functioning as an international community, now requires more

Thomas Odhiambo is Director of the International Centre of Insect Physiology and Ecology (ICIPE) in Kenya.

than ever before to find a new positive leadership in all sectors of human endeavor that is totally dedicated to building bridges to a more humane, fulfilling, productive, and reintegrated human family as we approach a new millennium. Such bridge-making requires not only a politico-financial strategy, but also a long-range science policy and strategy that will together transform our perceptions of each other. It is becoming apparent that the contemporary regional conflicts, and those that are likely to erupt in the near future, are likely to turn out to be conflicts on the management of large natural resources and perceptions as to who should ultimately control them. Leadership of an anticipatory kind, and the rational modulation of a people's perception of such issues, are likely to become the cornerstones of the resolution of these conflicts. Alex Keynan (1991) says it very well:

> In dealing with theories of international conflicts, scholars have found that such conflicts can be best understood by realizing that each side in a conflict reacts more to its image, or perception, of the other side than to any reality, however it is defined. This is probably also true of the normal interaction between people, organizations, and nations: the images held by each partner of its other partners might be as important as, or even more important than, objective, measurable attributes.[1]

Let us then begin from the beginning. Poverty stalks the great majority of the households of the developing world, but much more starkly in Africa.

II. DISPARITIES IN THE HUMAN CONDITION

However "development" is defined — whether as "the conscious promotion of economic growth with social fairness"[2] or as a process "to enlarge the range of people's choices to make development more democratic and participatory"[3] — the element of human development is central to it. It is the reason why one needs to recognize, as profoundly significant, two successes of the development process among the development regions over the last 30 years. In that period, adult literacy has jumped by 40%, and the average life expectancy has increased by 16 years. In the case of Africa, it has actually moved up from 40 to 52 years. But other aspects of the human condition in the developing regions of the world demonstrate a wretchedness on a scale and depth that is clearly an affront to our collective sense of equity and humanity.

Over 1.2 billion people live in absolute poverty now; by the end of this decade, it will have climbed to 1.3 billion. While Asia has the largest number of poor people at the present time, standing at some 500 million, Africa's share is more severe proportionately, and will grow ever more rapidly during the 1990s. Africa's current burden of the world's poor people is 30%; it is destined to grow to 40% by the end of this decade. Indeed, more than half the continent's population is absolutely poor, and that proportion will increase on present projections. The impact of such wretchedness in the developing world can be seen in the abysmal level of their health services. Over 1.5 billion people do not enjoy primary health-care. As a result, nearly 3 million children die each year from diseases which can easily be eliminated by well known and effective immunization programs; and about half-a-million women die each year from preventable complications associated with pregnancy and childbirth.[3] On a related matter, some 180 million, one in three, suffer from serious malnutrition, and they may never be able to enjoy a full intellectual self-realization.

If ever there is to be a new frontier in this contemporary world for intrepid spirits and dedicated pioneers, it is certainly the challenge to transform the South, particularly the almost impossible basket-case of Africa, from the present agonizing depth of wretchedness to a population that can again dream a future of prosperity and well-being. One possible scenario for translating that challenge into action is in regarding Africa (and other large areas of absolute poverty in other developing regions) as a disaster and deprived zone; and then mounting a specific rehabilitation and reconstruction program of a scale equivalent to the Marshall Plan for the reconstruction of Europe immediately after the end of World War II and its traumatic destruction. The terrible devastation of the economies of the poor South, and the attendant pillage of the natural resource base, have created conditions of despair, lack of direction, and of a vision-poor future.

For such a reconstruction scenario to reach the realm of possibility, there needs to be a closing of the gap of our perceptions as to what "our common future" means to us during the 1990s and beyond. To the North, it should continue to mean an inherited future; but that the North should begin to pay particularly keen attention to the unravelling of its social fabric, due to the accelerating erosion of its cultural and social norms. This has led to a profound change in the well-being of the Northerner: numbing self-isolation, homelessness, drug addiction, and suicide rates of unusually high levels.[3] To the South, "our common future" should begin to mean an invented future, founded on the resilient and inherited culture whose strength and continuity lies in the extended family and traditional prudence in the utilization of natural resources, but which grafts onto this solid rootstock a modern culture of science-led economic development. To both the North and the South, "our common future" demands the creation of a genuine partnership, because the synergy emanating from a functional bipartisanship will create more well-being for this reintegrated human family than each party attempting to arrogate to itself all of the political, economic, and social space.

A view from the marketplace, as exemplified by the conclusion of an international conference convened by business leaders in March 1990 in Vancouver, Canada, transparently enjoins us to have the two large economic groupings synergistically work together:

> This path to a common future requires that we
> live within the constraints imposed by ecology
> and resources. It also involves narrowing the
> widening gap between the rich and poor of the
> planet. Human poverty and environmental
> degradation are inextricably linked in developing
> countries. The pursuit of sustainable
> development incorporates and balances the
> concerns of economics, ecology and ethics.
> Striking this balance must involve all interests
> and parties, including both the public and

private sectors, environmental organizations
concerned about the impacts of growth, and local
communities directly affected by change.[4]

Africa, and other regions of the developing world, are being
weighed down to a standstill by the crushing burden of external
debt and internal debt. External debt of many developing countries (for instance, Mozambique, Laos, and Bolivia) now exceeds
their total gross national product (GNP). In some countries (such
as India, Malaysia, and Singapore) internal debt has grown larger
than the external debt. Many countries find the servicing of these
debts almost crippling: for instance, Jordan is expending 36% of its
GNP on debt servicing. These outgoings are made more critical by
capital flight which, in many countries, is escalating. For instance,
between 1962 and 1986, The Philippines experienced a capital
flight approximating 80% of its outstanding debt within that
period.
     No doubt, a more effective management of the national
economy, a more participatory style of governance and national
planning, a staunching of capital flight and corruption in the
public sector, reformation of public enterprises (including
privatization of non-strategic public enterprises), and a restructuring of the capital markets, are all measures that have become the
new imperatives of this decade. But all these efforts will come to
naught unless a fundamental step is taken to deliberately create
and nurture a capacity to fuel a science-led development in the
South, and particularly so in Africa, and to manage the dynamics
and direction of this change.

III. CAPACITY FOR LEADERSHIP AND
     ENTREPRENEURSHIP

     One can, in truth, state that the developing countries have run
a large internal capacity debt, particularly glaring in Africa. No
longer is the juxtaposition of a plentiful supply of land, labor, and
capital a sufficient formula to guarantee national development.
Otherwise, Africa in the heyday of foreign aid during the 1960s
and 1970s, with their abundant natural resources and plentiful
labor, would be now a developed region to contend with. No

longer is the ability to purchase state-of-the-art technology an adequate premise for industrializing a developing economy on a sustainable basis. Otherwise, the oil-rich Middle East would have been, by now, a shining example of a modern industrializing region.

The recent examples of Singapore and South Korea in industry, and those of India and Brazil in the green revolution technologies, overwhelmingly demonstrate that these profound transformations have been set in motion and sustained in reaching their goal by three key factors. First, a vision-rich geopolitical and geoeconomic leadership which carefully selects a beacon, and then sets an unwavering direction to reach that beacon. Second, a creative, dedicated scientific leadership, that imaginatively develops and implements a concentrated program of work which translates the national objectives into achievable landmarks. And, third, an entrepreneurial and managerial community, which empowers all the necessary linkages and core contributors from all sectors of the national economy to enrich it. This realization makes it essential for Africa (and other areas of gross underdevelopment) to adopt a radically new developmental paradigm which puts capacity building and its sustenance at the center.

The conventional university and polytechnic institutions in Africa have produced a very large number of governmental officers, administrators, planners, teachers, technical experts (in medicine, agriculture, engineering, business, banking, accounting, etc.), and individuals trained in extension and social services of various sorts over the last three to four decades. But it has hardly developed the kind of pioneer leaders, the frontiersmen, that Africa so desperately needs. Thus, resource industries, in which Africa should otherwise be able to play a dominant and competitive role in the world, and where the continent can learn to muster its engine for change in respect to sustainable development, the peoples of Africa have yet to find a means of guiding national development policies and the practice of resource industries so as to occupy the same locus.

This lack of internal capacity has led Africa to overly rely on technical assistance to manage and direct its development process. The continent now receives each year a total of US $6 billion in technical assistance.[3] The irony for Africa is that the largest proportion of this foreign aid is spent on the employment of foreign expertise; only a negligible amount is devoted to mobilizing national specialists. Almost nothing is devoted to building domestic centers of excellence. This is an intolerable situation that cries for immediate change.

Three imaginative experiments in creating an internal leadership capacity in Africa are worth reviewing briefly. They need the widest partnership support that they deservedly expect.

The first experiment is that of the African Capacity Building Initiative (ACBI), which is jointly sponsored by the World Bank, the United Nations Development Programme (UNDP), and the African Development Bank (ADB). The ACBI became functional in 1990, and has its executive office headquartered in Harare, Zimbabwe. The Initiative is destined to systematically enhance the capacities of the continent in two specific areas: those of policy analysis and economic management. Both are of crucial importance in today's Africa in relation to its own poor internal performance in the economic field, as well as in the overall global context. A new ethic and a problem-solving enterprise is required so that a more systemic attack on the poverty syndrome be activated and sustained, and so that the economic mainstream of Africa's development business becomes a long-range commitment. In the words of Sadler and Hull (1990):

> ...[The] real opportunity for change [to
> sustainable national development] lies in
> mustering and linking together political will,
> individual responsibility, business acumen and
> technological ingenuity.[4]

The ACBI intends to mobilize a fund of about US $1.2 billion. But in the first instance, it has planned for a more limited existence, during which an experimental period of 5 years will provide a reaffirmation whether it should become a more permanent feature of the continent's joint venture to uplift itself by its own built-up professional and ethical strength.

The second novel experiment in capacity building in Africa has a slightly longer history. The International Centre of Insect Physiology and Ecology (ICIPE), based in Nairobi, Kenya was

224   *Thomas R. Odhiambo*

founded in April, 1970, specifically to undertake mission-oriented fundamental research in insect science which would lead to the replacement of conventional, ecologically damaging pest control techniques, dominated by the widespread use and abuse of chemical insecticides. The pest management technologies that would result from such scientific discoveries and subsequent technological innovations would be those that are rational, that would be soundly based on our holistic understanding of the target insect pests and disease vectors in relation to their total environment, which would be long-term, and which would directly respond to the resource-poverty of the vast majority of the pan-tropical developing regions. In 1981, the African Advisory Committee, which consisted of independent African thinkers and scientists, strongly recommended to the ICIPE the elaboration of a curriculum and delivery mechanism for an African Regional Postgraduate Program in Insect Science (ARPPIS), for the education and training of selected candidates for the Ph.D. degree in Insect Science. Such a Program was intended to create a critical mass of new leadership in this field for the university system in Africa, the R&D institutions, pest management projects, and the extension services.

ARPPIS received its first 7 Ph.D. students in April 1983; and now selects between 10 and 15 students each year from all parts of Africa. ARPPIS is a consortium program between the ICIPE and selected African universities, now numbering 24 from all regions of Africa, cutting across erstwhile language and cultural barriers. Course-work and research project supervision is undertaken by joint teams of ICIPE senior scientists and university professors, while the execution of the Postgraduate Program is concentrated at the ICIPE. An Academic Board, consisting of representatives of each of the Participating Universities and the ICIPE, meets regularly twice a year, selecting students, monitoring performance, and setting achievement goals. Apart from the core courses in modern insect science, the ARPPIS students take additional courses in research management. They are constantly reminded of their responsibility in science, of their readiness to improvise and to flourish within their contextual circumstances prevailing in Africa, and of their need to build linkages between themselves on qualifying. So far, 56 of these students have completed their

5

courses; all are still working within Africa, and sustain a high level of mission and morale.

Over the last three years, a running debate has ensued whether or not the interim success of ARPPIS can be given depth, by beginning a process which would lead to the gradual emergence of research universities in Africa on the one hand, and of enhancing the Ph.D. program at the ICIPE itself as a possible model for other advanced research centers in Africa to adopt in regard to other priority fields of science and technology. This debate culminated in two important meetings this year to consider these options: a planning meeting, in June, at the Rockefeller Foundation Conference and Study Center, located at Bellagio, Italy; and a planning conference of Vice-Chancellors, in August, at the Jomo Kenyatta University College of Agriculture and Technology, located at Juja, Kenya. The two meetings strongly recommended the establishment of four Sub-Regional Centers for the Master's Degree in Insect Science; and the upgrading of the existing Ph.D. program into an ICIPE Graduate School to continue to concentrate on and enhance Ph.D. education and training in insect science. This set of decisions is a unique opportunity for Africa and its international partners to test fully their joint commitment to uplift the direct involvement of the continent in creating a new cadre of science leaders and technology managers in a field which has a burgeoning interest for the continent.

The third experiment is in the planning stage. It is to form an African Foundation for Research and Development (AFRAND), in order to provide resource continuity in vital areas in which Africa has an apparent comparative advantage or where there is need to enlarge a window of opportunity. A Pre-feasibility Study was completed, under the auspices of the African Academy of Sciences, by three consultants in September, 1991. A review of the Consultants' Report clearly shows that there is a good case for initiating a substantive planning process; and the Academy is now gearing itself to launch a full-scale Feasibility Study early in 1992.

Already, it is clear that AFRAND must install a medium-term test period, during which the African Foundation can be put through its paces. It is equally clear that policy prudence requires that, even in this limited trial period, AFRAND must, while only a modest institution, be independent from all institutions that

226   *Thomas R. Odhiambo*

could possibly derive benefit from its programs: this stricture includes the Academy and the ICIPE. And, finally, it is clear that financial probity demands that the management of the AFRAND investments be closely administered by a credible continental institution, such as the African Development Bank. Fortunately, the Bank's president is a member of the Task Force that initiated the proposal on AFRAND. The idea of such a Foundation is both ambitious and audacious. But, then, Africa now requires, more than ever before, bold new initiatives, that are at the same time implementable.

It is our sincerest hope that AFRAND, and the other experiments already highlighted, will prove to be breakthroughs in planning and in implementation as well as instruments for closing the chasm that divides the human family into two disparate groupings.

Let us now get to work, within a transparent partnership, because our joint futures are locked into the future of this one planet. Let us say, with Rutledge and Allen (1989), that we have the incentive to work and we are, together, building up the capacity and talent to do it:

> Common sense tells us there are only two
> questions worth asking when trying to forecast
> a country's future living standards. Do the
> people want to work? Do they have the tools
> they need to make their work productive? If
> people have the incentive to work and the
> proper tools to work with, they will find a way
> to get the job done.[5]

Let us get the job done regarding sustainable development!

REFERENCES

1. KEYNAN, A. (1991) The United States as a Partner in Scientific and Technological Cooperation: Some Perspectives from Across the Atlantic. New York: Carnegie Commission on Science, Technology and Government.

2. CLEVELAND, H. and LUBIS, M. (1990) The Future of "Development." Minneapolis, Minnesota, USA: University of Minnesota Hubert H. Humphrey Institute of Public Affairs.

3. UNDP (UNITED NATIONS DEVELOPMENT PROGRAM) (1991) Human Development Report 1991. Oxford and New York: Oxford University Press.

4. SADLER, B. and HULL, B. (1990) In Business for Tomorrow: The Transition to Sustainable Development. Ottawa: Conference Board of Canada and Globe '90.

5. RUTLEDGE, J. and ALLEN, D. (1989) Rust to Riches: The Coming of the Second Industrial Revolution. New York: Harper & Row.

An Institutional Response

Thomas F. Malone

I. INTRODUCTION

Institutions do not respond to opportunities or problems. Individuals do — working together within institutional frameworks. Institutions are not creative and dynamic; individuals are both. The test of the efficacy of suggestions for institutional reform, renewal, or innovations is the degree to which they enhance the effectiveness of individuals.

As Mostafa Tolba, Executive Director of the United Nations Environment Programme, pointed out in his 1990 Huxley-Baer Lecture, there are already some 10,000 international organizations concerned in one way or another with the matters being discussed at this Forum. Each organization has its uncritical lovers and its unloving critics. Changes in these institutions in response to Global Change must be supported by persuasive arguments. Proposals for innovation must have a compelling rationale. Papers presented at the Forum provide the context for both.

II. THE CONTEXT

The last half of the second millennium has been a turbulent era characterized by confrontation and conflict on an increasingly global scale. Nations and empires experienced ascendancy and decline in response to evolving economic and technological developments interacting with changing social structures, political systems and military power. Among the many developments that held portent for the human prospect, three — and their interaction — were particularly relevant to the topic at hand.

The first was development of a capability to tap the solar energy accumulated over billions of years in fossil fuels and to use it to augment the daily ration of solar energy that bathes our planet

Tom Malone is Distinguished University Scholar at North Carolina State University and a former President of Sigma Xi.

each day and sustains life through the process of photosynthesis. The power that this made available for human use was a catalyst for explosive technological innovations that dramatically expanded the potential for converting natural resources into the goods and services that satisfy basic human needs and the wants that provide meaning to sheer existence.

The second development was the advent of the scientific and technological era in which the human intellect was empowered to approach an understanding of natural phenomena through a systematic and rational process of observation, identification, description, experimental investigation and theoretical enquiry and to transform this knowledge into the technical infrastructure that supports modern society.

The science and technology of information were developed with dizzying speed during the present century. The information revolution led to a multiplication by many orders of magnitude in the capacity of the mind to deal with knowledge, just as the energy revolution increased millions of times the power of the human muscle to do work.

Meanwhile, the social sciences were making steady progress in understanding the nature and structure of the socio-cultural system and the relationship among people, the human mind and this system. They are now poised ready to play a key role in charting a course for society to cope with global change.

The third development of the past few centuries, sharply escalating in recent years, was the elevation of the role and importance of the individual in society, an increasing emphasis on democratic institutions and the diminution in the role of authoritarian rule. The seeds of human rights and equality, and of personal freedom and responsibility within a social community were planted, sprouted, and emerged as fragile but promising seedlings.

The fund of human knowledge that is now more than doubling each decade, and the social changes that are underway, have placed the world for the first time in its history in a position to influence human destiny and create an ever-expanding menu of feasible opportunities for human betterment. The time is propitious to summon our collective wisdom and will to achieve our full potential as human beings.

The developments described above have had a major influence on human activity on planet Earth. During the twentieth century, world population will increase by about 4 1/2 billion — a fourfold growth to the more than 6 billion anticipated by the end of the century. The annual output of the energy- and technology-driven world economy has grown dramatically and is expected to soar to $28 trillion — by the end of this century.

Projections into the next century suggest a doubling — or even trebling — in world population and a four- to five-fold growth in the annual production of goods and services. The consequence of this explosive demographic and economic growth is that human activity has emerged as a driver of global change. Most of the economic growth, however, will occur in the industrialized countries (North) while the surge in population will occur in countries which are at an early stage of industrialization (South).

The quality of life depends on more than the gross domestic product per person (e.g. health, education, freedom) [1]. It is clear, however, that there are distinct, socially destabilizing inequities in the production and consumption of goods and services between the north and south. Substantial efforts to reduce this "gap" during the last fifty years have fallen far short of their goals. Innovative approaches are required to supplement existing programs.

The exponential growth in an already substantial capacity for production in the north, and seemingly insatiable demands there for consumption, lead to global environmental impacts (e.g. greenhouse-gas warming and depletion of stratosphere ozone) that affect individuals everywhere. Exponential growth in the already large population in the south, where industrial capacity is still small, leads to local and regional environmental degradation and resource depletion that have global implications.

Given the projected population level in the south, if industrialization equal to that in the north were to take place, and in the same way in which that industrialization evolved, grave global environmental impacts could be expected that would affect both north and south. Yet it is unthinkable to expect the south to forego the economic development that would ameliorate poverty and enhance the quality of life. Tragically, in a world profoundly influenced by science and technology, less than six percent of the world's scientists and engineers are found in the South, which has eighty percent of the world's people.

An extrapolation into the next century of past economic growth in the north, where the current level is already high, raises serious questions with respect to both global environmental impact and equity in demands made upon the global life-support system. Yet to expect a reversal or even a cessation of growth is not acceptable or even practical.

In neither north nor south are present trends sustainable without jeopardizing the human prospect for all. Thus, an entirely new era of global interdependence is emerging, demanding a higher level of international cooperation.

The time has clearly come when the intertwined issues of environment and economic development must be considered together. This was argued persuasively in the Brundtland Report, *Our Common Future*, prepared by an independent commission on this subject appointed by the United Nations [2].

These topics will be the centerpiece of the Earth Summit convened as the United Nations Conference on Environment and Development in Rio de Janeiro in June, 1992. But even these broad and complex issues cannot be addressed in isolation. They are inextricably linked to the issues of population, science, technology and equity which are under scrutiny at this Forum in the context of the human prospect.

III. THE CHALLENGE

In broad terms, the world today stands at a strategic crossroads, in large measure as a result of the impact of the energy revolution and the striking advances in science and technology. Three possible options loom ahead:

1) Civilization could be snuffed out by a large-scale exchange of nuclear weapons.

2) Civilization could be strangled by a mindless continuation of unsustainable, exponential growth in both the number of people and the demands each person makes on planet Earth's life support system, with the inevitable conflict that would

rise from the strikingly different rates of growth between north and south in population and in the energy- and technology-driven economic systems.

3) A third — and much more attractive option — is to envision a possible world much to be preferred over the probable world, and then to pursue that vision by a long series of deliberate decisions and a successive sequence of discrete, wise and imaginative actions.

That vision may best be described as a sustainable and equitable world. In the spirit of the Brundtland Report, it may be defined as a world in which the legitimate needs and aspirations of the present generation are met without foreclosing options for future generations. This carries with it the concepts of intra-generational and inter-generational equity. It is a world that accepts and welcomes diversity in aspirations and accomplishments; it distinguishes fundamentally between equity and complete equality.

This vision has the implication of ultimate stabilization of global population through economic development, family planning and responsible parenthood. It is a world in which steady progress is made in transforming the energy- and technology-driven economic system into one that reduces to an acceptable level its impact on the environment. It is a world that addresses forthrightly the large sectors of absolute poverty in the south and the equally blighting pockets of poverty in the north. It is a world that discriminates sensitively between growth that seeks more of everything and human development that is a process that creates an environment enabling people, individually and collectively, to develop their full potential with a reasonable chance of leading productive and creative lives in accord with their needs, interests and talents. In this sense, both the north and the south are still immersed in the process of development. It is now timely that new partnerships of effort be forged to assure a human prospect that is shared in common by both. The scientific community, by tradition and proclivity, is in a unique position to contribute to this effort.

IV. INSTITUTIONAL INNOVATION

Particular urgency exists for institutional innovation to link industrialized and industrializing countries in the task of bringing knowledge to bear on assuring equity in the access to the life-supporting resources of planet Earth. The case was set forth persuasively by the World Commission on Environment and Development, in the report *Our Common Future*, in these words: "A major reorientation is needed in many policies and institutional arrangements at the international as well as national levels because the rate of (global) change is outstripping the ability of scientific disciplines and our current capabilities to assess and advise. A new international programme for cooperation among largely nongovernmental organizations, scientific bodies, and industry groups should therefore be established for this purpose."

In response, the conferees at the Second World Climate Conference [3] in November 1990 proposed as a priority item the establishment of "a special initiative (that) would create a network of regional interdisciplinary research centers, located primarily in developing countries, and focusing on all the natural science, social science, and engineering disciplines required to support fully integrated studies of global change and its impact and policy responses . . . and (to) study the interaction of regional and global policies."

A month later, the Scientific Committee for the International Geosphere-Biosphere Programme of the International Council of Scientific Unions set in motion a process to establish a global system of regional networks dedicated to analysis, research and training [4]. Identified by the acronym START (SysTem, Analysis, Research, Training), the network undergirds an ambitious program to describe and understand the interactive physical, chemical, biological and social processes that determine the unique environment for life on planet Earth and the changes that are occurring in the total Earth system as a result of human activity. It could be readily adapted to embrace the broad array of issues embraced by the term global change.

An imaginative initiative is now under intensive study by nations in the Western Hemisphere. It is to establish a network to be known as the Inter-American Institute for Global Change Research "to conduct and facilitate scientific, social and economics research on global change issues that are both unique to the region and important to the world" [5]. Sparked by a Workshop in Puerto Rico in July, 1991, a preliminary research agenda and organizational structure have been prepared. An Interim Working Group has been established to develop detailed final plans by April/May, 1992. The Institute would be linked to similar networks in other parts of the world.

In essence, the view is emerging that a habitable planet Earth will be the aggregate of an array of perhaps a dozen or so diverse but closely linked habitable regions. The entire array would be pursuing the common objective of a sustainable and equitable world. In a world in which confrontation and conflict are moving from a bipolar mode to decentralized regional levels, the need for unifying themes in pursuit of a common regional vision in the global context would have a salutary effect.

Some tasks would be best carried out as internationalized endeavors. The effective utilization of the enormous power of remote sensing from space, to understand and anticipate changes in the physical characteristics of the earth, will require an internationalization of space programs which will challenge the organizational and political capacity of sovereign nations. That could well be one important heritage of the International Space Year in 1992.

Other activities will be shared responsibilities. The ultimate transition to a post-fossil-fuel society will require combining diverse regional studies and an international effort of an unprecedented dimension to develop and articulate a world energy strategy. To reconcile world energy needs with sound environmental practices in a world undergoing nearly daily political change will require an effort in technological innovation that could serve as a unifying activity to replace preoccupation with competing interests.

The task of understanding reproductive biology and applying that knowledge to the stabilization of world population in a manner compatible with evolving individual mores is a formidable challenge. It will require the cooperation of every field of intellectual inquiry.

Preoccupied for centuries with the ebb and flow of economic and military power, the world has not yet addressed the potential of knowledge — its extension, integration, application and dissemination — as a vital contributor to enhancement of the human prospect [6].

It is time to do so, and to put in place the institutional arrangements to realize that potential. This needs to be done nationally, regionally and internationally. It is timely for the community of natural, social and engineering sciences to address this matter. The complex issues of global change require a profound change in our way of thinking — *metanoia*. The Age of Global Responsibility emerging from new dimensions of global interdependence will require a unifying global ethic as the basis for a sustainable and equitable world.

A compelling argument exists for institutional innovation that would consolidate the analysis, research and training on topics of environment and economic development in a three-tiered network at national, regional and global levels. The overarching and unifying questions would be those addressed at this Forum: What kind of a (country, region, world) do we have? What kind of a (country, region, world) do we want? What must we do to get the (country, region, world) that we want? Knowledge generation and policy formulation would be linked at regional levels where many critical decisions are made.

The conceptual foundation laid by the START and Inter-American Institute initiatives for dealing with the issues of environment, constitutes an appropriate point of departure. Existing institutions could be built upon while new dimensions of interdisciplinary research, analysis and training could be fostered. The role of the world's religions in participating in developing a "global ethic" deserves attention.

A pressing need exists during the 1990s — *The Decade for Decisions* — to forge new partnerships of effort among (a) governments charged with attending to the commonweal, (b) business and industry responsible for the production of goods and services, and with special interest in technological innovation and (c) universities and research institutions which serve as generators and custodians of knowledge.

The quality of scholarly work need not suffer because it is specifically directed toward societal needs. The pursuit of knowledge for the sake of that knowledge will remain a powerful motivation for scientific research. The research enterprise will be enriched by tithing of some percentage of each researcher's time and talent devoted to extending the frontiers of knowledge and using this tithed time to become informed on and active in issues arising from the interaction of science, technology and society. The psychological reward to the individual researcher is a powerful motivator.

The crucial involvement of individuals could be assured by an internationalized version of the proposed legislation to establish the National and Community Service Act of 1990, introduced last year into the Congress (S-1430). Conducted under the aegis or through scientific and professional societies, such an act would foster the concept of 'tithing' by underwriting the cost of voluntary participation in the global network of Global Change Institutes.

The institutional framework at the global level has yet to be spelled out, but it would involve a cooperative effort among a greatly strengthened International Council of Scientific Unions, Third World Academy of Sciences, International Social Science Council and the World Federation of Engineering Organizations.

Funding and oversight could be shared by individual countries, regional consortia of nations, and such international funding agencies as the Global Environmental Facility, the United Nations Development Program and the World Bank.

An initial step might be to convene representatives from business and industry, government, the research community, and private foundations to give form and substance to this concept. The catalytic role of private foundations in establishing the Consultative Group on International Agricultural Research provides a model which might be adapted to transform this concept into reality. The magnitude of the task should not be underestimated. It is matched only by the magnitude of the opportunity for enhancing the human prospect.

REFERENCES

[1]   United Nations Development Program, *Human Development Report* 1991, Oxford University Press, 1991.

[2]   World Commission on Environment and Development, *Our Common Future*, (The Brundtland Report), Oxford University Press, 1987.

[3]   Jäger, J. and Ferguson, H.L., *Climate Change: Science, Impacts and Policy*, Proceedings of the Second World Climate Conference, Cambridge University Press, 1991.

[4]   Eddy, J., Malone, T.F., McCarthy, J.J. and Rosswall, T., *Global Change System for Analysis, Research and Training (START)*, IGBP Report No. 15, UCAR Office for Interdisciplinary Earth Studies, Boulder, CO, 1991.

[5]   *Development of a Western Hemisphere Institute for Global Change Research*. A Report of a Workshop in San Juan, Puerto Rico, 15-19 July 1991 (Available from the U.S. Interagency Committee on Earth and Environmental Sciences, Office of Science and Technology Policy, Executive Office of the President, Washington, DC).

[6]   Boyer, E.L., *Scholarship Reconsidered*, The Carnegie Foundation for the Advancement of Teaching, Princeton, N.J., 1990.

The UNCED Process

Joseph C. Wheeler

On June 1-12, 1992 the United Nations Conference on Environment and Development, sometimes called UNCED or the Earth Summit, will convene in Rio de Janeiro. The world has never held a full-fledged United Nations conference at the summit level before, so this global meeting may turn out to be the conference of the century.

You might ask why this conference is taking place. The immediate reason is that the General Assembly of the United Nations decided to convene it in its Resolution 44-228 of December 22, 1989. The consensus behind that resolution reflected a growing awareness that, as we approach the 21st century, the human family is on an unsustainable course. It will take profound changes in behavior and the full application of the best in science to change direction.

Such a change in direction will need not only the wise decisions of nation states but also the full and constructive participation of all levels of society. Only by forging a grand partnership for a change in course can we hope to hand over to our great-grandchildren a world where people are using the natural systems on which human life depends in a sustainable way.

In numerical terms, Homo Sapiens became significant only a few thousand years ago. By 1950 we had reached a global population of 2.5 billion. Before 1950 development had been remarkable and great civilizations had been born, many to thrive. But the pace of change before World War II seen from today's vantage point was down-right slow compared with the explosive development of the past half century. This speeded up process was largely driven by science and technology. It is only in the past quarter century that most of us have come to realize that what we called progress was accompanied by serious dangers. As a world community, we focused on these dangers, especially at the United

Joseph Wheeler is Director of Programme Integration for the 1992 United Nations Conference on Environment and Development (UNCED).

Nations Conference on the Human Environment held in Stockholm in 1972. More recently, our sense of urgency has gained momentum with the publication of *Our Common Future*, the report of the World Commission on Environment and Development, and the subsequent reports of scientists revealing depletion of the ozone layer and the buildup of greenhouse gases.

Other reports raised concerns about biological diversity and the health of the oceans. There are worries about fresh water supply and its quality, about disposal of all kinds of wastes, about air pollution, and about soil and forest loss and desertification.

Even with the rising concern about what may be happening to the global and national environment, as might be expected, people everywhere continue seeking to better their condition. The damages to the global ecological systems came mostly from activities of industrial countries as they achieved unprecedented high living standards. This now leads to a basic ethical question. Will all 10 billion people expected fifty years from now have an equal right to share the limited environmental room which nature provides us? The answer can only be "yes."

This means that all parts of the world, both industrial and developing, must redefine progress. The industrial world will have to undergo an extraordinary transition, especially in energy sources and consumption patterns, to maintain and improve standards of living with a fraction of the present pressure on the environment. The developing world, while redefining development goals in parallel with the industrial world transition, will need quickly to achieve the efficiencies in production and allocation processes which will provide improving standards of nutrition, health and education without continuing to damage the environment. These are the tasks of the next fifty years. Just as science made possible the successes of the past, science will again play a leading role in achieving the development goals of the decades ahead and in solving the serious problems which have emerged.

The outlines of the programs needed to achieve these transitions have been glimpsed in the debates of the UNCED Preparatory Committee. This Committee, which consists of delegations from each of the Members of the United Nations, has so far met three times. The fourth and last meeting will be in New York beginning on March 2, 1992 and will run for five weeks. The small Secretariat in Geneva, of which I am a part, is headed by Maurice Strong of Canada and his Deputy Nitin Desai of India. We serve the Preparatory Committee.

Our first task as a Secretariat was to prepare background papers which illuminated the problems and possible solutions. Then we were asked to suggest action programs. Now we are completing this task. We expect to put some 125 draft action programs to the New York preparatory meeting. Together they will constitute an agenda for the 21st century - Agenda 21. These programs will cover the whole gamut of environment and development subjects. It is the formidable task of the fourth Preparatory Committee meeting to reach consensus on each of these programs. Together, if adopted and then implemented successfully, they could provide considerable momentum for the change in course required for the transition to sustainable development.

The preparatory phase of the Earth Summit is actually following the structure of your forum. First, the background papers addressed "What kind of a world do we have?" Now the Preparatory Committee must answer "What kind of a world do we want?" and "What must we do to get there?"

The answer to your second question on "What kind of a world do we want?" will be in the Rio Declaration, or Earth Charter. While the Secretariat is providing background staff work, we have not been asked to articulate a draft of a global charter for the 21st century. This is a task for the Preparatory Committee itself and will be the subject of negotiation in its Working Group III, which will start work right from the beginning of the New York meeting. This document must express a vision of what kind of world we seek.

Agenda 21 is meant to answer your third question: "What must we do to get there?" I have said it will run the whole gamut. I will expand on this.

The assumption of Agenda 21 as it is taking shape is that there are no simple one-dimensional prescriptions for changing the world's unsustainable course. Instead, we have highlighted the interrelationships among issues. For example, population growth is affected by education levels. Both population and education levels are affected by health. Child spacing improves health. All affect and are affected by improved nutrition and increased food production. And unless the multiple facets of poverty are dealt with, we have little hope of reducing the environmental damage of people eking out a living on fragile ecosystems. This is a conference about environment <u>and</u> development. The two are seen as two sides of the same coin.

This does not mean there are no choices or no priorities. First, developing countries have choices among strategies between those favoring existing elites and those favoring the whole population. Donor agencies have choices on aid priorities. We all have choices between military and economic priorities. We all can drive for more efficiency in use of resources. In science, we can favor research relevant to efficient reduction in poverty and to the development of environmentally benign technology. Agenda 21 should help us think about those choices.

Agenda 21 will deal with many issues of particular environmental relevance, including atmosphere and energy; agricultural development, land use and fragile ecosystems; biotechnology and biodiversity; oceans and coastal areas; freshwater quality and quantity; sanitation; and toxic chemicals, hazardous wastes and solid wastes. These are the issues which were concentrated on in the first three sessions of the Preparatory Committee.

Now the preparatory process has come to focus increasingly on what are called cross-cutting issues. First, there are the broad economic and social issues dealing with poverty, including employment, production, nutrition, health, science, human settlements and education. Then there are international policy issues, such as trade, debt, economic instruments, consumption patterns and demographic trends. Finally, there are the measures related to implementation: finance, capacity building, training, technology transfer, data and information. Agenda 21 will have something to say about each of these. I will say a few words about several.

While enormous progress has been made in developing countries over the past half century, still we recognize that much more attention is needed to <u>capacity building</u>. We will suggest a process for improving the use now made of technical cooperation funding, some $15 billion annually, with the hope that partner networks can be enhanced, better strategies can be developed and improved coordination achieved. We will propose more emphasis on strengthening of institutions.

Closely related to capacity building is technology transfer. In this connection, I read with great interest the recent article in *Science and Public Affairs* by your Past President, Tom Malone, in which he allowed himself the luxury of a journey to the end of the third millennium. Looking back he saw Sigma Xi in a coalition with engineers, social scientists and humanists. The scientific community entered into a massive international effort to bring into use energy technologies to replace carbon derived fossil fuels and to redress the growing socio-economic disparities between industrialized and non-industrialized countries. Tom Malone's vision is worthy of careful study by each of us.

We are also looking to the results of the International Conference on an Agenda of Science for Environment and Development into the 21st Century which will be convened in Vienna later this month. I have already seen excellent papers prepared for that conference.

Information systems and data development and availability are also important. New technology should make it possible for planners everywhere to access expanding data bases including geographic information systems. Technology improvements can be disseminated quickly as computer costs come down.

One other aspect of the UNCED Preparatory process is the National Report. Each Member State is expected to prepare one. We are expecting to receive the United States Report any day now. The National Reports, which often reflect a process of extensive consultation with interested groups in society, can be the basis for national Agenda 21 programs later on.

Finally, there is the question of finance. Financing begins at home in each Member State with improved revenue systems and more efficient use of funds. But international financing for developing countries needs to be increased too. Efficient mechanisms are needed to disburse funds. Interested parties need to be adequately represented in making policies. And, in the end, industrial countries must review priorities to consider whether aid funds are being sensibly allocated and where additional funds will come from. UNCED's original mandate, Resolution 44-228, called for new and additional resources to respond to initiatives to carry out Agenda 21 programs.

I have discussed two products of the Rio Summit: the Earth Charter and Agenda 21. The Summit is also the place where we hope to sign two important conventions, one related to climate change and the other to biodiversity. Negotiations on these very important conventions are following separate processes. The action programs of Agenda 21 will be meshed to avoid inconsistencies. Earlier there had been discussion of a third convention on forestry, but instead Members have decided to negotiate a set of principles. If a convention is needed, it will come later.

We must see the Rio Summit as a part of a process. If we succeed, as we must, in articulating a vision for the 21st Century in an Earth Charter, an action program in the form of Agenda 21, and conventions on climate change and biodiversity, surely Member States will wish to urge the General Assembly and the Secretary-General of the United Nations to establish a follow-up process. Again, this is a subject to be negotiated by Member States without a formal suggestion from the Secretariat. There is strong support among Members for establishing a system for monitoring and follow-up to the Rio consensus.

What can Sigma Xi and its colleagues do to help the UNCED process? First let me tell you that yesterday was our internal deadline for submitting our Agenda 21 programs to the Secretary-General of the Conference, Maurice Strong, for his approval. So get the results of your deliberations here to Maurice Strong immediately, because he must send Agenda 21 to New York by December 6 to assure its timely translation for our meeting beginning March 2. Second, express your views to your governments, since they are the ones who will negotiate in New York. Third, if you have applied for accreditation, you may wish to come to New York to make your views known in the corridors. The UNCED process has probably been the most participatory in the UN's long history of global conferences. We need your views, and we welcome them.

For me it is a pleasure to have had this chance to talk about the UNCED process. We live in a world of almost unimaginably rapid change. With your help, the United Nations Conference on Environment and Development can chart the necessary transition strategies toward a sustainable and fulfilling future for us and for our great-grandchildren.

UNESCO's Scientific Contribution

Adnan Badran

I. INTRODUCTION

One of the first international meetings on the global environment was sponsored by UNESCO in 1968, and the international scientific community collectively advised governments of the world of the rapid deterioration of the environment and the serious negative impact and consequences of global change. Before that, scientists focused their efforts on accumulating data on one species or another and tried to resolve the fauna and flora interaction, but had not considered human beings as an integral part of the ecosystem, contributing greatly to the disturbance of its equilibrium. As a consequence, UNESCO launched its widely recognized program of Man and Biosphere (MAB) in 1971, to avoid further degradation of our planet.

Earth is our natural capital, on which human kind depends for food security, medicine, shelter, and industrial products. Biological diversity, which has developed through evolutionary processes over millions of years, is threatened by the world's population, which stands now at 5.3 billion but is predicted to rise by the turn of the century to 6.3 billion. Of the extra billion people over the current population increase after 40 years, 900 million will be in the third world — a world which already has problems of food sufficiency. To keep pace with population growth, food production has to triple over the next forty years. There is a growing concern that the extinction of species will deprive future generations of new medicines and new strains of food sources. With as many as 50 plant species disappearing every day, it is estimated that 10% of plant biodiversity will be wiped out by the year 2015.

Threats to the world's gene pool come from the expansion of human activity, which ignores the value of the planet's ecosystem and undermine the importance of genetic biodiversity to man-

Adnan Badran is Assistant Director-General for Science at the United Nations Educational, Scientific and Cultural Organization (UNESCO).

kind. The economic value of genetic biodiversity is unmatched, not only as part of the ecological biosystems of which man is an integral part, but by the addition of direct economic value. It has been estimated that crop gains in the United States at the present time have one billion dollars annually of added value to U.S. agricultural output by the widened genetic base. So global strategy of protecting diversity is an important step toward protecting our genetic and natural heritage.

Health services are dependent on the wild species. Over 40% of all U.S. prescription drugs depend on natural sources derived from the wild and are estimated at over 40 billion dollars a year. Many of the genetic blocks needed to produce new strains for food and medicine, which are resistant to pests and of higher yield, are only available in the wild.

The rate of environmental destruction is terrifying. It is running at 25,000 times its natural rate. It is estimated that by the second half of the next century, over half of the earth's species will have become extinct. Although tropical forests cover 14% of the earth's land surface, they contain over 50% of the world's natural gene bank. However, the 1990s offers us a very small window of hope to "save the planet," its genetic biodiversity, its atmosphere from the greenhouse gases, its water resources from depletion and pollution vis a vis the preservation of our ecosystem from destruction. At the United Nations Conference on Environment and [sustainable] Development in Rio de Janeiro, Brazil, June 1992, there will be an "Earth Summit" to agree on an "Earth Charter," where all governments of the world will take on global responsibility for future generations. The world community must share resources and work together to safeguard the planet from destruction.

We are at the crossroads for a new world of shared responsibility. A world which requires from every country a commitment to international multilateral cooperation to achieve human basic needs and sustainable development. A world which appreciates cultural diversity and lives in harmony with nature. A world which ensures human rights and stresses the work of individuals toward society.

II. KEY QUESTIONS

In speaking before the Scientific Research Society of Sigma Xi, we at the United Nations Educational, Scientific and Cultural Organization (UNESCO), have been guided by three questions of the highest pertinence suggested by the chairperson of your Steering Committee, Thomas Malone. In the context of Global Change and the Human Prospect, let me try to respond to these questions and explain how UNESCO is contributing to the responses. Tom Malone has asked:

- What kind of world do we have ?
- What kind of world do we want ?
- What must we do to arrive there ?

First, the world we have. This can be stated succinctly. The 20th century, ensuing directly from the scientific and political revolutions of the 1700s and the industrial revolution of the 1800s, has been characterized almost everywhere by phenomenal growth in both population and technology. The new nations of the world, born after the Second World War, are striving tirelessly to catch up with the industrialized regions. But new technology everywhere (based primarily on science) has also become, despite its advantages otherwise, a force menacing the globe's habitability — a threat to every region of the planet.

The kind of world we have made could thus prove to be the greatest challenge to be faced by mankind in the 21st century, in both the industrialized and developing regions. This prospect refers us immediately to the second question, about the kind of world we desire.

The World Commission on Environment and Development perhaps capsulized best the answer to the question in its Tokyo Declaration of February 1987. This Declaration called for strengthened international cooperation so as to ensure :

- revival of economic growth and
- concomitant change in the quality of growth;
- conserving, while enhancing, the natural-resource base;
- ensuring a sustainable level of population;

- reorienting technology while managing its risks;
- integrating environment and economics in decision-
  making; and
- reforming the world's economic relations.

This statement of intentions is, in fact, the rationale behind the forthcoming UNCED; it should guide the work of governments, UN agencies, and other bodies.

III. UNESCO'S ROLE

Our institution, UNESCO, the principal scientific and educa-tional arm of the UN, is closely associated with the work of the intergovernmental UNCED Preparatory Committee in formulat-ing specific proposals to help all nations achieve a world that we want.

Strategic issues and goals of UNESCO, within the UNCED context, demand that our programs be in tune with new trends in the environmental sciences. Parallel with the emergence of a political consciousness of the global nature typifying many envi-ronmental problems is the new interdisciplinary research on the whole-earth system and global change — research for which worldwide cooperation is a prerequisite.

The World Climate Research Program therefore combines the support of the World Meteorological Organization, and UNESCO's Intergovernmental Oceanographic Commission (IOC), together with ICSU's International Geosphere-Biosphere Program on the Human Dimensions of Global Change. Social scientists, I hasten to add, are much involved in global change investigations.

At UNESCO's 26th General Conference, which closed only last week, the following declaration was adopted:

> *The General Conference welcomes the significant*
> *contribution of UNESCO to the preparation of*
> *[UNCED] and the excellent working arrangements*
> *established between the Secretary-General and the*
> *Secretariat of UNCED and UNESCO. The General*
> *Conference emphasizes that UNESCO's areas of*

competence, particularly education, science and
technology, and culture, will be essential for
environmentally sound and sustainable development.

In approaching the response to our last question, "How do we get there?" I must now put on my hat of scientist and scientific administrator. You probably recall that UNESCO has had a scientific mission since its founding in 1945, and that indeed its first head, the biologist Sir Julian Huxley, was a practicing scientist. During the nearly half-century that has elapsed, the organization has built its reputation both on the teaching of teachers and on using a multidisciplinary-multisectoral approach to the solving of problems, combining those in education and research with those in communication and culture.

Besides its responsibilities to help overcome illiteracy and assist the newly independent countries that have proliferated since about 1960 to establish viable educational systems, UNESCO has concrete obligations in the world of scientific knowledge. Not the least of these is the education of scientists and engineers, their continuing education included.

Our responsibilities also call for persuading governments to inculcate scientific and environmental consciousness through the education of students at primary and secondary levels, and helping develop appropriate curricula and vocational training. At the university level, we champion the teaching of science to general-studies classes and students of the humanities, as well as exposing most students to problems and solutions relating to development and environment in their countries. At the same level and higher (I should like to concentrate on the third cycle and postgraduate levels of education), our programs become highly specific — as I shall make clear.

The cornerstone of a program meant to help reduce the gap between industrialized and developing countries is, more than ever before, that of promoting the basic sciences: physics, chemistry, biology and biotechnology, and the mathematics that are the universal means of expression for all of these. About 5,000 specialists are being trained or supported within the framework of such annual basic-science programs: 95% of this activity takes place in developing nations. UNESCO is preparing an input, for example, in cooperation with the Florida Institute of Technology, to the 1992 World Congress on Nonlinear Analysis in Mathematics.

Cooperation with Member States can be truly efficient, however, only if it is based on wide involvement by teaching or research institutions at the national, regional and global levels. Currently there are 15 such active regional networks in the biosciences, including the high-impact Molecular and Cell Biology Network (MIRCEN), the Regional Network for Microbiology in Southeast Asia, and the Network for the Chemistry of Biologically Important Natural Products.

In the implementation of both training and research, UNESCO also involves appropriate non-governmental bodies — among which a long-standing partner is the International Council of Scientific Unions (ICSU). UNESCO and ICSU sponsor fellowship and lectureship programs, too, some conducted in part with the Third World Academy of Sciences. ICSU and its Unions are cooperating actively with UNESCO.

Our organization, together with the International Atomic Energy Agency, also oversees the International Centre for Theoretical Physics in Trieste (Italy). Many American physicists know this center of excellence — now processing annually as many as 3,000 theoretical and mathematical physicists, coming mostly from developing countries, who visit the Centre for periods of several weeks.

Elsewhere, annual schools of physics include the Iberian School of Condensed-Matter Physics, the International School in China on Recent Advances in Physics Research, and the Southern European School of Physics. Only this past September the new International School of Physics was organized under the combined aegis of UNESCO, the American Physical Society and the Physical Society of the U.S.S.R.

Since the inception in 1962 of the International Cell Research Organization, UNESCO has helped ICRO organize more than 300 training courses in 72 countries. Total participation thus far: more than 7,000 specialists. Similarly, UNESCO's work with the International Brain Research Organization (IBRO), has underlined the need for collaborative, multidisciplinary investigation in the neurosciences, currently under way by talented researchers from many countries.

UNESCO's Global Network for Molecular and Cell Biology, begun in 1990, encompasses 58 leading research institutions managing 10 cooperative research projects among Europeans, Latin Americans, Asians and experts from the United States. Among the Network's American centers are the Harvard Medical School, The Johns Hopkins University, Baylor School of Medicine in Houston, the University of California at Berkeley, and the National Cancer Institute in Bethesda.

Following an appeal made by scientists, including members of the international HUGO project, UNESCO launched its Human Genome Project two years ago. This is aimed at exchange of costly information and experience in mapping the human genome. This is an undertaking already showing much promise in the genetic identification of diseases and should help cure or eradicate some of them.

An important additional dimension of this activity is international analysis of the ethical and other social implications of genome study. American specialists, notably Professors Watson and Gilbert, have cooperated and we are grateful for their roles. Now what we must do is focus on developing a viable South-North dialogue in this field, beginning with a conference to be held in Cashambu (Brazil) in 1992.

Biotechnology, already mentioned, calls for specific skills cutting across many disciplinary boundaries. Intensive training schemes are especially needed in developing countries. UNESCO's Biotechnology Action Council (BAC), only a year old, has taken a lead in plant and aquatic biotechnologies, already training 85 young men and women and placing another 15 in established laboratories in developed countries.

Most of us here are scientists, but I cannot disparage our engineering colleagues — without whom many of today's problems would remain unsolved — by omitting reference to technological education.

There can be no effective strategy for sustainable development, it is certain, unless both the natural and engineering sciences collaborate to create "ecotechnologies." Here the goal of UNESCO is to re-orient traditional emphasis in the engineering sciences, generating new teaching/learning curricula, methods, and materials designed to train engineers and technicians (including environmental technicians) adequately for the 1990s and beyond. Specifically, research and development related to renewable energy sources needs strong encouragement. In July 1993 UNESCO will launch a World Decade of Renewable Energy during a major congress to be held in Paris, with the theme "Sun in the Service of Mankind."

Cooperation between universities and industry to advance technological research and development, furthermore, should be seen as an essential mechanism for the achievement of many of sustainable development's goals. In this respect, UNESCO is placing special emphasis on world regions where progress of this kind has been slow, beginning with Africa.

IV. UNESCO'S ROLE IN THE ENVIRONMENT

Now let me move much closer to research and education dealing directly with the environment.

The significance, in time, of biological diversity and conservation of the natural heritage marks another priority area. UNESCO's endeavor here comprises three sets of interlinked activities — two representing major instruments evolved during the 1970s and 1980s and a third, exciting new research project.

The International Network of Biosphere Reserves now numbers 300 sites in 76 countries: 77 of these sites are in the United States, and they stretch from the southern Appalachian Mountains to the Aleutian Islands. This overall effort is the world's only intergovernmental network of protected ecosystems seeking to combine the conservation of genetic material, long-term research, and monitoring of environmental change, while demonstrating practical approaches to sustainable development.

The second instrument is the Convention for the Protection of the World's Natural and Cultural Heritage. Its 119 signatory countries stand behind an impressive international protocol intended to support national efforts to safeguard mankind's total heritage.

At the roots of this accord are leading American personalities, such as the distinguished Russell Train. In a tribute to this pioneering role in the launching of the Convention, the United States has invited UNESCO's World Heritage Committee to hold its 20th anniversary session at Santa Fe in December, 1992.

The third component of UNESCO's work on the natural heritage concerns biological diversity and its scientific underpinnings. Diversity can be perceived from many angles: scientific and technological (of course), but also economic and utilitarian, legal and regulatory, ethical and religious, aesthetic and even emotional. Arguments for conserving the diversity of species include the importance of safeguarding products and services — possible, yet undiscovered — that diverse species may provide: food and medicine, fiber and feed, fuels, and vital ecosystem services such as biological control.

Yet much of the debate now raging about biological conservation is based on scant scientific information. Few studies have documented the relationships between ecosystem disruption and species loss. Little is known, too, about the functional role of biological diversity, or the acceptable degree of species redundancy, or how diminishing biodiversity affects the operation and viability of the terrestrial and aquatic ecosystems upon which we all depend. Only integrated research can provide the answers.

A novel initiative by UNESCO and two non-governmental scientific bodies — ICSU's Scientific Committee on Problems of the Environment and the International Union of Biological Sciences — is intended to establish the ecological significance of biodiversity. At a workshop held at Harvard Forest only last July, twenty-five hypotheses were reviewed to determine how they might be tested in field studies and experiments, and a coordinating committee has been named to oversee this collaborative project. The entire program is part of the draft "Agenda 21" on biodiversity being prepared for next year's UNCED "Earth Summit."

The impact of any major UN meeting is best measured by how effectively its resolutions are transformed into action at both national and international levels. To help decision makers at the national level better understand environmental problems and solutions, we launched only this past summer a new advisory series called *Environment Brief*. The *Brief* is intended primarily to assist policy planners and decision makers in their difficult tasks at national and regional levels.

When one measure threats to the environment, of no less importance to the global environment than biological diversity is the world's oceans. The holism characteristic of UNESCO's approach in this respect includes especially public awareness: the need to think globally and act locally.

To this end, the scientific community has the obligation to express itself understandably and strongly regarding the fundamental processes that determine the changeability of the earth's climate and conditions of life. An anticipated result is that scientifically sound advice can be provided, both on the exploitation of resources and on individual and societal behavior affecting our environment.

Sound scientific information is therefore vital for making well-grounded choices regarding the environment and sustainable development, and it needs to be combined with corresponding considerations for the legal, economic, cultural and other human undertakings of society.

There is no doubt, you will agree, that the oceans play a decisive role in changing climatic conditions and in the support of life of all kinds. Many countries still lack, however, the capability to acquire the needed scientific base, both to ensure public awareness and to provide for appropriate policy and action based on such knowledge.

Tropical forests and agriculture change, too; they affect the climate significantly, although the impact of the changing marine environment may be larger by several magnitudes. Recent research shows, for example, that only very small modifications in ocean circulation account for the wide range of the globe's temperature changes over the past 80 million years.

It is essential, furthermore, that we proceed to improve our understanding of ocean processes dominating the fluxes between atmosphere and lithosphere everywhere on the planet. This will require, among other things, putting in place a global ocean-observing and monitoring system with free access for all to the data collected. This would help equate regular "ocean reports" in the future with today's weather reports available to everyone via the mass media.

UNESCO's Intergovernmental Oceanographic Commission is proceeding, therefore, together with the World Meteorological

Organization, the U.N. Environment Program and ICSU, to develop the Global Climate Observing System, of which the future Global Ocean Observing System will be a major component. These were reasons, too, for UNESCO's participation in the Second World Climate Conference in autumn 1990.

ˌ Today water, in all its forms, is an urgent preoccupation of many countries, beyond the confines of the oceans and of arid lands such as the Sahel in Africa or the western United States. The mission of UNESCO's International Hydrological Program (IHP), for the rest of the decade and beyond, is to help Member States develop the scientific and technological capacity and exchanges permitting better national management of water resources, in terms of both quantity and quality.

UNESCO's water program has three objectives. The first is to promote hydrological research in a changing environment. Given anticipated climate change, water specialists must begin to design water-management schemes that take a flexible approach to coping with limited water resources. Scientists, working through IHP, are studying the effects of storm surges and saltwater intrusion in estuaries and coastal aquifers which would result from global warming and rising sea levels.

The second aim is the management of water resources for sustainable development. Populations in many developing countries may double by the year 2002, and more people will mean a demand for more water. Thus, water-management strategies need to balance available resources with future requirements. To accomplish this, we need to improve methodologies for evaluating current freshwater resources and predicting the likely impacts of water development projects. National water-management authorities will have to assign, therefore, high priority to water protection and conservation.

The third goal combines improved education, training, knowledge transfer, and public information. Better management and conservation in a changing environment means upgrading considerably all education and training in hydrology and related sciences and technologies, especially in the developing world, using North-South transfers as much as possible. In parallel, there is a need for providing relevant information not only to planners, decision makers and specialists in related fields, but to the water-consuming public as well.

UNESCO's range of activities in broad applications of the geosciences has been conspicuous since even before its post-earthquake work 30 years ago at Skopje (Yugoslavia) and Agadir (Morocco). These experiences, among others, permitted the refinement of cooperative efforts for systematic monitoring of seismic zones, developing defensive measures to attenuate post-disaster catastrophe among the affected populations, while helping minimize serious damage to mankind's great cultural monuments.

Only two weeks ago, the U. S. Geological Survey and UNESCO agreed, at meetings held in Reston, Virginia, and in Paris, to expand their already close cooperation in eight major areas:

- development of hazard zoning strategies;
- production of training materials for disaster reduction, especially from earthquakes and floods;
- promotion of interdisciplinary research, in conjunction with engineering designers and health-care workers, on earthquake risk;
- improved monitoring of seismic phenomena by instruments;
- cooperation in reducing volcanic disaster;
- promoting cooperation to reduce flood cataclysms;
- development of new strategies to reduce post-disaster effects worldwide, with a planning meeting to be convened in 1992; and
- publishing authoritative material on the environment, development, and related natural hazards for the guidance of decision makers.

Responding to ever-growing demand, UNESCO continues to assist developing countries in strengthening their scientific-technological capacities by providing advisory services concerning the development of human resources. Research and information exchange in this field of resource-building is handled through existing networks in Asia and the Latin American-Caribbean region; networks for Africa and the Arab States are to be established in 1992 and 1993.

When it comes to strategies for management in research and technology, UNESCO has supported the Club of Rome in a study on mobilizing science and technology to meet global challenges. It also commissioned the International Council for Science Policy Studies to carry out a corresponding analysis devised to aid the developing countries.

In light of recent developments in Eastern and Central Europe, a meeting was organized toward the end of 1990 to develop a restructuring of science and technology systems in these regions to facilitate transition to a market economy. A similar conference was held, roughly at the same moment, for all the countries of Central and South America and the Caribbean.

In the sphere of scientific culture — what you call scientific literacy here, UNESCO will be managing the awarding of six prizes for research or popularization, publishing the quarterly journal *Impact of Science on Society* in seven languages, co-sponsoring the first world congress of science journalists (Tokyo in 1992), producing a videotape series called "Science in the 90s," launching a new *Yearbook of Science* intended largely for use in developing countries, and supporting regional networks in Asia, Africa and Latin America for the training of young communicators of science, especially women.

In the complex domain of ethics, UNESCO continues its active collaboration with the Pugwash Conferences on Science and World Affairs. The ethical component of our work, I should like to add, is being strengthened as both experience and resources become available, an expansion intended especially to help the industrializing nations develop their own information systems on a democratic basis.

V. CONCLUSION

I trust that I have been able to give you a bird's-eye view of the meaning of the letter S in UNESCO, "science" signifying an active, utilitarian synergy between the natural, engineering and social disciplines — and how these should interact throughout the world, now and in the future, more and more beneficially for the human race.

Appendixes

Appendix A

Breakout Group Conclusions and Recommendations

The forum's ten breakout groups were each charged with developing no more than three conclusions and three recommendations in one of ten crucial areas of global concern for the 21st century and beyond. Areas of concern were: Food & Nutrition, Public Health, Urbanization, Population Growth, Industrial Metabolism, Habitable Biosphere, Industry, Science, Education, and Institutional Change. The following are the conclusions and recommendations from the participants. They do not necessarily represent the views of the moderators, panelists, Sigma Xi, or other sponsoring organizations.

Food & Nutrition

Moderator: **Pierre Crosson**, Senior Fellow, Resources for the Future
Panelists: **Dennis Avery**, Hudson Institute
Gary Evans, Special Assistant, Global Change Program , USDA
Li Zhensheng, Vice President, China Academy of Science
Rapporteur: **Susan Malone Back**, Research Consultants

Conclusions

1. Problems of achieving a sustainable agriculture arise from underinvestment in the rural infrastructure and from inadequate education of rural people in developing countries.

2. Poverty and inequity of income, which often are exacerbated by political instability, are among the chief causes of inadequate food intake and nutritional status.

3. Although per capita global food production has increased, there is no assurance that it will continue unless there is continued research, education, and development in food production, distribution, and post harvest technology. Culturally appropriate technology transfer geared to the needs of local food producers and delivered by those who are from the local area can be effective in improving farming when coupled with indigenous knowledge.

Recommendations

1. Educate the public to appreciate the importance of agriculture and the value of farmers.

2. Increase investment in transportation and distribution of food and in education of rural people within developing countries.

3. There should be sustained investment in research, in culturally appropriate extension programs, and in environmentally friendly food production and post harvest technology.

Public Health

Moderator: **Stephen S. Morse**, Assistant Professor, Rockefeller University
Panelist: **Rita Colwell**, President, Maryland Biotechnology Institute
Rapporteur: **Paul S. Berger**, Senior Microbiologist, U.S.E.P.A..

Conclusions

1. Health has a major impact on, and is affected by, virtually all of the ecological factors considered at this conference. Ecological and environmental factors drive both the emergence and dissemination of infectious disease, as well as affecting many non-infectious diseases.

2. A continuing effort to bring all people of the world to an acceptable minimum standard of health, defined as healthy adulthood, should be an immediate goal. To achieve this goal, adequate nutrition, sanitation, and pre- and perinatal care should be assured. Eradication is not possible for many diseases, but effective control should be employed.

3. An interdisciplinary approach is needed for evaluating the effects of ecological factors on disease emergence and spread. Suitable incentives and funding should be developed to encourage this approach.

Recommendations

1. Aggressively pursue global immunization programs for serious diseases, especially major childhood diseases, including both immediate and efficient worldwide deployment of cost-effective vaccines, and incentives for development of new or additional preventive measures.

2. Facilitate the sharing and coordination, at all levels and on an interdisciplinary basis, of data and expertise relevant to public health (*e.g.*, also

agriculture and demography) by establishing a coordinating body (linking existing computer systems where possible). Establish a pro-active surveillance program for serious diseases on both a regional and global scale, to be coordinated with this system.

3. Develop continuing cooperative arrangements for global transfer of technology, technical and management expertise, and materials (*e.g.*, vaccines). We envision that this would operate through regional centers that would, in turn, train and educate local officials and populations and provide the needed resources. As an example, minimize the inappropriate use of drugs (especially antimicrobial agents) and pesticides through educational efforts on a global scale.

4. Donor agencies should ensure that health impact assessments (analogous to environmental impact assessments) are completed before providing financial assistance for development projects.

Urbanization

Moderator: **Richard Rockwell**, Executive Director, ICPSR, University of Michigan
Panelists: **Lourdes Arizpe**, Director, International Union of Anthropological Sciences
Tom Kingsley, Urban Institute
Rapporteur: **Charlotte Zieve**, Institute for Environmental Studies, University of Wisconsin

Conclusions

1. Urban growth cannot be stopped. Government can do little to control or direct it. The problem is to make cities work better and with less environmental damage and less damage to people from intense point sources of pollution. We must find ways to assist cities to work with less environmental damage, in more sustainable ways.

2. It is clear that "city" is not the same thing around the world. Cities differ in topography, soil, hydrology, and ecosystem—not to speak of economic base, economic development, and rate of growth. Therefore, sweeping statements about cities are not likely to be possible or helpful. The group was not prepared to declare *a priori* that mega-cities are necessarily disasters, although we suspect that it is perhaps not size but rate of growth that makes these cities vulnerable and unlivable.

3. In dealing with problems of cities, we have also to deal with problems of the hinterlands—i.e., issues of equity, economic growth, population, racism,

and cultural differences. The group emphasized opportunities for the exercise of foresight, better management, better planning, the need for appropriate studies to provide the "best guess" about the likely consequences of alternative policy actions, because scientific uncertainty should not be used as a reason for inaction.

Recommendations

1. Sigma Xi should recognize its obligation to provide the training needed for local scientists to establish data bases for dynamic environmental modeling and analytical systems focusing on trade offs.

2. Work out relationships between regulation and market-driven growth of cities in order to establish a culturally appropriate balance between such policies and between the city and a sustainable agro-ecosystem so that effective management of these forces can be developed.

3. Redesign aspects of urban infrastructure and urban metabolism for the environmental, economic, social, and political sustainability of the city-hinterland system so as to avoid economic, cultural, health, or ecological disasters: for example, the use of inexpensive but reliable materials that can be designed and installed by local effort.

Population Growth

Moderator: **Tom Merrick**, President, Population Reference Bureau
Panelists: **Perdita Huston**, Author of *Third World Women Speak Out*
                  Carole Jolly, Committee on Population, National Academy of Engineering
                  John Langan, S.J., Rose Kennedy Professor of Christian Ethics, Kennedy School of Ethics, Georgetown University
                  Caroly Shumway, AAAS Science, Engineering, and Diplomacy Fellow, Office of the Environmental Coordinator,U.S.A.I.D.
Rapporteur: **Judith Herzfeld**, Department of Chemistry, Brandeis University

Conclusions

1. No one knows the human carrying capacity of the Earth, and it is dangerous to test it empirically as we are now doing. In the face of serious signs of environmental strain and accelerating depletion of biological and other natural resources, it is far safer to stop human population growth as soon as possible, at as low a level as possible (now believed to be 7-8 billion), rather than later, at a higher level.

2. There is an unmet and growing demand worldwide for family planning services. Family planning services would be most effectively expanded in the context of reproductive health programs. These programs include research and services in the areas of contraception, prevention and treatment of sexually transmitted diseases, and maternal and child health.

3. Our present and future welfare depends on the health of the global environment. We must develop a greater appreciation for the effects of human practices and numbers on the biosphere.

Recommendations

1. Everyone, at all levels, should do their utmost to decrease worldwide population growth as fast as possible. This should include allocation of increased funding, the exercise of greater political leadership, and efforts to improve the opportunities and status of women.

2. Increase funding to realize the universal right to comprehensive reproductive health care enunciated in numerous international declarations.

3. Increase public education (in and out of the classroom) regarding the impact of human activity on the biosphere and foster greater understanding of the interdependencies in nature which connect species, transcend national boundaries, and link successive generations.

Industrial Metabolism

Moderator: **Brad Allenby**, Senior Attorney, AT&T Corporation
Panelists: **Ben Cooper**, Staff Director, U.S. Senate Energy Committee
             Jae Edmonds, Technical Leader, Economic Programs, Battelle
             Deanna Richards, Senior Program Officer, National Academy of
             Engineering
Rapporteur: **Bernardo F. Grossling**, Research Geophysicist, U.S. Geological
             Survey

Conclusions

1. It is important to consider consumer behavior and industrial activity as an interactive system.

2. It is important that international equities, economic competitiveness, and trade considerations be integrated with environmentally preferable practices.

3. Products should be designed in a framework which includes all of the appropriate environmental factors to the extent possible.

Recommendations

1. Environmental industrial policies should be designed to take into account new data, to be performance oriented, and to be consistent with the goal of achieving sustainable and equitable societies.

2. The global scientific and technical communities should: a) develop methodologies and data for defining and implementing environmentally preferable industry practices, and b) work with other sectors to develop efficient and socially acceptable decentralized incentives and constraints to encourage private firms to internalize environmental considerations.

3. Recognizing that gross national product (GNP) per capita has become the defacto indicator of societal well-being, the scientific and technical community should help industry and commerce by developing new numerical measures of quality of life which emphasize human development as distinguished from the simple consumption of goods and services.

Habitable Biosphere

Moderator: **V. Kerry Smith**, University Distinguished Professor, Resource and
Environmental Economics Program, North Carolina State University
Panelists: **Herman Daly**, Senior Economist, The World Bank
David Galas, Associate Director for Health & Environmental Research, U.S. Department of Energy
John Knauss, Administrator, National Oceanic and Atmospheric Administration
Diane Lowrie, Vice President, Global Tomorrow Coalition
Rapporteur: **Steven Shaw**, Director of Community Education, Jewish Theological Seminary

Conclusions

1. Uncertainty will not be resolved in time to fully understand all the implications of human activities on biodiversity and the global ecosystem; therefore, we need to act and learn simultaneously.

2. There is a need to transform the values that motivate and direct research, policy, and economic activities, reflecting values for stewardship of the natural environment.

3. Balance is required to connect the need for action, the will to act, and the costs of action for the developed and developing worlds, so that actions to modify economic activities can be sustained.

Recommendations

1. Sigma Xi should recommend periodic review of research funding and priorities by non-governmental and scientific-based groups to assure that there is a balance between basic research and policy-directed research. Sigma Xi should further recommend that where policy-motivated research is undertaken, especially integrated environmental science, that the science be connected to policy recommendations.

2. Sigma Xi should endorse recognition of non-use values for environmental resources as reflections of stewardship for the environment and thus account for all sources of the value of natural assets. Sigma Xi should explicitly incorporate environmental values both as damages and as values of the services of preserved environments into the signals and incentives given to consumers and producers whose decisions influence available environmental services. Values should not be limited to damages or to values that can be measured but can be reflected by establishing permits or quotas for materials and energy inputs.

3. Policy should be directed at slowing use through incentives and endorsing the International Biosphere Research Project. Greater attention should be given to education or public communication about environmental sciences and values.

Industry

Moderator: **U.V. Henderson**, General Manager (retired), Environment and Product Safety Department, Texaco

Panelists: **Lewis Branscomb**, Director, Science, Technology and Public Policy Program, John F. Kennedy School of Government, Harvard University
Joseph Norbeck, Manager, Chemistry Department, Ford Motor Company
Bill Nitze, President, Alliance to Save Energy

Rapporteur: **Roger Chiarodo**, U.S. Department of Commerce

Conclusions

1. Multinational companies are already actively engaged in all the dimensions—economic, political and environmental—of global change. Many of these companies are signatories to the principles stated in the "Charter for Sustainable Development" of the International Chamber of Commerce.

2. Environmental considerations are increasingly entering the mainstream of industrial manufacturing processes and product development. Consortia to address common environmental problems are becoming increasingly acceptable.

3. The majority of scientists and engineers are employed by industry and are uniquely positioned to influence programs and policies consistent with environmentally sound sustainable growth.

Recommendations

1. The U.S. should develop an energy policy which includes conservation, the efficient use of current energy resources, and due concern for the development of renewable energy for sustainable growth. Environmental control should, to the extent possible, be based on market mechanisms. U.S. industry and government should develop strategies for superior environmental technologies for worldwide use. We strongly recommend that all U.S. companies endorse the Charter for Sustainable Development of the International Chamber of Commerce.

2. Professional societies should encourage their members, working and retired, to provide their expertise to solving problems related to the environment and sustainable growth. Governing boards of societies and companies should be broadened to include knowledgeable people from a variety of disciplines. Maximum utilization of the knowledge and skills of the entire U.S. workforce is essential to environmentally sound manufacturing processes and sustainable growth.

3. Decision frameworks and risk assessments used for private and public policies and programs for sustainable growth should include all relevant external costs. The public and private communities should develop accounting systems which more adequately address measures of sustainable growth, including considerations of public health and welfare.

Science

Moderator: **Eric Leber**, Executive Director, Council of Scientific Society Presidents

Panelists:　**Ronald Abler**, Executive Director, American Association of Geographers

　　　　　Richard Gowen, President, South Dakota School of Mines

　　　　　Peggie Hollingsworth, Professor, Department of Pharmacology, University of Michigan Medical School

Rapporteur: **Evan Ferguson**, Director of Programs, Sigma Xi

Conclusions

1. Scientific and professional organizations have been too insular, too non-communicative to their members, students (all levels), and to the general public about global change issues, and they are too discipline-oriented. They have not been sufficiently aggressive in motivating and mobilizing their members to resolve global change issues.

2. Scientific and professional organizations have not adequately addressed and assessed their own missions, priorities, goals, values, and their role in science policy issues concerning global change problems.

3. Scientific and professional organizations need to place paramount importance on multifaceted environmental issues, including the human dimensions of the problem, education (members, students, and the general public), multiplicity of approaches (i.e., multidisciplinary) from both basic and applied sciences, ethical considerations involving both basic and applied research values, as well as a reconsideration of our institutional structures, and then take appropriate steps to enhance human diversity, including representatives from all races and both genders in the decision-making process.

Recommendations

1. Scientific and professional organizations must be restructured to address environmental problems. This restructuring should involve a reassessment of their missions, priorities, activities, communications and inter-relationships with other organizations (other societies, industry, and government).

2. Scientific and professional organizations must actively involve their memberships in the pursuit of environmental goals. Such efforts should include developing and distributing information and resource kits for scientists, engineers, educators, students, and the public about environmental problems; increasing interaction with policy makers on these issues; increasing scientific and technical literacy among students and the public; and improving cooperative programs with industry and other professional organizations.

3. Scientific and professional organizations must join together to develop a shared agenda and to provide a unified effort on relevant global issues directed at policy makers, educators, students, the public, respective society memberships, and political candidates.

Education

Moderator: **William Hoyt**, Western Center Director, Program for Leadership in Earth Systems Education
Panelists: **Frank Huband**, Executive Director, American Society for Engineering Education
Jim Rutherford, Director, AAAS Project 2061
Rapporteur: **Whitman Cross**, Director, Red Mountain Museum

Conclusions

1. Professional societies can have a positive impact on science education by becoming actively involved in global change issues.

2. All learning impacts global change issues.

3. Individuals can be a valuable resource by sharing their expertise with centers of learning.

Recommendations

1. Professional societies should support science education at all levels by reviewing and revising their mission statements and by examining the composition of their boards to reflect the high priority of science education in general, especially in response to global change.
2. Global change studies should be integrated into school and college curricula at all levels and in cross-disciplinary perspective (natural sciences, social sciences, and humanities—specifically including ethics), with sensitivity to the diverse values and perspectives within the international community.

3. Scientific society members should become actively involved with K-12 schools to bring scientists and engineers to the students to further enhance a sense of the excitement and wonder of science by involving them in investigative, participatory science, mathematics, and engineering. Scientific society members should actively attempt to attract and maintain the interest of underrepresented groups in mathematics, science, and engineering, and they should encourage science centers, parks, and museums to serve as advisors for the improvement of exhibits and the coordination of public programs.

Institutional Change

Moderator: **Thomas F. Malone**, Past President, Sigma Xi
Panelists: **Ambassador Eduardo MacGillycuddy**, Uruguay
Nancy Maynard, Assistant Director for the Environment, Office of Science and Technology Policy
Stephen Klein, U.S. UNCED Coordination Center
Zell Steever, U.S. UNCED Coordination Center
Rapporteur: **Elizabeth Kirk**, International Programs, AAAS

Conclusions

1. Extension, integration, application, and dissemination of knowledge is an essential element of the response to global change.

2. New modes of interaction are needed among the natural, social, and engineering sciences, the humanities, and decision makers in the public and private sectors.

3. Institutional arrangements are needed to ensure cooperation among: a) the community responsible for generating and conserving knowledge, b) business and industry that produce goods and supply services, and c) government, which attends to the commonweal.

Recommendations

1. We recommend that regional networks such as START, the Inter-American Institute for Global Change Research, and the Third World Academy of Sciences Centers, as well as centers established for related purposes, reflect the interdependence of environment and human development.

2. The International Council of Scientific Unions' Initiative for Cooperative for Planet Earth is endorsed and encouraged to reflect the interdependence of environment and human development. Cooperation and collaboration with the World Conservation Union (IUCN), World Federation of Engineering Organizations, and International Social Science Council should be encouraged.

3. Sigma Xi should pursue modes of cooperation among the industrial, scientific, and governmental sectors of the community—nationally, regionally, and globally.

Appendix B

Summary
Prepared by *Charles Blackburn, Sigma Xi*

Global Change: Eight Key Points from the Forum

Eight major points emerged during the Sigma Xi Forum on Global Change. They are outlined below as an aid to discussion, followed by brief summaries of each major theme. The summaries are based entirely on information and views presented by the speakers in the plenary sessions, as well as by members of the audience and participants in the breakout sessions.

1. Global Trajectory

Global trajectory, i.e. the projected quality of human life on Earth in the 21st century and beyond, is determined by the great forces of population growth, poverty, economic development, and environmental stress. Many indicators suggest that the world is currently on an unsustainable path, but the prevailing view at the Sigma Xi Forum was that we have the knowledge and technical ability to change our course, if we do not delay.

2. Global Progress

Progress has been made in some parts of the world on some global change problems. Fertility is declining, inroads have been made against many serious health problems, and environmental planning is at least gaining lip service. Science and technology offer new options for solving human problems.

3. Poverty

However, poverty is stark for many — more than a billion people — and health problems and strains on resources are still enormous. As the growing billions in the less developed countries struggle to achieve an adequate standard of living, the strains on the environment may be unbearable unless new approaches are found for development. The issues of human development and environment are inextricably linked. Empowering people with knowledge gives them the best chance for a better life in harmony with the ecosystem.

4. An Equitable World

The world is not at a crisis stage, but the mere recognition of global problems is not enough. These problems are in urgent need of attention, before they progress beyond our control. However, it seems possible to shift the globe's temporal trajectory from the unpalatable future of swamped overpopulation, stark poverty, and environmental ruin, to one of an equitable society. To do so will require decades of effort by individuals and governments, but the task is possible. A fundamental, widespread change in attitudes and values is a vital part of the solution.

5. Partnerships

Partnerships are needed between industry and government, between the public and private sectors, between society and the research community, between the northern and southern hemispheres. Government programs must address social stresses, health problems stemming from poverty, poor or nonexistent education, and malnutrition. Growing interdependence among the nations of the world is giving added validation to the concept of a global community, diminishing the value of isolationism as a national policy.

6. Breaking Barriers

Barriers must be broken between regions — North and South, East and West — and between countries. Support for regional institutions in the developing world is necessary. These institutions would develop national talent, rather than relying on outside experts. Outdated attitudes and perceptions must be overcome if the global community is to thrive.

7. Economic Development

Environmentally sound industrial growth is required for economic development, which will provide long-term solutions to many of the problems the world faces. Population stabilization will require economic development and an equal role for women in society.

8. Professional Tithing

People are willing to work at local levels and in professional associations. In addition to pressing for governmental actions, members of scientific and engineering societies should devote a portion of their time to working at the local level on the issues addressed at the Forum. Among valuable activities, members can improve college curricula, support introduction of Forum information into local schools, and initiate public discussion of these topics.

Global Trajectory

If we do not change our direction, we are likely to end up where we are headed.
—Chinese Proverb

By any standard, remarkable progress has been made in improving health and economic well-being in many developing countries since World War II, but the global community is still struggling with widespread poverty, disease, malnutrition, ignorance, and injustice. As the standard of living has risen in industrialized nations, the gulf has widened between the "haves" of the northern hemisphere and the "have-nots" of the southern hemisphere.

A composite of statistics cited at the Forum presents a stark picture of the human family. Seventy-seven percent of the world now earns 15 percent of the total global income. Two out of every 10 people on Earth go hungry daily. UNICEF estimates that each day nearly 40,000 babies die of starvation or its complications. Twenty-four million young people die from preventable causes every year. More than 1.3 billion people in the world are without potable water. More than 1 billion people in developing countries are trapped in absolute poverty.

All of these problems are likely to be exacerbated by a projected doubling of the world's population, from 5 billion to 12 billion (World Bank estimates), by the end of the next century. Unless population stabilizes sooner rather than later, progress in such areas as public health could be overwhelmed by sheer numbers. An estimated 3 billion people will be added to the world's population in the next three decades alone, and 90 percent will be born in the developing countries.

Population growth, poverty, economic development, and environmental stress will be the key factors in determining the human prospect in the next century. It has become increasingly apparent that these issues are all closely interrelated.

The developing world has the responsibility to ensure that future generations will have a chance to hope for a better life. Economic development is widely seen as the means to that end. An increase in per capita income and social programs that promote comprehensive reproductive health care could well do more for population stabilization than programs that focus strictly on population control. At the same time, economic development is the primary cause of the environmental degradation that has been a byproduct of prosperity in the industrialized North.

That the world is not headed in a sustainable direction is becoming accepted dogma. In the coming decades, unless trends are reversed, the arable acreage that will be lost due to soil depletion and erosion will be equivalent to that which today feeds 84 million people. The area of rain forest that the world loses every year is comparable to the U.S. losing the state of Washington. The loss of biodiversity is a fast-moving problem; it is clearly a near-term problem compared to global warming. Eighty percent of the planet's biodiversity is in the developing nations and is vulnerable to increased development. In many parts of the world, environmental problems such as deforestation are frequently the byproducts of extreme poverty, born of slash-and-burn economies, in which cashing in natural resources is the only way impoverished people can eke out a living.

In Mexico, for example, Dr. Lourdes Arizpe of the National University of Mexico said that poverty is the driving force behind migration from cities to the rain forests, where poor people hope that logging and agriculture will provide a better life. In the course of time, soil depletion and/or a fall in agricultural prices drive the next generation to forsake the subsistent life of the forest for what they hope will be a better life in the city, and the cycle begins again. Within a few generations, as the population rapidly increases, this cycle could take an enormous toll on rain forests.

Meanwhile, the already crowded cities of the world appear destined to become mega-cities. Population density is enormous now in some cities: 88,000 per square kilometer in Calcutta, 45,000 in Manila, and 30,000 in Cairo. The population of Mexico City could reach 30 million by the middle of the next century. City growth is being driven by economic necessity. If capital investments do not flow to the people, the people will flow to the capital investments. If rural livelihood continues to disappear, migration will continue, and the major cities will become so large that the people cannot be fed. In the future, famine may be largely an urban problem.

Overconsumption in the North is seen by many as the critical component in an environmental equation whose three major factors are population size, consumption, and production. Yet policies in the North are concerned with population control in the South rather than with curbing overconsumption. We should think of our natural resources—the forests, ozone, coral reefs—as assets comparable to man-made capital in their ability to provide services over time. Too often, the proceeds from environmental degradation are consumed rather than invested. When we look at the capital base of society to judge whether we are on a sustainable course, it is clear that we are living off our assets.

We have been burdened with a consistent failure to recognize the systemic nature of environmental problems and their causes. We cannot completely eliminate the problems of global change through science and technology, and there is real danger in thinking that "science will save us," because runaway population growth, injustice, maldistribution of resources, and inappropriate economic theories will soon pass the point at which science will be able "to deliver the goods."

The United Nations should develop an integrated approach to environment and development. Human ability to manage natural resources is improving technically. There are well-managed, clean industries, but environmentally responsible development will require a change in attitudes in industrial countries, as well as environmentally friendly policies and practices in developing nations.

While the problems associated with global change are in urgent need of attention, it is not too late to take action. The decade of the 1990s presents a window of opportunity to change the global trajectory. The challenge is to rectify our inability to harmonize population growth with the rate of resource depletion, and raise the standard of living within the global community, while preserving the ecosystem.

Global Progress

Progress in world health over the last 25 years
is one of the most remarkable success stories in human history.
—Dr. Dean T. Jamison

Progress on a variety of issues related to global change is being made in many developing countries, as well as in the industrialized North.

There is still wide variation in public health among developing nations, but dramatic improvements overall can be linked to increased per capita income, which has grown at the rate of 2.5 percent a year in developing countries (with the exception of Africa, where per capita income has declined). Two-thirds of the world's people now have access to some form of health care. Infectious diseases are in decline, which has, in turn, led to reductions in the fertility rate, down from five children per female in 1950 to between three and four today. World population growth is expected to peak in the very near future at 100 million per year and then decline steadily. Even so, large numbers of people will be added to the population in the next few decades. Infant mortality has declined dramatically in many parts of the world, and life expectancy has increased steadily. In China, despite widespread poverty, life expectancy is now only six or seven years less than it is in the United States. Life expectancy in Africa is up from 40 to 52 years.

With declines in fertility and mortality, global demographics are shifting toward an older population, which presents new problems. Dr. Dean T. Jamison, of the University of California at Los Angeles School of Public Health, said that chronic diseases have emerged as a leading cause of death in the developing world, just as they are in the industrialized nations. In Asia (including India and China) the incidence of circulatory disease is expected to rise from 0.6 percent in 1985 to 2.8 percent in 2015. The enormous problems inherent with chronic diseases must be addressed by research and public policy, or our health care systems will not be able to keep pace. Jamison said we are not acquiring the intellectual capital today that will be required to deal with these health problems in the future.

However, recent initiatives in Africa promise long-term, positive impact on domestic problems by developing and nurturing local expertise, an approach that could have widespread applications throughout the developing world. One such effort is called the African Capacity Building Initiative, funded by the World Bank and the United Nations. Another is the International Centre of Insect Physiology and Ecology, which is devoted to fundamental research in insect science, using a holistic approach for long-term solutions. The Centre has a postdoctorate program for Africans. A cooperative effort among 24 African universities has led to a Ph.D. program that has awarded 50 doctorate degrees since 1983, and all of the recipients have stayed in Africa. This effort may ultimately result in the development of research universities in Africa. An African Foundation for Research and Development is also in the planning stages. In Singapore, South Korea, Brazil, and India, profound transformations have been possible due to visionary political leaders, creative, dedicated scientists, and entrepreneurial and management leadership.

There are many cultural traditions throughout the world aimed at preserving the rain forest and other natural resources, traditions that have been established over thousands of years. National research centers could be in a position to promote such traditions while seeking to improve the quality of life within the region. Perhaps the best way to promote conservation is to give people the capacity to think for themselves, to empower them with knowledge. Education has many hurdles to overcome in the developing world. For example, only 1 percent of the textbooks used in Africa are written by African authors in national languages. But these obstacles are not insurmountable. A science book fair for African children, as well as a children's newspaper, are among recent innovations that promise long-term remedies.

Even a little knowledge can make a profound difference in quality of life, as has been illustrated by the introduction of intercropping in some areas of Africa. This relatively simple idea has led to a new level of affluence that has allowed some families to build homes for the first time.

Some of the problems in the developing world do not require high-tech solutions. To combat the tropical guinea worm, a parasite that infects about 10 million people a year through drinking water, Du Pont is donating 1 million nylon filters a year to place over water jars, a simple solution that is having a very positive effect on public health.

On the environmental front, nearly all countries have laws and policies protecting natural resources. Emission controls are becoming more stringent in many countries, and there has been progress in reducing sulfureous emissions. But perhaps the most heartening development has been a growing awareness that belief systems that value profit over everything else have detrimental effects on the environment. A spontaneous change in attitudes among many young people bodes well for the future. It is time to establish a better measure of progress than Gross National Product and redefine human success in terms of every single member of the human family having the chance to live up to his or her potential.

It is becoming clear that economic policies, if carefully thought through, can contribute to sustainability. A number of countries are developing environmental incentives. Scandinavia has developed environmental taxes. There has been a call to tax all carbon-based fuels in Europe within the next two years. Japan enacted a recycling law in April of 1991. Ms. Mayumi Moriyama, Senior Director of the Special Committee on Environment for the Japanese House of Councillors, said in her talk that in 1988 Japan recycled 50.5 percent of paper, 45 percent of aluminum cans, and 43 percent of steel cans. She said Japanese women have been very influential in establishing more environmentally friendly policies. No phosphate detergents are made now in Japan, and the reuse of paper has become economic. In the international arena, debt is being used to some extent as a means of securing global environmental gains; lending nations are occasionally writing off Third World debts in exchange for conservation projects.

Political independence following World War II has meant an end to colonialism but has not led to the betterment of the masses. The need now is for freedom from within. The poor have the right to enjoy the fruits of political independence, but they lack the economic and intellectual capital necessary to build a better world. During this same period of history, there has been tremendous growth in organized human knowledge in the form of science for humane purposes. Science and technology offer new options for solving the world's problems.

> *There is growing awareness that belief systems that value profit over everything else have detrimental effects on the environment.*
> —Dr. David A. Munro

Poverty

*We do not wish to impoverish the environment,
but we cannot forget poverty.
Are not poverty and need the greatest polluters?*
—Indira Gandhi

Because economics and environment are inextricably linked, efforts to curb environmental degradation are unlikely to enjoy widespread success until the standard of living improves within the global community.

Poverty stalks most of the households in the developing world. More than 1.2 billion people earn less than $1 a day. More than 500 million are seriously malnourished, receiving less than 80 percent of the UN's minimum caloric intake per day. Firewood remains the chief fuel for 1.4 billion people. The children of the rain forest will ultimately decide its fate, but there are few teachers to educate them. Human development is essential to successful economic development.

Indeed, many parts of the world could be characterized as human disaster areas and should be treated as such. The transformation of the South represents an enormous challenge. The monumental nature of the task will require massive commitments of resources and expertise, on a scale similar to the Marshall Plan that rebuilt Europe following World War II. We must stem the flight of capital from the developing countries. Six billion dollars a year goes to Africa in the form of technical assistance, but most is spent on the employment of foreign expertise. None is spent on centers of domestic excellence.

We should not expect significant investment by countries that labor under severe economic hardship. The developing countries are burdened with $200 billion in debt service alone. But with the end of the Cold War, it is time to turn swords into plowshares. In 1987, the developing countries received about $34 billion in foreign assistance, while at the same time spending $34 billion on military arms.

In our efforts to solve the problems of global change we should take those prudent measures which are good in their own right, such as conservation, but we should avoid drastic measures, for which we don't have a solid scientific basis and which would place great economic burdens on developing countries. Alternative energy sources, such as solar power, could be enormously important to countries that do not already have centralized energy systems, but many countries simply do not have the capital to pursue the development of alternative energy. This is an area in which the industrialized nations, which have the financial and intellectual capital to invest, can and should take the lead.

The governments of the South know it will be to their advantage to stabilize population growth as soon as possible. There have been 50 studies of family planning programs in India and why they do not work. Poverty, illiteracy among women, and other factors undermine such programs. At the same time, there is a rising tide of expectations and demands by the developing countries who are tempted by the affluence of industrial nations. The poor in all countries aspire to the life of the rich in their cities, and the countries of the South aspire to the life of the rich in the North.

Poverty stalks most households, especially in Africa.
—Dr. Thomas R. Odhiambo

Dire poverty and the hope of a brighter future are strong motivators. As conditions worsen in many parts of the world, more people will pull up stakes and seek a better life elsewhere. The lure of the North will become even stronger. California, for example, will have 7 million new low-paying jobs in the 1990s that will encourage immigration.

The human family must learn to live within the constraints of its economy and its resources. We are creating the conditions for despair. The world is suffering from poverty of spirit as well as from a lack of basic human necessities. In the affluent North, the erosion of cultural and social norms is manifesting itself in drug addiction, homelessness, and suicides. The South must invent a future based on its own culture, on the extended family. As Dr. Thomas R. Odhiambo said, "If people have the tools, they will find a way to get the job done."

To those who live in the rain forest it is not a matter of population versus environmental degradation; it is "us or the trees."
—Dr. Lourdes Arizpe

An Equitable World

Global equity is widely seen as a matter of ethics—simple justice.
—Dr. David A. Munro

Equity is a unifying theme for many of the issues that will affect the human prospect in the next century. Global equity implies that every member of the human family should at least have a chance to fulfill his or her potential. The concept also embraces the idea that global equity involves a contract between present and future generations, particularly in regards to the legacy of natural resources and biodiversity that one generation leaves another. Achieving economic, social, political, and environmental equity within the global community will take decades of effort by individuals and governments, but it is a reasonable and attainable goal.

In the closing decade of the 20th century, however, global change issues have reached the point that it is not sufficient merely to recognize that problems exist. It is time to do something about them. The nations of the world are becoming increasingly interdependent, and the attitudes, policies and actions of one country can have an impact far beyond its borders. The complexity of the problems related to global change will require a concerted effort from the entire global community.

Global inequity is growing. The net flow of resources is from the poor of the South to the rich of the North, like a transfusion from the sick to the healthy. Seventy-seven percent of the global population is using about 20 percent of the world's industrial energy, a statistic that speaks volumes about the maldistribution of industrial development worldwide.

Will all 10 billion people who will be on Earth in 50 years have the same right to enjoy our planet's natural resources? The answer must be "yes," both in terms of access and availability. But biodiversity is dwindling rapidly. The loss of species is not an academic issue. Of the 20 largest selling prescription drugs in the world, all either came from natural sources, or the molecules of the drug were patterned after natural sources. A drug derived from the Madagascan periwinkle, for example, has improved the survival rate for a form of childhood leukemia from 1 in 10 to 19 out of 20.

> *We are throwing away our biological patrimony,*
> *for which future generations will never forgive us.*
> —Dr. Peter H. Raven

We are living in an interdependent ecological system, in which upsetting one part can upset another. The North must change its patterns of energy use to maintain its standard of living and, at the same time, decrease environmental damage, because the unsustainable consequences are not borne by those who cause them. In the case of air pollution, the world has seen a three-fold increase in carbon dioxide emissions since the 1950s; the United States, with 5 percent of the world's population, contributes 25 percent of the world's carbon dioxide.

With regard to equity for women, a recent survey conducted by USA TODAY on what American industry is doing for females provided a commentary on the attitudes that must be overcome. In the survey, 46 percent of respondents indicated child care was a female issue. In discus-

sions about stabilizing population growth, not much emphasis is placed on
male responsibility. There are some exceptions. Family planning in India is
aimed at men as well as women; the largest component of the program is
male sterilization. But overall, there is clearly a need to raise the status of
women and ensure their rights and independence, then family planning can
be more of a partnership, a shared responsibility.

Illiterate, rural women want to space their children,
but it will require educating their husbands, who deny them contraception.
—Perdita Huston, journalist

We must empower underrepresented groups, particularly women.
We need to accelerate the transfer of environmentally friendly technology to
developing countries to empower them with knowledge. Many of the
problems related to global change fall into the realm of human and social
relations. Scientific and technical goals should be derived from overarching
social goals, such as economic strength, security, freedom, and education.
As Dr. Peter Raven, Director of the Missouri Botanical Gardens, said, "We
must base our actions on a love of humanity and all the good things of planet
Earth." To which U.S. Rep. George E Brown Jr. (D-California) later added,
"We must learn how to husband and share the bounty of this planet, and in
the marketplace of human aspirations, lead to change by example."

There is enough for everyone's need, but not for everyone's greed.
—Mahatma Gandhi

Partnerships

The UNCED conference in Brazil has the immodest task
of changing the course of history.
—Dr. Joseph C. Wheeler

Many of those concerned about global change are optimistic that
the United Nations Conference on Environment and Development
(UNCED), scheduled for June of 1992 in Rio de Janeiro, Brazil, will lay the
groundwork for building the international partnerships necessary to alter
global trajectory. Other conferences have defined the problems; UNCED
will seek to establish an agenda for international action. UNCED was
designed to bring presidents and prime ministers together to talk about
environment and development. More than 50,000 people are expected in
Rio for the conference, with huge delegations from each country.

UNCED delegates will consider 125 draft action programs as an agenda for the 21st century. Agenda 21 will encompass the atmosphere, energy, agriculture, land use, fragile ecosystems, biotechnology and biodiversity, oceans and coastal areas, fresh water, sanitation, hazardous wastes, and solid wastes. Organizers of the conference caution that there is no simple prescription for changing the world's unsustainable course. It is their hope that UNCED will chart the necessary strategies for a sustainable world for present and future generations.

However, it will be up to individual governments, organizations, and people to provide the political will, motivation, and human energy to make whatever changes are necessary to ensure a bright prospect for humankind. There is growing sentiment that the time has come to do more than acknowledge the consequences of our actions; we must change our behavior. In that context, *Think Globally/Act Locally* is more than a snappy slogan for a bumper sticker. The phrase embodies the sort of change in attitudes that will be needed to solve the problems of global change.

The dominant imagery of the international dialogue on global change is one of the fractured human family, in which the nations of the world have drifted away from acting as an international community. The U.S., Mexico, and Canada are heading for a trading block similar to the European block. A Pacific Rim block is talked of, as well as an African economic community. We need new positive leadership dedicated to building bridges and reintegrating the human family. UNCED may well begin the process of reuniting the human family. But the tasks before us require a long-range science policy that will essentially transform our perceptions of each other. Indeed, the image held by global partners may be more important than objective measures. We must close the gap in understanding of what our common future means. The motto of the French Revolution—Liberty, Equality, Fraternity—was proposed by Dr. M.G.K. Menon, President of the International Council of Scientific Unions, as a fitting one for a new international order, a compact between the North and South.

In this new era of partnerships, it is vital that we take full advantage of those resources that already exist and forge new links among them. Institutional cooperation is essential to effect change. Linking research centers around the world in global networks is fundamental to attacking the problems of global change and monitoring progress. We need to reach out beyond our individual disciplines and strengthen international science communication and cooperation. New ideas are needed, including bringing in non-Western science.

We need to revitalize elementary-through-undergraduate science education to expand scientific literacy and meld with the humanities to develop the perspective to make wise decisions. We should begin earlier in the educational process to generate interest in science by promoting interaction between pre-college students and researchers. The physical science community needs to become more involved with social sciences, business, schools, and politicians. In other words, science must become more worldly. The complexity of the problems related to global change require interdisciplinary research and new cooperative modes of interaction among individual researchers and professional societies.

On the international scene our overarching challenge is to bring to bear our store of knowledge through expanding democratic institutions. We must forge new partnerships of effort among governments, business, industry, and universities, as well as within the research community. Sustainable development will require a mix of market structures, with governmental guidance and incentives. Market mechanisms, such as emissions trading rights, in which everyone is allocated a certain amount of atmospheric loading, present a highly efficient means of effecting change. Institutional innovations are needed to link the industrialized and industrializing countries to bring their resources to bear on the problems of global change. The International Council of Scientific Unions, for example, has proposed a global system of regional networks.

A primary challenge for the scientific and technical community is to conduct systems analysis and design policy for science and technology and institution building. It is essential for scientists and engineers to recognize that political changes are propelling them into a unique position as a bridge across diverse realms. The scientific and technical community has a unique international span and responsibility. Increasingly, science cannot afford to leave value judgments to politicians, who are apt to use data any way they choose.

The industrialized nations could be of enormous help to developing countries by providing them with the know-how to leapfrog into the future, using environmentally friendly technology that was unavailable until recently to foster sustainable development and improve their standards of living. This will require more rapid and systematic technology transfer from North to South. A good deal of technology that is in the public domain could be of inestimable value to developing countries, who have only 6 percent of the world's scientists and engineers. Well over 100 countries have no scientific or engineering base at all, yet we are asking them to sign international environmental treaties. They cannot effectively cope with the issues involved without strong scientific and technical support from the North.

*The fractured human family has drifted away from acting
as an international community. We need new ways to build bridges
to get back to an integrated human family. We need a genuine
partnership between the North and South.*
—Dr. Thomas R. Odhiambo

Ultimately science is a method in society, and the link between science and society should be strengthened. A number of signs suggest that the social contract forged more than four decades ago between the research community and society is up for renewal. Some of the terms are becoming clear. They will involve summoning our individual and collective wisdom and will to influence global change in the interests of the human prospect.

Breaking Barriers

*We need more societal transformation than we need science.
The time for a paradigm shift is upon us.*
—U.S. Rep. George E. Brown, Jr.

The barriers that stand in the way of a favorable human prospect are not insurmountable. As was proven by worldwide response to ozone depletion, international cooperation can accomplish sweeping reforms. History has shown that if people are given sufficient motivation, they have the capacity to make remarkable changes.

There are those who say evidence concerning the ultimate effects of global change is insufficient to draw meaningful conclusions at this time. Science, by its nature, involves healthy skepticism and the demand for hard data. Yet clean air legislation was an example of public policy being driven by popular opinion. Action to protect the ozone was data driven, and it is not clear yet what will drive global climate issues. While more data and more research are needed on many global change issues, the question is, can we afford to delay action until we have conclusive data?

Deferring all decisions until the edifice of knowledge has been completed will not correct the flawed trajectory of human progress. The art of decision making under uncertainty has a long history. We must not be driven to poor choices by emotional convictions, but we must not be deferred from action by rigid ideological beliefs.

National and regional barriers must also be transcended if we are to alter the unsustainable course of human activity. With the end of the Cold War, we are witnessing basic changes in the nature of society. Domestic democratization and the rise of transnational players—corporations, the scientific and technical community, and religious organizations—have led to a proliferation of actors on the international stage. The growing significance of public/private relations has meant that the very scale of technical innovation leads to the public sector's calling on the private sector. This bodes well for the role of the scientific and technical community in overcoming nationalistic barriers to our common interests.

As the world moves away from bilateral relations between superpowers, the soft power realm will become more important, characterized by negotiation rather than threat, in which one nation tries to promote its own agenda by convincing others that its goals are really in their best interest. This approach strengthens the power of analysis over the power of weapons, giving added influence to research.

The impact of global change on the world of the future is potentially so profound we cannot afford to take an isolationist approach to it. For example, in the discussion about global warming, claims that the U.S. could cope with a 1.5 to 4 degree Celsius increase in temperature ignore the fact that a rise in temperature could alter patterns of rainfall globally, with potentially devastating consequences for agriculture and the global economy.

According to Dr. William C. Clark, of Harvard University's John F. Kennedy School of Government, the world sees the U.S. as enormously laggard about doing its share to solve the problems of global change, which undercuts our international influence. At the moment, Americans spend an average of $40 per capita a year in foreign development assistance, the least of any of the industrialized nations, in spite of what we would gain by global stability. On the plus side of the ledger, the American people have begun to recognize that the ability to realize their national interests depends increasingly on what other nations do to realize theirs.

We can develop plausible, measurable national goals. From 1957-1970, electricity use in the U.S. grew 2.1 times faster than the Gross National Product. From 1973-1988, the ratio was essentially 1:1. Dr. John H. Gibbons, Director of the Congressional Office of Technology Assessment, said that a combination of actions to increase efficiency in energy conversion and use (by about 2 percent per year), along with shifts of energy supply toward natural gas, nuclear, and renewables, could reduce carbon intensity by about 10 percent a decade. "This may not be fast enough," Dr. Gibbons said, "but it is a start."

Many of the problems the world faces in the next century
will require a profound change in our way of thinking—a metanoia.
—Dr. Thomas F. Malone

Economic Development

There is something fundamentally wrong in treating the Earth
as though it were a business in liquidation.
—Herman Daly

Ultimate population stabilization will require economic development as well as family planning. It will require human development, the
objective of which is to expand individual capacity to influence human
destiny by providing access to income and employment opportunities,
education, health, a clean and safe physical environment, and political
freedom.

Everybody's self interest is in advancing worldwide prosperity
without ravaging the globe. We need to develop ways to achieve global
prosperity without upsetting Mother Nature. Environmental activists must
accept that the poverty-stricken nations of the world need industrial development, and industrialists must understand that such development must
produce durable, recyclable goods, while limiting waste, better using non-
renewable resources, and increasing use of renewable resources. There is
growing market appeal for recycled products, and although environmental
disregard characterized the industrial revolution in the U.S. and Europe, the
developing countries might be able to leapfrog the environmentally degrad-
ing side effects of progress with scientific and technical assistance from the
North.

Multinational corporations are in a good position to practice
widespread environmental stewardship and share their knowledge in the
countries where they do business. And, in fact, individual companies are
responding to the environmental imperative. The lessons learned from
ozone depletion may be useful for future protocols. The response, based on
hard scientific evidence, was global, required leadership from large corporations that had significant financial resources, and resulted in concerted steps
to solve the problem.

Some companies have set challenging goals for reducing waste and
are making substantial investments in research to eliminate it altogether.
Large, multinational corporations can create the conditions for finding the
right technology and for making the right decisions. Du Pont, for example,
has tied manager incentive pay to environmental stewardship.

Governments must recognize that all economic policy has an
impact on the environment. Environmental degradation is truly damaging if
it hurts our chances for sustainable development. Nations are no different
from individuals. They must replenish their capital through investment and
the creation of new capital, and this applies to natural capital as well as other
forms.

In Nigeria, for example, 17 percent of the Gross National Product is lost each year to soil erosion; 2 percent, or $100 billion, is lost to erosion annually in the United States. Yet many politicians treat the environment as an addendum, something to consider when it gets bad and only if we can afford it. The challenge to economic and ecological science is to ensure that development is encouraged in a way that minimizes its environmental harm. Whatever system of national accounting is used should incorporate environmental degradation into the equation, since natural resources are national assets.

According to Professor David Pearce of the Centre for Social and Economic Research on the Global Environment, the prospect of a sustainable world does not depend on curtailing the scale (human numbers and GNP) of economic activity. Rather, he proposes that such measures are not *necessary* for a livable world provided the thermodynamic link between economy and environment can be reduced. This link can never be completely broken, but the scope for 'decoupling' is enormous. Strong financial incentives to decouple economic activity from its effect on the environment, combined with a firm policy on containing population growth, is Pearce's recipe for sustainable development without sacrificing the legitimate aspirations of people to improve their standard of living.

The World Conservation Union emphasizes that development should not come at the expense of other groups or generations. The United Nations might be the logical body for beginning to establish market-like incentives that are more global in character, such as: No industrial plant should be built without waste management plans, and no country should apply green protectionism, i.e., requirements imposed on international firms but not on domestic companies.

To many the issue is saving the planet; to us, it is the human prospect.
We need to develop ways to achieve global prosperity
without upsetting Mother Nature.
—Dr. Elwood P. Blanchard Jr.

Professional Tithing

The concept of tithing is central to the involvement
of busy scientists and engineers in the process of influencing
the forces that determine global change.
—Dr. Thomas F. Malone

Institutions do not respond to problems or opportunities, individuals do. We have fantastic reservoirs of creative talent in scientific societies, and the 1990s present a window of opportunity and a decade of decision for changing humankind's unsustainable course.

The three basic questions posed by the Sigma Xi Forum provide a framework for reflection for each individual on his or her personal role in extending, integrating, applying, and disseminating knowledge. This framework is also applicable to every aspect of daily life — individual development and goals, consumer priorities, civic responsibility, personal behavior and procreation.

The impact of individuals is leveraged through associations and professional societies. The themes outlined at the Forum provide an agenda deserving continuing attention during the decade of decision. Each organization can determine its own mode of response. There is great strength in diversity.

The research enterprise will be enriched by tithing of some percentage of each researcher's time and talent devoted to extending the frontiers of knowledge and using this tithed time to become informed on and active in issues arising from the interaction of science, technology, and society.

The chapters and clubs of Sigma Xi have a special opportunity and responsibility by virtue of their unique geographic outreach into every sector of society. Sigma Xi culminated its centennial observance with a commitment to enlarging its mission to embrace the challenge of fostering a dynamic and creative interaction among science, technology, and society.

The solutions are not easy. It is not clear that there are solutions—
but the Forum will provide a path for us to follow.
—Dr. Rita R. Colwell

Appendix C

Exhibitor List

The following had exhibits at the Sigma Xi Forum.

AAAS/Project 2061
1333 H Street, NW
Washington, D.C. 20005
Tel: (202) 326-6648
Fax: (202) 842-5196

American Geophysical Union
2000 Florida Ave., NW
Washington, D.C. 20009
Tel: (202) 462-6900
Fax: (202) 328-0566

American Scientist
P.O. Box 13975
99 Alexander Drive
Research Triangle Park, NC 27709
Tel: (919) 549-4691
Fax: (919) 549-0090

The American Society of Mechanical Engineers
22 Law Drive
P.O. Box 2900
Fairfield, NJ 07007-2900
Tel: 1-800-843-2763
Fax: (201) 882-1717

Committee for the National Institutes for the Environment
730 11th Street, NW
Washington, D.C. 20001-4521
Tel: (202) 628-4303
Fax: (202) 628-4311

Ford Motor Company
Scientific Research Lab
P.O. Box 2053, Rm E-3172
Dearborn, MI 48126
Tel: (313) 337-4040

General Motors Research Laboratories
Environmental Services Department
30500 Mound Road
Warren, MI 48090-9055
Tel: (313) 986-1622
Fax: (313) 986-1910

Island Press
1718 Connecticut Ave., N.W.
Suite 300
Washington, D.C. 20009
Tel: (202) 232-7933
Fax: (202) 234-1328

The MIT Press
55 Hayward Street
Cambridge, MA 02142
Tel: 1-800-356-0343

NASA/Goddard Space Flight Center
Code 900
Greenbelt, MD 20771
Tel: (301) 286-3411
Fax: (301) 286-3884

National Academy Press
2101 Constitution Ave., N.W.
Washington, D.C. 20418
Tel: (202) 334-2728
Fax: (202) 334-2793

National Marine Fisheries Service
1335 East West Highway
Silver Spring, MD 20910
Tel: (301) 427-2299

National Oceanic & Atmospheric Administration
Office of Global Programs
Suite 1225
1100 Wayne Avenue
Silver Spring, MD 20910
Tel: (301) 427-2089
Fax: (301) 427-2082

Naval Research Laboratory (NRL)
Code 4811
Washington, D.C. 20375-5000
Tel: (202) 767-2541
Fax: (202) 767-6991

Penn State Press
Suite C
820 North University Drive
University Park, PA 16802
Tel: (814) 865-1327
Fax: (814) 863-1408

Princeton University Press
41 William Street
Princeton, NJ 08540
Tel: (609) 258-4900
Fax: (609) 258-1335

Sigma Xi, The Scientific Research Society
P.O. Box 13975
99 Alexander Road
Research Triangle Park, NC 27709
Tel: (919) 549-4691
Fax: (919) 549-0090

University of Minnesota Press
2037 University Ave., S.E.
Minneapolis, MN 55414
Tel: (617) 624-2516
Fax: (617) 626-7313

University of Wisconsin Press
114 N. Murray Street
Madison, WI 53719
Tel: (608) 262-6438
Fax: (608) 262-7560

Yale University Press
Box 92A Yale Station
New Haven, CT 06520
Tel: (203) 432-0969
Fax: (203) 432-0948